A Dusty Grey Pony

A Dusty Grey Pony

A Dusty Grey Pony

Book 1
Volume 1

Tearna Goldston

A Dusty Grey Pony

A Dusty Grey Pony
Book 1, Volume 1

ISBN: 978-0-646-90464-1 (Paperback)

Notes: Includes bibliographical references and index.

Subjects: Connemara pony.
Ponies--Australia.
Ponies--Pedigrees.

Copyright 2013 by Tearna Goldston

Author	: Goldston, Tearna, author.
Cover creation and formatting	: RW Marketing
Front cover pony image	: 'Glenormiston Slipper' by Peter Brown
Back cover photograph	: 'The author with Clairvale Padraic and geldings' by Isobel Goldston.
Dewey Number	: 636.16

No part of this book may be reproduced or transmitted in any form or by any means, electronic or mechanical, including photocopying and recording, or by any information storage and retrieval system, without permission in writing from the publisher.

Sue Clarke riding Domo Cavallo Praize with
daughters Sarah and Sophie.

This book is dedicated to the memory of Susan Clarke, Connemara Pony enthusiast, breeder, inspector and judge. Sue gave so much to the breed in Australia through the importation of ponies, her dedicated and well-considered breeding program, and through her promotion of the pony both competitively and through the media. I am forever indebted to Sue for taking the time to recall her memories of the ponies for use in this book, and also for allowing me to go through the many publications, photograph albums and scrapbooks in her extensive library. This series of books would be very much poorer without her encouragement and contribution.

Acknowledgements

I would like to thank the many people who have contributed so much to the content of this book: professional photographers Satu Pitkanen, Cheryl Heynemann, Wildwych Photography, Helen Sloane, Julie Wilson, Fran Adam, Brigitte Heyer, Geoff Garrett Photography, Anthony Reynolds Photography, Sports International Photography, Hoofbeats Photography, Chris Ros Photography, Doug Jervis of Pro Photographics International Inc., James Manifold Photography, Agile Photographics, Suzanne Coutanceau, Lian Shaw of Shawshot Photography, Manfred Grebler and the family of the late Jo Heard. Jenny Hagenblad provided me with much extended pedigree information and encouragement and Lucy McEvilly supplied Clifden Show results from the show's inception. Many Irish and British breeders extended their hospitality to me in 2011, and provided me with information and access to their archives. These were Blanche Miller, Pat Lyne, Benita Sanders, Anne Rolinson, Eileen Simpson, Kerry Wainwright, and Lady Anne Hemphill. In particular, Anne Rolinson, who has had an enormous impact on the Connemara Pony in Australia, through the ponies she bred and exported to this country and by acting as an agent for Australian buyers; and Benita Sanders, who allowed me to scan a Connemara Pony enthusiast's treasure – a hand-written original Irish stud book with photographs of many ponies from that era.

Thanks must also be extended to the Connemara Pony Breeders' Society of Australia, the Connemara Pony Breeders' Society and the British Connemara Pony Society for allowing me access to and use of photographs and information from newsletters, studbooks and the Connemara Chronicle, and to Beatrice Milleder and the German Connemara Pony Association for allowing me to use photographs from their annual magazine. So many Australian, Irish, British and American breeders and enthusiasts have been generous with material, memories and photographs, or have hosted me while I interviewed them and viewed their wonderful ponies (one of my great pleasures of writing this book), that I would not dare list them for fear of leaving someone out. I have very much appreciated all the help and it has certainly added to the comprehensive nature of this book.

A special thanks to Su Moore who not only provided so much help in writing this book but allowed me the opportunity to breed from her wonderful mare Tinderry Enya. And lastly to my family, my husband Christopher in particular, who have supported me through this rather lengthy obsession!

Prologue

This journey really began in 1982. I was a pony-crazy girl growing up in country Queensland, and regularly letting my parents know about my greatest wish – for a pony of my own. My father made enquiries as to where I could get riding lessons, and so it came about that I learned to ride at Shelford Downs Connemara Pony Stud. My first three ponies were Shelford Downs ponies and I have nursed a passion for the Connemara Pony ever since.

Many years later a question was posed on an international Connemara Pony internet forum as to whether or not grey ponies were more typical than their non-grey counterparts. This led me to research the Connemara Pony families in Australia, and I began looking at photographs to try to establish an 'eye for type'. I continued researching and visiting pony breeders, eventually deciding that I should do something with the information that I had so that other enthusiasts could access it. It is amazing what small decisions such as this can lead to! With ten years of working on the book in my spare time with a young family, ponies to work and regular moves as a defence family, one book became three, and then the first book required dividing into two!

I hope I have done justice to the pony and to the work and enthusiasm of Australia's breeders and owners over the years. For various reasons I have sometimes found it difficult to obtain the information and photographs I would like for the books and it may at times seem that I have focused more on some pony families than others. This was, however, never my intention. I have simply presented the information I have been able to gather in a format that I find easy to read and interesting. It may also seem unbalanced that I have used the stallion lines as a focus for the books as, of course, a pony is the result of all the ponies in its pedigree. It was a decision made purely to give structure to the books, and I have included as much information on the mare line of all ponies as I have been able, including the mare families of our imported mares to current entries in the studbook in further volumes of this series.

The author receiving riding instruction from Jack Conroy on the imported mare Chiltern Saffron at Shelford Downs Stud in 1982.

Photo: Russell Smith

This book would be much diminished without the photographs included, and I have endeavored at all times to locate, contact and give credit to the photographer. If however a mistake or omission is noted, I would appreciate being contacted to rectify the error and to compensate the photographer.

A Dusty Grey Pony

Contents

Part 1: An Introduction to the Connemara Pony in Australia p1

Part 2: The Cannon Ball Line Pre-Imports p9

Chapter 1: Cannon Ball to Rebel p10

Chapter 2: The Inchagoill Laddie – Gil Line Stallions p13

Chapter 3: The Inchagoill Laddie – Tooreen Laddie Line Stallions p25

Chapter 4: The Lavalley Rebel Line Stallions p30

Chapter 5: Calla Rebel Line Stallions p41

Part 3: The Cannon Ball Line Stallion Families in Australia p43

Chapter 6: The Cannon Ball Line Stallion Families p44

Chapter 7: The Island King Stallion Family p45

Chapter 8: The Innishgoill Laddie – Gil Line Stallion Families p62

Chapter 9: The Inchagoill Laddie – Tooreen Laddie Line Families p95

Chapter 10: The Lavalley Rebel Line Stallion Families p120

Chapter 11: The Calla Rebel Line Stallion Family p148

Chapter 12: Conclusion p155

Index p156

Reference List and Recommended Reading p170

Part 1

An Introduction to the Connemara Pony in Australia

Home Vale Quantas (106) mustering cattle with John Moore in the Australian high country.

Part 1   An Introduction to the Connemara Pony in Australia

The Connemara Pony has a history that reflects the landscape and climate in which it developed, the people who relied upon it throughout the centuries, hard facts and a sprinkling of romantic notions. It is easy, as I quickly discovered, to be caught up in the desire to delve more deeply to understand the roots of this most wonderful of large pony breeds and see how it has developed into the modern athletic family pony of today.

Connemara is an area of Ireland, west of the city of Galway and bounded by the Maamturk Mountains, Lough Mask, Lough Corrib and the Atlantic coast. It is easy to understand how the pony developed its reputation for thriftiness and hardiness when we consider its native environment which varies from mountainous areas with stony outcrops, to lakes, bogs and wind-battered shorelines. It is understood that the early native ponies of the western seaboard of Ireland were very similar to those of Shetland, Norway and Iceland before the introduction of ponies, most likely Barb, brought to the region by the Celts in the fourth and fifth centuries BC. There is a legend that Andalusian stallions from the Spanish Armada swam ashore from wrecks, and bred with the local ponies. However Ireland enjoyed excellent trade relations with Spain through the centuries, with Galway city being an important trading centre. Wealthy merchants imported fine horses with Barb, Arabian and Andalusian blood that would have influenced local stock to varying degrees. These influences can still be noted in the modern Connemara pony, along with later infusions of 'outside blood'.

A number of excellent publications precede this one, explaining in-depth the origins of the pony, and I shall not venture into details better explained by those far more learned and well-researched than myself. Suffice to say that in the latter part of the nineteenth century, it was noted by the government that the number and quality of ponies in the Connemara region had deteriorated due to the impoverishment of the agricultural community. The government, through the Congested Districts Board, instigated a scheme to improve local horse breeding by making quality government-owned stallions available to local mare owners, with a view to increasing the value and marketability of local stock. The

'Bring in the Turf' by Basil Bradley 1842-1904. This painting shows the creels (baskets) used for transporting turf, seaweed, produce etc in Connemara at the time.

Part 1   An Introduction to the Connemara Pony in Australia

stallions used included Thoroughbred, roadster, Hackney, Clydesdale and Welsh Cob. However, according to a number of concerned locals at the time, this scheme failed miserably in its aims, further degenerating the local stock and rendering many ponies useless for their daily tasks. These included being the main mode of transport, both ridden and driven, being used for ploughing, carting peat, seaweed and produce, and in the case of mares, breeding a foal each year to sell at market. As such, it was imperative that the resultant stock from these outcrosses be thrifty, sure-footed and strong, with a good temperament and work ethic.

Fairyhill Madonna surveys her native Connemara environment.

A survey and report on the Connemara pony was conducted by Professor JC Ewart in 1897 for a Royal Commission examining horse breeding in Ireland. He stated in his report, published in 1900, that the Connemara pony was "capable of living where all but wild ponies would starve", and that the pony had strength, endurance, easy paces, intelligence, docility, and a "capacity for work under conditions which would speedily prove disastrous to horses reared under less natural conditions". Ewart made three recommendations in his report: that the best Connemara sires should be acquired, a register of pure-bred mares should be prepared to provide material for a studbook, and that farmers should be encouraged to use the stallions selected. He also noted five separate 'types' within the breed: the Andalusian type, the Eastern type, the Cashel type, the Clydesdale type, and the Clifden type. The Andalusian type was considered to be the original, or old type of pony, shorter in the neck and legs, deeper in the girth, shorter in the ears and with powerful jaws, and many being 'yellow-dun'.[1] The Eastern type showed greater Arabian influence while the Cashel type was similar to the Andalusian type but with longer legs and powerful loins. The Clydesdale type had strong limbs, a great depth of girth and powerful loins, and abundantly feathered fetlocks. Lastly, the Clifden type was larger than the Andalusian type, had beautifully moulded heads, well arched ribs, good shoulders, well-developed

---

1 R4 p43

Part 1   An Introduction to the Connemara Pony in Australia

Competitors and spectators at an early Clifden show.

loins and hindquarters and short legs, and were, according to Ewart, the best kind of Connemara.[2]

In 1911 a Connemara Pony Committee held a meeting in Clifden, drawing up a description of the pony: "The Connemara Pony should be intelligent, active, and enduring, presenting the outline of a long, low, powerful animal, covering a lot of ground. The action should be good and straight. The hobby should be of a yellow dun, grey, or bay colour, from 13 to 14 hands high, having the croup as high as the withers; the head should be larger than fine, with large jaws; the ears small and pointed; the distance from the occipital crest to the eyes relatively great, and the distance between the eyes from 7½ to 8 inches. The neck should be strong, and of medium length, the shoulders somewhat straight; the withers of moderate height; the body, long and deep (girth from 63 to 70 inches), mounted on short, stout legs (foreleg measuring from 31 to 33 inches from elbow to ground), a good back; powerful loins, slightly drooping, rounded quarters; well-developed breech; short below the knee, with flat, hard bone (measuring from 6½ to 7½ inches under the knee); wide, open, well-formed hoofs."[3]

Michael O'Malley attended this meeting and wrote extensively both before and after detailing his thoughts on the native pony of Connemara. He wrote that from his own observations he considered that either a "large and coarse head," or a "small and fine head," is quite characteristic of the pure Connemara Pony". He also noted that "You will get one pure Connemara Pony with a rather big, coarse head and stout legs, and another that is not one whit the more impure, with a small, fine head, and fine legs." Mr O'Malley added roan, strawberry and black to the usual colours of the breed, and regarding height wrote that "Experience teaches that liberal and careful feeding will be quickly and remarkably responded to by the pure Connemara Pony, inasmuch as he will far exceed the maximum height (14 hands) with which he is credited".[4]

In 1923, the Connemara Pony Breeders' Society was formed, with the policy of the first council being to "encourage the breeding of Connemara ponies and

---

2   R4 p43-48
3   R49 p12-13
4   R49 p14

Part 1 An Introduction to the Connemara Pony in Australia

their development and maintenance as a distinctive breed". A studbook was formed with those ponies to be included being required to be presented for and pass inspection. For Volume I of the studbook only nine stallions passed from sixty-five presented, and thirty-six mares from four hundred and thirty-six mares presented! The low number of ponies successfully entering the studbook was a disappointment to the society, and it was not long before the number of stallion lines was found to be too narrow. Consequently, the society allowed the introduction to the studbook of the crossbred progeny of some non-Connemara stallions out of registered Connemara mares. Particularly influential have been the Thoroughbred stallions Little Heaven and Winter and the Arabian stallion Naseel. We also see the occasional influence of the Irish Draft stallions Skibbereen, Hillside Rover and May Boy, and another Thoroughbred, Thistleton. The studbook was finally closed to any pony of unknown or crossbred breeding in 1964.

Five established Connemara pony stallion lines have remained unbroken in Ireland, these being the lines of Cannon Ball (Ire 1), Connemara Boy (Ire 9), Mountain Lad (Ire 32), Carna Dun (Ire 89), and Clonkeehan Auratum (Ire 104). With the variety of 'types' noted in the breed preceding the formation of the CPBS, and the addition of outside influences to the studbook in later times, it has been an ongoing struggle for breeders and enthusiasts to develop an eye for 'ideal type', and also to breed a consistent type using the available bloodlines. The inspection process in Ireland has played its part in the continued development of the breed, as has showing and the sale of performance ponies locally and internationally. The first society show was held at Roundstone in 1924, and the Clifden Show has been held on the third Thursday in August every year since 1947. Winning stallions have been very well utilised by breeders, however in some cases this has been to the detriment of the gene pool.

With both pure and partbred Connemaras becoming renowned in hunting and jumping circles, and international performances by the partbreds Dundrum and Stroller in jumping and eventing, and Little Model in dressage, the breed's profile increased markedly. Marketed as a good all-purpose family pony, exports from Ireland increased to the United Kingdom, Europe, the USA and as far afield as South Africa.

Dundrum (Little Heaven x Evergood) with Tommy Wade

Part 1   An Introduction to the Connemara Pony in Australia

The first Connemara pony imported to Australia, the stallion Island King (1) who arrived in 1963, and Ardan (1001), the first imported mare, are from the Cannon Ball line, the focus of this first book. Although his purchase and importation was intended to improve the size, bone and temperament of the Australian Pony, Island King and his owner Dr Fred Wiltshire soon inspired others to devote their loyalty to the breed, and quite a number of ponies were imported in the late 1960s and throughout the 1970s.

With Fred's infectious enthusiasm, it was decided that an Australian Connemara Pony society should be formed and as such an inaugural meeting was held at Lancefield on the 17th of March, 1971. With Mr Clive Cochrane as Chairman, a formal motion to set up the CPBSA was put forward by M Kelly, and seconded by Fred Wiltshire. The first AGM was then held on the 21st of September, 1973. In the early years of the society a studbook was set up, and this included a 'breeding-up' program designed to increase numbers of purebred stock in the country. There are only a few remaining 'bred-up' pony families in Australia, and these appear in the final volume of this series. The CPBSA studbook was eventually closed to new 'outside blood' in 1984.

The tragic passing of Fred Wiltshire in 1973 due to a tractor accident was a terrible blow to the Connemara community, however the CPBSA struggled on. One difficulty the society faced after his death was the refusal of the CPBS to recognise the Australian bred ponies in their studbook, Fred having been seen as an accepted inspector of ponies in this country. An inspection program was therefore, for better or worse, put in place to allow the Australian ponies recognition by the mother society. Fortunately it was decided that mandatory inspections were only necessary for colts as with the difficulties involving the distances between ponies in this country, and the availability of inspectors, it may well have been the end of CPBSA registered ponies if it had also been necessary for fillies.

In recent years, with changes made to the Irish studbook born from pressure from EU laws and support from members of the International Committee of Connemara Pony Societies (ICCPS), we now have a studbook that recognizes all ponies as purebreds that have been bred from two purebred parents. This includes a section for inspected and approved ponies, one for those uninspected or having

A group of Connemara pony enthusiasts ready for a trail ride at Barwidgee in the 1970s.

Photo: M Kelly

Part 1   An Introduction to the Connemara Pony in Australia

failed inspection but passed a vet check, and another section for those that are uninspected and/or failed a vet check. This allows much greater scope for breeders to fully utilise the bloodlines we have available in Australia.

In the early days the CPBSA set up a 'Connemara of the Year' competition to promote the pony, and some results of this scheme are noted within the pages of these volumes. Recently this has been replaced with a performance register. The ponies receiving the most points in each state are rewarded with prizes each year and points are accrued toward bronze, silver and gold awards. The society also issues the 'Jo Heard Trophy' each year to a nominated pony that is promoting the breed, and not necessarily through conventional means such as competition. There are a number of Connemara Action Groups throughout Australia that hold regular activities including displays, shows and hunter trials.

An Australian party visiting Tulira. Ken and Breda Wiltshire, the Jacksons and their children and the Baldwins.

Photo: Hemphill Archive

Over the years a number of major activities have been held, including a Native Pony field day at Bowral in 1980, with Connemara breeder, judge and author Pat Lyne as a guest judge, and a Mountain and Moorland pony festival at Brookfield in 1987, with Connemara pony breeder, native pony judge and author, Anne Rolinson as a guest judge. In 1988 the CPBSA held a Silver Jubilee All-Connemara Show, judged by Blanche Miller of the Rosenaharley Stud in England. More recently a number of Connemara enthusiasts from Victoria have organised regular Connemara Showcases, which are a great boost for the breed.

Sadly, a number of stallion and mare lines of imported ponies have disappeared since our first imports. There are many different reasons for this, either tragic or mundane, regarding both the ponies and their custodians. Many lines have flourished, and all of the lines of the imported ponies in Australia up to the time of writing are contained within the volumes of this series for readers to view their success or otherwise. This first volume includes all of the imported stallions and their families of the Cannon Ball stallion line. This has been a very successful line in Australia, and as such this entire book is devoted to it. The second volume contains the imported mares from this line, and the final volumes contain ponies from the Connemara Boy, Mountain Lad, Carna Dun and Clonkeehan Auratum lines, plus some additional ponies from smaller lines such as Snowball, Winter and our Australian bred-up mare lines.

Part 1   An Introduction to the Connemara Pony in Australia

Lineup of ponies at the 2013 Victorian Connemara Pony Showcase held at the National Equestrian Centre at Werribee.

THE CPBSA'S DESCRIPTION OF THE CONNEMARA PONY

Height: not exceeding 14.2hh at two years of age or at the time of inspection.

Colours: Grey, Black, Bay, Brown, Dun (Buckskin), Roan, Chestnut, Palomino and Dark-eyed Creams.

Type: Compact, well-balanced riding type with good depth and substance and good heart room, standing on short legs, covering a lot of ground.

Description:

Head: Well-balanced head of medium length with good width between large kindly eyes. Pony ears, well-defined cheekbone, jaw relatively deep but not coarse.

Front: Head well-set onto neck. Crest should not be over-developed. Neck not set on too low. Good length of rein. Well-defined withers, and good, sloping shoulders.

Body: Body should be deep, with strong back, some length permissible but should be well-ribbed up and with strong loins.

Limbs: Good length and strength in forearm, well-defined knees and short cannons, with flat bone measuring at least 18cms.

Hind Quarters: Strong and muscular with some length, well-developed second thighs (gaskin) and strong low-set hocks.

Part 2

The Cannon Ball Line Pre-Imports

A group of two-year-old Connemara Colts in 1939.

Part 2   The Cannon Ball Line Pre-Imports

Chapter 1
Cannon Ball to Rebel

Cannon Ball (Ire 1)
↳ **Rebel (Ire 7)**
  ↳ Innishgoill Laddie (Ire 21)
    ↳ Gil (Ire 43)
      ↳ Cill Ciarain (Ire 78)
      ↳ Carna Bobby (Ire 73)
        ↳ The Admiral (Ire 201)
        ↳ Leam Bobby Finn (Ire 297)
          ↳ Cocum Hawkstoone (Ire 570)
          ↳ Kirtling Brigadoon (Ire 625)
        ↳ Ballydonagh Rob (Ire 321)
        ↳ Killyreagh Kim (Ire 308)
          ↳ Kings Ransom (Ire 584)
          ↳ Truska Pimpernel (Ire 618)
          ↳ Wise Cygnet (Ire 544)
        ↳ Coosheen Finn (Ire 381)
    ↳ Tooreen Laddie (Ire 86)
      ↳ Tooreen Ross (Ire 99)
        ↳ Bridge Boy (Ire 124)
          ↳ Marco Polo of Clonkeehan (Ire 236)
          ↳ Tulira Colman (7)
            ↳ Calmore Swagman (Ire 5329)
        ↳ Tulira Mairtin (Ire 214)
          ↳ Tulira Nimble Dick (Ire 426)
  ↳ Lavalley Rebel (Ire 24)
    ↳ Inver Rebel (Ire 93)
      ↳ Wisbridge Golden Rebel (Ire 130)
        ↳ Wisbridge Whiskey Flake (UK 4486)
        ↳ Wisbridge Erinmore (Ire 484)
      ↳ Rory of Millfields (Ire 158)
      ↳ Rebel Wind (Ire 24)
        ↳ Errislannon Sparkler (Ire 210)
        ↳ Island Baron (Ire 327)
        ↳ Roundstone Oscar (Ire 337)
        ↳ Ocean Minstrel (Ire 420)
      ↳ Greaney Rebel (Ire 186)
    ↳ Corrib (UK 3891)
  ↳ Calla Rebel (Ire 38)
    ↳ Strongbow (Ire 90)

Part 2   The Cannon Ball Line Pre-Imports

There is absolutely no question that the Cannon Ball line has had a greater impact on the Australian Connemara pony herd than any other stallion line. Twenty-six imported or imported in-utero (iiu) stallions, and the sires of forty-five of the imported or iiu mares, are direct male-line descendants of **Cannon Ball (Ire 1)**. He is also represented in other branches of the pedigrees of all of our imported ponies. There would not be a Connemara pony living today that does not carry his legacy.

Cannon Ball (Ire 1)

Cannon Ball was a grey stallion of 13.3hh foaled in 1904 out of an unregistered native Connemara mare. According to Bartley O'Sullivan (1939) he was by a stallion named Dynamite. Dynamite was a very well-regarded chestnut pony who frequently won trotting races and also in-hand in Ireland before being exported to the USA. He was also out of an unknown Connemara mare and by the Welsh Cob stallion Prince Llewellyn, and thus we find a Welsh influence in the foundation of today's Connemara pony.

Cannon Ball was an extraordinary pony by all accounts. He did not have an easy life by modern standards – pulling the plough, hauling turf and rocks as well as performing his stud duties. He was a legend at the local races, having never been beaten in the 'Farmers' Race'. His owner, Harry (Henri) Toole of Oughterard, had a special bond with him, and Connemara locals recalled the pair's regular safe and steady journey home with Cannon Ball pulling the cart or side-car in which Henri slept soundly after a visit to the local pub.

A wonderful description of Cannon Ball given by Valentine Boucher reads as follows: "By some trick of nature he was born, if not bred, an aristocrat. The snow- white of his coat, the proud carriage of his head, the short back and splendid muscle of his quarters raised him above the level of his kind of life, and, in death, made him a legend." On his death, Cannon Ball was given a wake befitting his status in life, and he was buried standing up in a hay-lined grave facing the Oughterard race course.

As indicated by his standing as the first stallion classified and entered into the newly formed CPBS's studbook, the qualities Cannon Ball possessed were those the CPBS regarded as ideally representative of a Connemara stallion.

Part 2   The Cannon Ball Line Pre-Imports

As he was such a popular sire locally, and many of the original ponies entered into the CPBS Studbook are registered without known parentage, it may well be that more ponies than we know have Cannon Ball in their ancestry.

Cannonball's son Rebel (a link established by Pat Lyne when she was researching for her book Shrouded in Mist) continues this line toward Australia's imports.

Rebel (Ire 7), a grey pony of 13.2hh foaled in 1922, passed CPBS classification in 1924 and was purchased by the society. He worked in harness and was ridden in the local races in addition to performing stud duties. Rebel was remembered as an attractive pony, much like his sire, and he did well in-hand including four wins at the society show. At sixteen years of age Rebel was euthanised due to ill-health, but left behind some good quality progeny including three influential sons, Innishgoill Laddie (Ire 21), Lavalley Rebel (Ire 24), and Calla Rebel (Ire 38). Each of these sons created branches in the Cannon Ball stallion line that are well-represented in the CPBSA studbook. I shall review these branches separately rather than strictly by generation for continuity of reading.

Rebel (Ire 7)

Photo: Sanders Archive

Chapter 2

Innishgoill Laddie – Gil Line

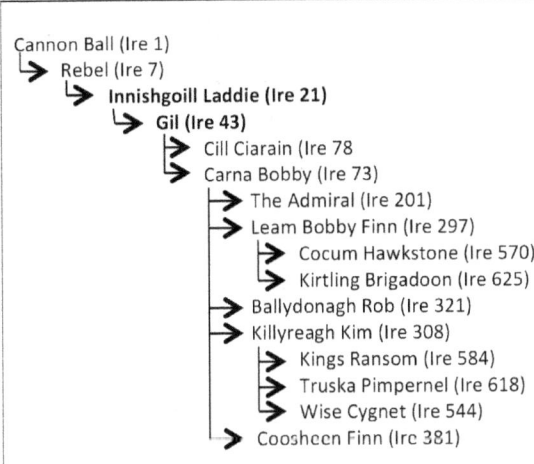

Innishgoill Laddie (Ire 21)

Rebel's first stallion son for review, Innishgoill Laddie (Ire 21), was a grey pony of 13.2hh, foaled in 1934 out of the mare Dooyher Lass (Ire 188) who has no recorded pedigree. He was bought by the CPBS as a foal and turned out to mature for two years on the island of Innishgoill in Lough Corrib (hence his prefix of Innishgoill – or Inchagoill as it is written in later CPBS studbooks). During his lifetime Innishgoill Laddie resided with a number of stallion custodians for the society, all of whom regarded him well. He was a winner of races like his sire and grandsire, a hard-working farm pony, and won in-hand at Clifden in 1938 and 1940. He was reportedly slow to mature and not quite even in his action, but left many good

Chapter 2   Innsishgoill Laddie – Gil Line

Golden Gleam (Ire 296)

Photo: CPBS Studbook Vol V

daughters and five stallion sons, two of whom have contributed significantly to the Australian studbook. These were Gil (Ire 43) and Tooreen Laddie (Ire 86).¹

Gil (Ire 43) was a grey pony of 13.3hh, bred by Dudley McDonagh of Maam Cross in 1938 from the well-regarded buckskin mare Golden Gleam (Ire 296). Golden Gleam won her class at the society show at Carna in 1938, 1942 and 1945. Anne Rolinson described her as an early example of the improvement in quality and riding type that the society and breeders were aiming for. Although not stated in the CPBS studbook, it has been documented by Pat Lyne and Susan Bowen that a palomino mare named Golden Glimmer (Ire 297) was her dam.²

Gil was purchased by the CPBS, and passed his classification as a three-year-old. He produced twelve stallion sons and fifty-nine daughters during his stud career, and won his class at Clifden as a ten-year-old in 1948. He remained on the CPBS's stallion list until 1952 when he was sold on.³

Gil's son Cil Ciarain (Ire 78) sired the imported mare Noreen Ban (Ire 2355). He was foaled in 1946, and was a strongly influenced Cannon Ball line sire as he was out of Irish Beauty (Ire 669) who was by Rebel. He was purchased by the CPBS after winning his foal class at the society show, and remained on their stallion list for many years after passing classification.⁴

---

1 R4 p151, R6 p122
2 R5 p67, R11 p25
3 R4 p155, R5 p67
4 R4 p159, R3 p72

Chapter 2   Innsishgoill Laddie – Gil Line

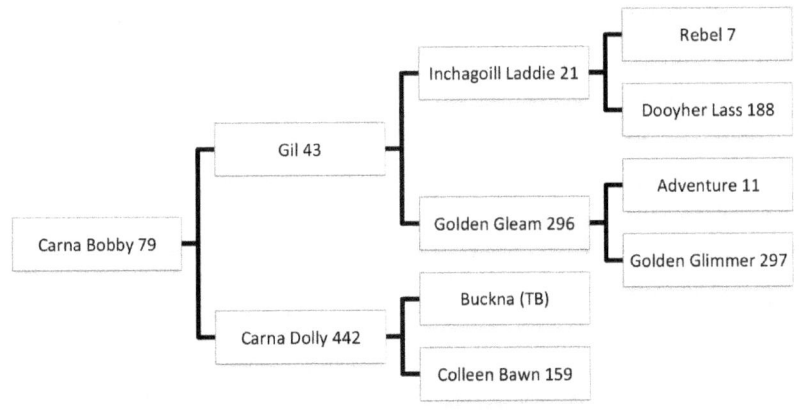

Carna Bobby (Ire 79) with Jack Bolger

Carna Dolly (Ire 442)

Carna Bobby (Ire 79) was Gil's second son to influence the Australian studbook directly and he has done so most surely! A grey pony of 13.3hh, Carna Bobby was foaled in 1946 out of the Mulkerrin family's hard-working farm pony and broodmare Carna Dolly (Ire 442), who was also shown successfully in-hand by the Mulkerrins, winning her class at the society show five times.[5] Carna Dolly was by the Thoroughbred stallion Buckna and possibly showed a little extra quality and presence in the showring that caught the judge's eye. Carna Bobby was bought by the CPBS as a foal, and remained with the Society until his fifteenth year when he was sold to Patrick Lally of Gort.

Carna Bobby was considered to be slow to mature and weak behind, but he had a presence and quality that ensured his success in the showring. He won first

---

5 R4 p207-208

place at Clifden five times (every time he was eligible and competed) before bowing to Clonkeehan Auratum's win in 1959. He stamped his progeny with quality, good movement and lovely heads, and continued to be popular with mare owners until his death in 1974. Three hundred and five ponies registered with the CPBS were by Carna Bobby, forty-seven of these being stallions, which shows his influence on Connemara pony breeding. The honour of being considered to be one of the 'great' sires is well-deserved.[6] The first Connemara Pony to be imported to Australia, Island King (1), was by Carna Bobby, as was the iiu stallion Blandings Bobby (44). Six mares by him were also imported, these being Silver Mill (1038), Knock Ina (1039), Ballydonagh Belle (1047), Abbeyleix Polly (1055), Abbeyleix Fiona (1151), and Abbeyleix Grey Pearl (1159). Further influence on the Australian studbook can be found through Carna Bobby's Irish and British sons The Admiral (Ire 201), Leam Bobby Finn (Ire 297), Killyreagh Kim (Ire 308), Ballydonagh Rob (Ire 321), and Coosheen Finn (Ire 381). Two of these stallions, Leam Bobby Finn and Killyreagh Kim, also have influential sub-branch families.

Cashel Kate (Ire 2030) at the 1967 Clifden Show.

Photo: CPBS Studbook

Ballydonagh Sticky (Ire 337) in The Netherlands

Photo: De Leliaard Archive

The Admiral (Ire 201) was a grey 14.0hh stallion foaled in 1961 out of the very well-regarded mare Cashel Kate (Ire 2030). Cashel Kate was a four-time Clifden champion and a dam of regular winners, including another member of this stallion family, Killyreagh Kim (Ire 308). Cashel Kate is listed in the CPBS studbook as being by the Mountain Lad line stallion Tully Lad (Ire 48), however it is a commonly held opinion that her sire was in fact the half-Thoroughbred stallion Carna Dun (Ire 89).[7]

The Admiral spent his lifetime as a teaser in Co. Westmeath, and therefore did not leave a large number of progeny, but he did produce a stallion son, the Clifden winner Mervyn Pookhaun (Ire 528), before he died in 1981.[8] His full-brothers Ballydonagh Rob (Ire 321) and Ballydonagh Sticky (Ire 377) and his full-sister Ballydonagh Deirdre (Ire 3423) have contributed

---

6 R3 p80 150, R5 p159, R6 p62, R14:1
7 R4 p215, R6 p75
8 R3 p110, R20:2

significantly to Connemara studbooks in Australia and The Netherlands. The Admiral's contribution to the Australian studbook was his daughter Shelford Downs Clairwood iiu (1176).

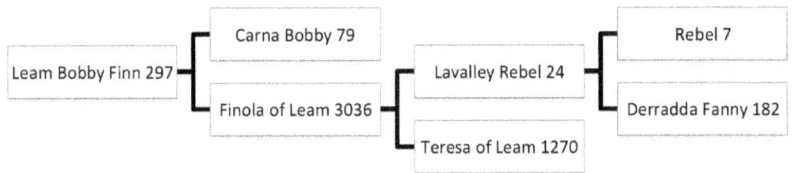

The second of Carna Bobby's sons to be represented directly in this line is Leam Bobby Finn (Ire 297), a grey stallion of 14.0½hh foaled in 1967. Leam Bobby Finn was bred by John and Phyllis Meade of The Glyn Farm in Wales out of their outstanding mare Finola of Leam (Ire 3036). The Meades travelled Finola to Ireland to visit Carna Bobby as they were convinced that he would be the ideal match for her. Their convictions proved to be well rewarded as her second colt foal, Leam Bobby Finn, was exactly what they had hoped for and he was retained as a stallion prospect. At two years old he was moved to The Glyn and stood at stud there until the Meades retired. At his first show Bobby Finn won the young stock class – the start of a glittering show career. He was Supreme Exhibit at the British Connemara Pony Society Breed Show in 1972, 1974 and 1975, and was also Champion Mountain and Moorland Pony at the Ponies of Britain Show in 1973 (the first time a Connemara Pony had won against all other Native Breeds in Britain) and again in 1975. Leam Bobby Finn's progeny followed his footsteps in-hand and he also produced saddle champions and exceptional performance ponies. He was very well regarded by British breeders, and was ultimately rewarded with Super Premium Stallion status by the BCPS. In 1985 he moved to The Leaze Stud and then to Julia

The handsome head of Leam Bobby Finn

Leam Bobby Finn (Ire 297)

Chapter 2   Innsishgoill Laddie – Gil Line

Greenwood in the north of England, where he resided until his death in 1993 at 26 years of age.⁹

Leam Bobby Finn sired the imported stallion Mylerstown Huckleberry Finn (89), and the imported mare Finchampstead Martha (1147); and further influenced the CPBSA studbook through his sons Cocum Hawkstone (Ire 570) and Kirtling Brigadoon (Ire 625).

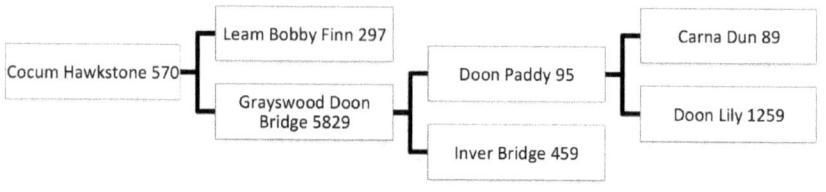

Cocum Hawkstone (Ire 570)

Grayswood Doon Bridge (Ire 5829)

Cocum Hawkstone (Ire 570), a grey stallion of 13.3½hh, was foaled in 1972 at John and Cecilie Williams' Cocum Stud in England, and was thus named as the Hawkstone Otterhounds were visiting Cocum Stud at the time. His dam, Grayswood Doon Bridge (Ire 5829), was by the Carna Dun line stallion Doon Paddy (Ire 95) and out of the mare Inver Bridge (Ire 459), who also produced the stallion Inver Rebel (Ire 93), to be reviewed later in this chapter. Grayswood Doon Bridge had been purchased by the Williams for their younger daughter, Bettina, to ride. She was also a very reliable driving pony before beginning her career as a broodmare.

Hawkstone has been described as having quality, depth, particularly good

9 R5 p25, R7 p76, R15:3, R25:1, R29:2, R33:1

movement and a kind temperament. He did very well for the Cocum Stud in the showring, standing supreme champion at the BCPS Breed Show in 1977 as a five year old and being awarded premium status by the BCPS. He was chosen in 1979 by the Royal Worcester Porcelain Company to be the model for their Connemara pony mould in a limited edition Mountain and Moorland Pony range, which is indicative of his presence and appeal. Hawkstone produced some excellent progeny including two stallion sons.[10] He is represented by two daughters in the Australian studbook: Cocum Raindrop imp (1103) and Sandy Park Kathleen Mavourneen iiu (1202).

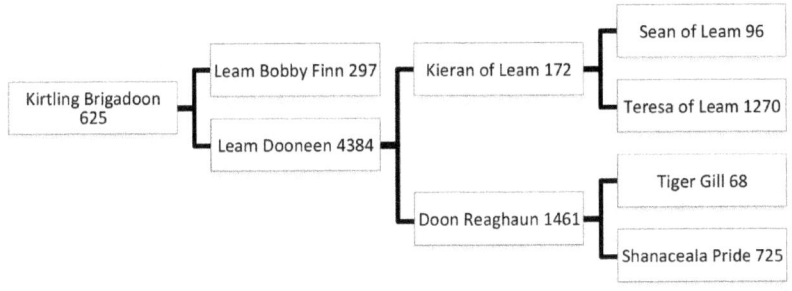

Kirtling Brigadoon (Ire 625)

Leam Dooneen (Ire 4384)

Leam Bobby Finn's second son with direct sire-line influence on the Australian studbook is Kirtling Brigadoon (Ire 625), being a grey stallion of 14hh. Brigadoon has been described as having "great presence and good bone with a strong hind leg and free movement. Like his sire well let down, the cannon bone short with nice flat (8½ inch) bone."[11] He also displayed a lovely temperament and manners when being handled or ridden by adults and children alike. Eileen Simpson notes that when being stood up at a show or at home he always stood perfectly due to his exceptional conformation, and when trotting out he "just floated"!

Brigadoon was bred in 1973 by Mrs Rachel Millet of the Kirtling Stud in Newmarket, England, out of Leam Dooneen (Ire 4384). This mare's dam, Doon Reaghaun (Ire 1461) also produced the Connemara

---

10 R5 p27, R7 p46, R17:2, R18:1, R38:1
11 R27:1

Chapter 2   Innsishgoill Laddie – Gil Line

Boy line stallion Whalton Sandune (UK 4411), who shall be reviewed later in this series.

In 1973 Kirtling Brigadoon was sold to Eileen Simpson for her Sydserff Stud in North Berwick, Scotland. Brigadoon did very well in the showring both in-hand and under saddle, winning the Cluggan Cup for Supreme Champion at the BCPS Breed Show in 1980 and 1983 as well as qualifying under saddle for Olympia in 1983. He was also a very successful stud sire for Eileen, and his progeny have done exceptionally well in-hand and as ridden show and performance ponies. As such, Brigadoon was also awarded Premium status by the BCPS.[12] Two stallion sons of Kirtling Brigadoon, the full-brothers Sydserff Brig-O-Doon (83) and Shelford Downs Berwick Boy (96), are included in the Australian studbook.

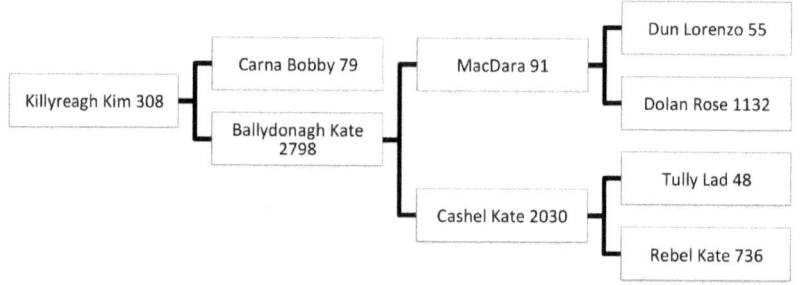

Killyreagh Kim at the 1983 Clifden Show

Dr Sabine Bachmann

The second son of Carna Bobby to have a sub-branch stallion family for review is Killyreagh Kim (Ire 308). Killyreagh Kim was a grey stallion of 14hh bred in 1967 by Col Michael Creighton of Co. Fermanagh in Northern Ireland. His dam, Ballydonagh Kate (Ire 2798), was purchased by Col Creighton in foal to Carna Bobby, with Killyreagh Kim being the resultant foal. As Ballydonagh Kate was a daughter of Cashel Kate, Killyreagh Kim is very closely related to The Admiral (Ire 201) and Ballydonagh Rob (Ire 321).

---

12 R5 p27, R7 p23 53 72

Chapter 2 Innsishgoill Laddie – Gil Line

As a yearling, Killyreagh Kim was shown for a second place at Clifden and was then donated to the CPBS. Described as a late maturer, a common theme with this line of ponies, he nonetheless continued his success in the showring with wins at Clifden including champion of the show in 1984. His progeny followed his footsteps and he was held in high regard as a sire, producing two hundred and forty-two registered progeny in his lifetime. Killyreagh Kim lived until the respectable age of twenty-five.[13]

No sons or daughters of Killyreagh Kim made their way to Australia, however three sons have contributed to our studbook, these being Kings Ransom (Ire 584), Truska Pimpernel (Ire 618), and Wise Cygnet (Ire 544).

King's Ransom (Ire 584) was a grey stallion of 14hh foaled in 1973. He won every class in which he was entered as a yearling, including at Clifden in 1974, and was sold to Sarah Hodgkins' Spinway Stud in England later that year, eventually taking over stud duties from Atlantic Rebel (107) who was sold and exported to Australia.

King's Ransom's dam was Errisbeg Rose (Ire 2895), a roan mare by Carna Dun (Ire 89) out of Dolan Rose (Ire 1132) and thus a half-sister to the Connemara Boy line stallion MacDara (Ire 91). Errisbeg Rose was an outstanding broodmare in Ireland, and also in England after Sarah Hodgkins managed to purchase her when she was nineteen years of age. She produced a number of stallion sons in addition to King's Ransom, and her progeny performed exceptionally well both in-hand and under saddle, leading to the BCPS awarding her Premium Mare status. Sarah described her as "the most correct pony, with lovely bone and an outstanding natural free mover, and still is at the age of twenty-six showing no sign of stiffness or wear or tear."[14]

King's Ransom became a top sire of both in-hand and performance ponies in Britain, and won the Cheyne Cup (sire's progeny group) at the BCPS Breed Show in 1982. In 1980 he was exported to France.[15] He is represented in the Australian studbook by one imported daughter, Spinway Fantasy (1143)

---

13 R3 p129 139 163 205 215, R5 p29 271, R6 p62
14 R30:2, R5 p281, R30:2
15 R7 p52

Chapter 2   Innsishgoill Laddie – Gil Line

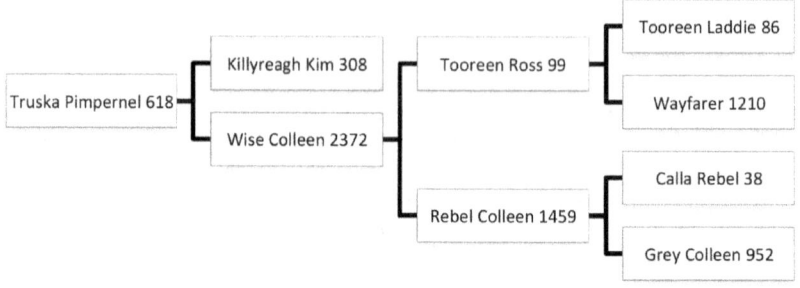

Truska Pimpernel (Ire 618)

Colleen Bawn (Ire 159) at 7 years

Killyreagh Kim's second son to influence our studbook was **Truska Pimpernel (Ire 618)**, another grey stallion of 14hh. Pimpernel was bred on the beach at Ballyconneely in 1972 by Thomas McHugh, out of Wise Colleen (Ire 2372), a mare whose dam line was founded by Colleen Bawn (Ire 159), dam of Carna Dolly (Ire 442). In 1973 Truska Pimpernel was purchased by Pat Lyne as a stallion prospect to use over her Island Duke (Ire 208) mares, and exported to Britain. Pat named him Pimpernel because a suitable colt fulfilling all of her criteria had proved to be quite elusive!

After producing well for the Chiltern Stud for three seasons, he was purchased by Mr and Mrs Benson to use as a teaser on a Thoroughbred stud. Pimpernel continued to stand at stud to Connemara mares, however, and was also shown very successfully in-hand, including winning the Snowball Cup (champion stallion) and best opposite sex to the supreme champion at the 1982 BCPS Breed Show. He was awarded premium status by the BCPS, and it was most unfortunate when the Bensons lost Pimpernel to founder at only twelve years of age.[16] His influence in Australia is through the imported stallion Tiercel Galloping Major (103), and the imported mares Chiltern Martina (1128) and Chiltern Variation (1129).

---

16   R5 p29, R6 p7

Chapter 2   Innsishgoill Laddie – Gil Line

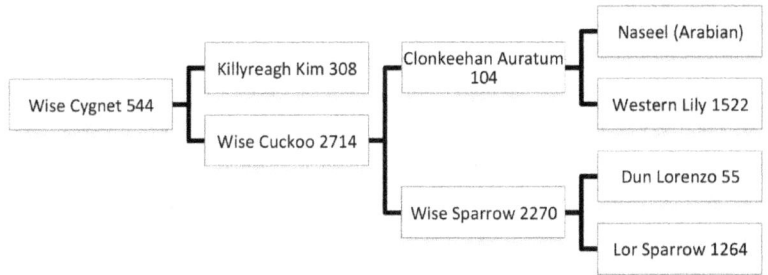

Wise Cygnet (Ire 544) ridden by Mary McCann

Photo: Lady Maria Lavinge

Killyreagh Kim's third son of influence is **Wise Cygnet (Ire 544)**. Wise Cygnet was a brown stallion foaled in 1972 out of Wise Cuckoo (Ire 2714). Wise Cuckoo was an outstanding broodmare for John Joyce, producing a number of stallion sons and prize-winning daughters, including the 1989 Clifden supreme champion Maureen's Cuckoo (Ire 8799).[17] Her dam, Wise Sparrow (Ire 2270), was the foundation mare for the Ashfield Stud and was out of another class-winner at Clifden, Lor Sparrow (Ire 1264) which indicates the consistent quality of this mare line.

Wise Cygnet was purchased from his breeder John A Joyce in Ballyconeely, Clifden, as a yearling by Lady Maria Lavinge. He won his yearling class at the Galway Show and was raised as a stallion prospect. Unfortunately only one of his testicles was a normal size, and he grew overheight to 15hh, so after covering two mares to produce two fillies at the Grange Stud, he was gelded. Wise Cygnet was subsequently sold to Mary McCann of Hartwell Stud in Kill, who produced him successfully under saddle before he was again sold on. He is represented in the Australian studbook by his imported daughter Grange Solitary Swan (1112).

Of Carna Bobby's stallion sons that have progeny directly represented in the Australian studbook, the first for review is Ballydonagh Rob (Ire 321). Bred by Mr Trevor Donnelly of Co. Wicklow in 1967, Ballydonagh Rob was a 14.1hh grey stallion out of Cashel Kate, and thus a full brother to The Admiral. A promising young colt, he placed third in his foal class at Clifden Show in 1967, and also placed third in the stallion class in 1975. He also sired youngstock who won and placed highly at Clifden.

---

17 R3 p100

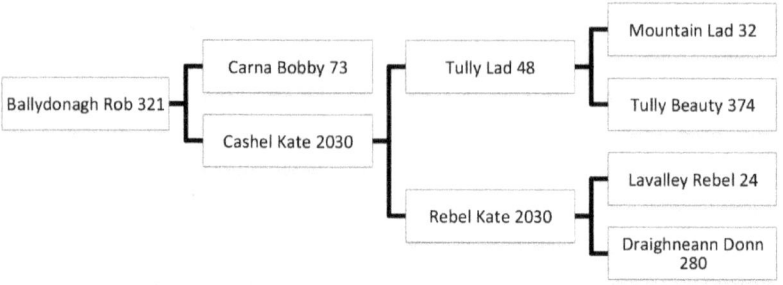

Ballydonagh Rob (Ire 321)

Coosheen Finn with Elizabeth Petch in 1983

Coosheen Finn enjoys a gallop in the sunshine

Ballydonagh Rob succeeded his sire Carna Bobby with Patrick Lally at Gort, before he was lost tragically to tetanus. Before his death, Lady de Vesci of the Abbeyleix Stud sent her lovely mare Finola of Leam (Ire 3036) to him. The result of this union was the imported Australian stallion Abbeyleix Finbar (93).

The last of Carna Bobby's sons to influence the CPBSA studbook directly is the 13.2hh grey stallion **Coosheen Finn (Ire 381)**, bred in 1968 by the Meades of the Leam Stud. He was the third colt born to Carna Bobby and Finola of Leam, and was foaled with Jack Bolger who had purchased his dam. Mrs Elizabeth Petch of the Coosheen Stud bought him from Jack as a foal and he rewarded her with a stallion class win at Clifden in 1978, and also by siring many top-quality and prize-winning progeny. Coosheen Finn was described to me by Martin Haller (author of "Ponys aus Irlands") as being "very typey, having good bone, a nice topline, a beautiful head, and oodles of charisma". In 1980 he was bestowed with the special honour of representing his breed on a stamp, one of a series of Equestrian stamps produced in Ireland.[18] Coosheen Finn is represented in the Australian studbook by his imported daughter Coosheen Laura (1084).

---

18 R3 p177 271, R6 p35, R20:1

Chapter 3

Innishgoill laddie – Tooreen Laddie Line

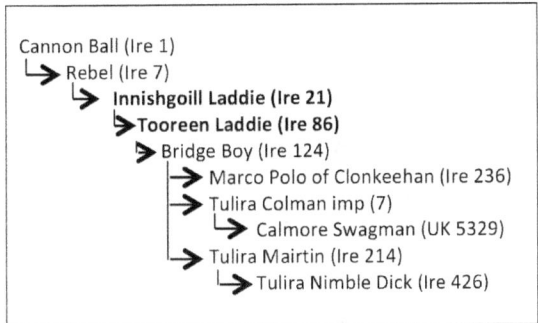

We now trace back up the stallion line chart to the last of Innishgoill Laddie's sons to be registered, and the second to establish a family branch impacting on Australian breeding – to **Tooreen Laddie (Ire 86)**.

A grey stallion of 13.3hh, Tooreen Laddie was bred in 1947 by Luke Nee of Letterfrack, out of the mare Grey Swan (Ire 457) who has no recorded pedigree. The CPBS purchased Tooreen Laddie as a two-year-old and used him for four seasons before he was sold. He subsequently made his way to Mrs Harris of Hideaway Stud in the USA in 1955. Patrick Joyce reportedly described him as of "the old-fashioned stock" – being strong boned, having a good head and shoulder and a kind nature.[1] Tooreen Laddie contributed to the Australian studbook through his son Tooreen Ross (Ire 99), and also indirectly but significantly through his daughter Leam Lassie (Ire 1838), dam of the imported mare Ardan (1001).

Tooreen Ross was a 13.3hh grey stallion foaled in 1954 out of Wayfarer (Ire 1210), another mare without a recorded pedigree. At four years old he was bought by the CPBS and included on their stallion list for five years, during which time he sired the imported stallion Cregmore Dun (Ire 223) and the imported mare Renvyle Rebel (1002). He was subsequently purchased by Mrs Duff in 1965 and exported to Britain, however it is considered that he was quite under-used

---

1 R4 p157, R5 p98, R7 p73

Chapter 3   Innishgoill laddie – Tooreen Laddie Line

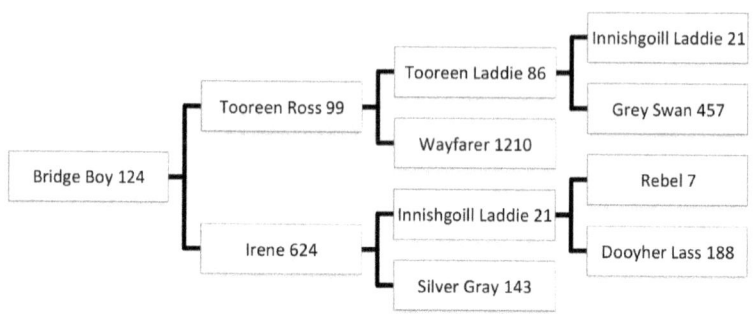

Bridge Boy (Ire 124) in 1974

as a sire after his export.[2] Tooreen Ross further influenced the Australian studbook through two sons, Bridge Boy (Ire 124) and Tulira Mairtin (Ire 214).

Bridge Boy (Ire 124), foaled under a bridge in 1959, was a grey stallion of 14.2hh (recorded as 138cm in the Danish studbook which appears to be more accurate than the Irish listing) bred by the Geoghegans of Oughterard out of their favourite mare Irene (Ire 624). Irene did well for the Geoghegans in the showring, but rewarded them even more fruitfully as an excellent broodmare. Bridge Boy had a powerful presence, which earned him wins in the stallion class at Clifden in 1963 over MacDara (Ire 91) and Carna Dun (Ire 89), in 1965, 1967 and 1969. He always put on quite a 'display' for the watching crowd, requiring a handler on either side to lead him, and remained with his breeders until 1976 when at seventeen years of age he was sold and exported to Denmark.[3]

Bridge Boy has provided Australia with quite a legacy, being the sire of the imported stallions Tulira Colman (7), Garafin Boy (28) and Glory Boy (31); the iiu stallion Connemara Park Seumas (3); and of the imported mares Sweet Sue (1012) and Boffin Heron (1051). He further influenced the studbook through his son Marco Polo of Clonkeehan (Ire 236) and through the English-bred son of Tulira Colman (7), Calmore Swagman (UK 5329).

---

2   R3 p111, R4 p160, R5 p140, R6 p65
3   R3 p131 159, R4 p162 204, R5 p187 272, R6 p64, R47:2

Chapter 3   Innishgoill laddie – Tooreen Laddie Line

Marco Polo of Clonkeehan (Ire 236) was a grey stallion of 13.2hh, foaled in 1966 and out of Canrower Lass (Ire 1977). Canrower Lass was by Carna Bobby (Ire 79) and out of Speculation (Ire 295), a mare with no dam recorded but by the half-Thoroughbred sire Adventure (Ire 11). Pat Lyne described Canrower Lass as a plain mare, but she produced well as a broodmare and was the dam of Pat's exceptional foundation mare Arctic Moon (Ire 2377).[4] Marco Polo is represented in Australia by his iiu daughter Coomel Prima Donna (1043).

Marco Polo of Clonkeehan (Ire 236)

Calmore Swagman (UK 5329) in England

Calmore Swagman (UK 5329) was a 14.2hh grey stallion foaled in 1970 and bred by Eileen Thomas of the Calmore Stud in Britain. He was by the Australian import Tulira Colman (7) and out of Scarteen of Calmore (UK 12600), dam of another Australian import, the mare Macaroon of Calmore (1079). Before being exported to France in 1975, Swagman left fourteen registered progeny, including the stallion Hinton Bush Law (UK 6765) who has, in turn, produced a number of prize-winning performance ponies in Britain.[5] Calmore Swagman is represented in Australia by his daughter Eaden Calypso (1150).

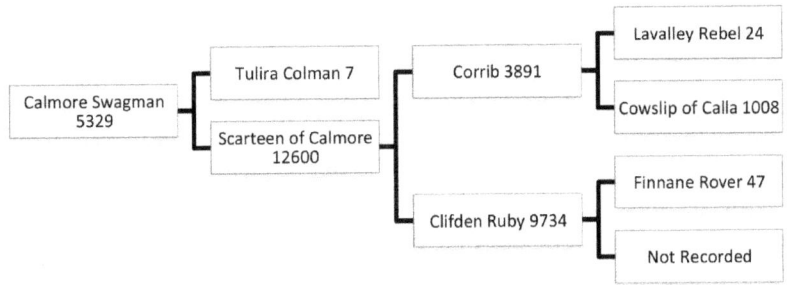

---

4 R4 p227, R5 p91
5 R5 p25 234, R7 p57 79

Chapter 3   Innishgoill laddie – Tooreen Laddie Line

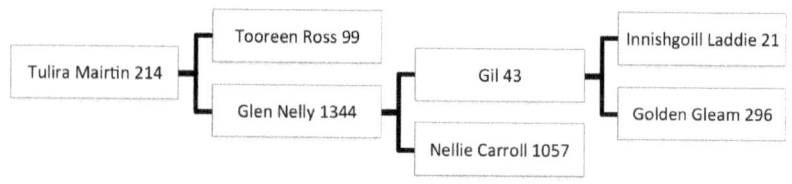

Tulira Mairtin (Ire 214)

Glen Nelly with Tulira Mairtin at foot.

Tooreen Ross's third son to influence our studbook, **Tulira Mairtin (Ire 214)**, was a grey stallion of 13.1hh foaled in 1965. He was bred by Lady Anne Hemphill of the Tulira Stud in Gort, Co. Galway. Lady Hemphill grew up with a love for Connemara ponies and hunting in particular. Although home-schooled in her youth, she recalls that much of her time was actually spent at the stables! Her first Connemara pony was an unregistered mare named 'Peggy', who had 'done everything'. Performance ability was always a top priority for Lady Hemphill, and this is reflected in the ponies that she bred.

Mairtin's dam, Glen Nelly (Ire 1344), and another mare Star of Fahy (Ire 1453), were bought by Lady Hemphill from film producer John Huston, and these two mares formed the foundation of the Tulira Stud. Lady Hemphill describes Glen Nelly as having been a lovely, quality mare with a wonderful temperament. She says that John had shown Glen Nelly and that she had often won. Mairtin himself was never shown. As a two-year-old he was brought in from the field and put in a stable when the vet was coming for a visit. Mairtin promptly jumped through a glass window, cutting himself badly which resulted in scarring.

He did, however, breed very well for the Hemphills and produced stallion sons as well as many daughters. One son, Tulira Finn MacCool (Ire 715)

Chapter 3   Innishgoill laddie – Tooreen Laddie Line

Tulira Nimble Dick (Ire 426)

out of Tulira Heather (Ire 4851), proved to be very successful in-hand, including being sashed champion stallion at Clifden in 1991.[6] Mairtin appears in the Australian studbook as the sire of the imported stallion Cregmore Galway (62); the imported mares Tulira Grainne(1111), Tulira Fuchsia (1131), Tulira Silver Gull (1193) and Tulira Mary Lou (1157); and the iiu mare Barwidgee Aran (1088). He further influences our studbook through his son Tulira Nimble Dick (Ire 426).

Tulira Nimble Dick (Ire 426) was a 14hh grey stallion foaled in 1970 out of Noreen Grey (Ire 2287). He was sold to Germany after passing his classification in Ireland, and was a very successful sports pony and sire there. Nimble Dick was described by Beatrice Milleder as "a great character; a charming pony and I will always remember his wonderful head with those dark and friendly eyes – those eyes that you luckily can find in all his progeny."[7] He is represented in the Australian studbook by his imported daughter Tulira Aileen (1115).

Lady Anne Hemphill, 8 years old, riding Peggy at her first hunt meet, with Paddy Daly (John Daly's father) riding a Thoroughbred.

---

6 R3 p199, R5 p29, R39:1
7 R36:3

Chapter 4

Lavalley Rebel Line

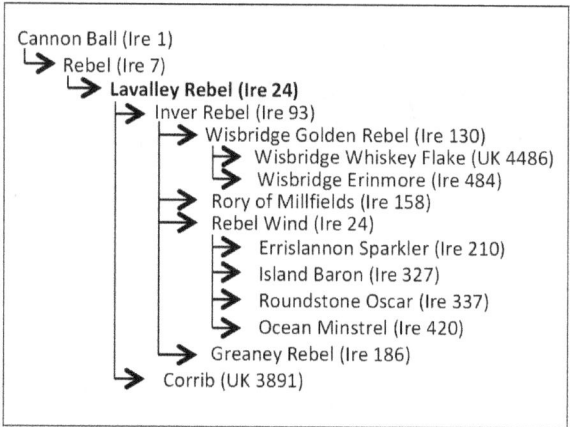

Returning again to earlier branches of Cannon Ball's stallion family, we find that Rebel's second son to produce a family influential in the Australian herd was **Lavalley Rebel (Ire 24)**. A grey stallion standing 13.2hh, Lavalley Rebel was bred in 1935 by Pat Flaherty. His dam was the Clifden class-winning mare Derrada Fanny (Ire 182), who has no pedigree recorded.[1] Lavalley Rebel was bought as a foal by the CPBS to raise as a stallion prospect. He duly passed his classification and remained on their stallion list until 1949. While owned by the CPBS, he worked hard in harness as well as performing stud duties on his routes. He had quality and presence and won the stallion class at the annual pony show at Carna in 1944 and 1946.

In 1949 Lavalley Rebel was purchased by the Meades of the Leam Stud and travelled to Britain where he proved to be a very popular and successful sire. His most lauded progeny was probably his daughter Finola of Leam (Ire 3036), dam of the stallions Leam Bobby Finn (Ire 297) and Coosheen Finn (Ire 381) and of the Australian imports, the stallion Abbeyleix Finbar (93), and mare Abbeyleix Fiona (1151).[2] Lavalley Rebel's direct stallion line influence in Australia is through his Irish son Inver Rebel (93), and his British son Corrib (UK 3891).

Foaled in 1950, **Inver Rebel (Ire 93)** was a grey stallion of 13.3hh, out of Inver Bridge (Ire 459) who has no recorded pedigree. He is another stallion to have been purchased as a foal from his breeders, the Mulkerrins, and raised by the CPBS. He passed classification and remained with the society until thirteen

---

1 R3 p41
2 R3 p63, R4 p153, R5 p17, R7 p11 26, R22:2, R36:2

Chapter 4   Lavalley Rebel Line

years of age when he was sold. Pat Lyne states that "he was a prolific stock getter and stamped his progeny with many of the truest and best Connemara characteristics."[3]

The remarkable impact of Carna Bobby on the Australian herd is well-known but it could easily be argued that Inver Rebel's influence easily matches, if not exceeds it. He is represented directly in the Australian studbook by his imported daughter Ardan (1001), one of our most influential foundation ponies. Four of Inver Rebel's sons have influenced our studbook through their progeny. Rory of Millfields (Ire 158) and Greaney Rebel (Ire 186) contribute to the Australian studbook directly, and Rebel Wind (Ire 24) and Wisbridge Golden Rebel (Ire 130) continue the stallion line toward Australian imports through their sons.

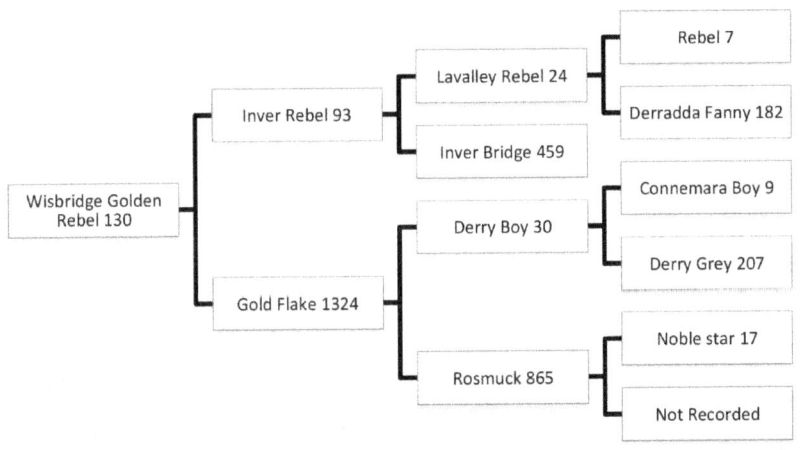

Wisbridge Golden Rebel (Ire 130)

Wisbridge Golden Rebel (Ire 130) was a 13.2hh buckskin stallion born in 1967.

He was bred by Thomas Conroy of Rosmuck from his roan mare Gold Flake (Ire 1324). Golden Rebel was bought by the CPBS as a yearling but sold as a two-year-old to Pat Piercy of the Wisbridge Stud in England. He is said to have been quite nervy when he arrived from

3 R4 p160

Ireland, but after settling in became renowned for his gentle and reliable nature. He did very well in the showring, both in-hand and under saddle, including winning the Leam Cup in 1962 and the Snowball Cup in 1969, but was probably under-used as a stud stallion due to his colour and the risk of producing a blue-eyed-cream (BEC) foal.[4]

Wisbridge Golden Rebel is represented in the Australian studbook by his imported daughter Emerald Cornelian (1048), and also through two sons, Wisbridge Whiskey Flake (UK 4486) and Wisbridge Erinmore (Ire 484).

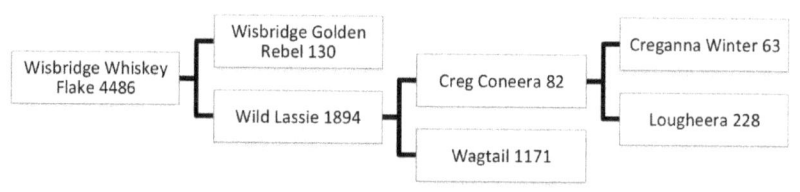

Wisbridge Whiskey Flake (UK 4486) was a 13.2hh buckskin stallion bred in 1964 by Mrs Piercy out of her mare Wild Lassie (Ire 1894). Whiskey Flake was sold by Mrs Piercy, who regarded him very highly, to the Bigger family of Keymark Stud as a four-year-old. In 1974 Mrs Bigger described him as "a very kind pony with good conformation and movement, producing lovely foals,"[5] and Pat Parker also remarked on his temperament and his beautiful head in a Connemara Chronicle article.[6] He always ran out with his mares, and his progeny did well in-hand, under saddle and in harness. Whiskey Flake lived to nineteen years of age and is represented in the Australian studbook by his imported daughter High Trees Kerry Blue (1083).[7]

---

4 R5 p21 30, R7 p37 54, R36:2
5 R13:1
6 R15:2
7 R23:1, R7 p56

Chapter 4　　　　　　　Lavalley Rebel Line

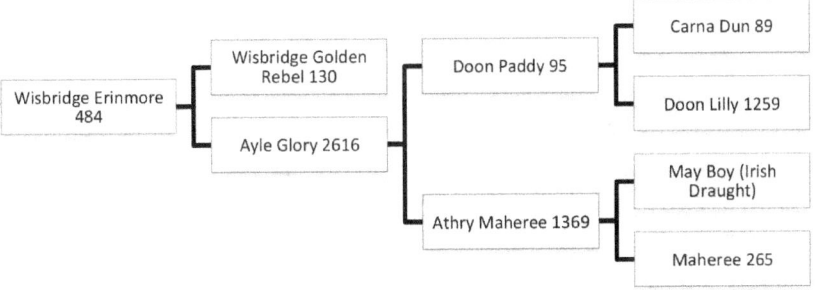

Wisbridge Golden Rebel's second son of interest is **Wisbridge Erinmore (Ire 484)**, a 13.3hh bay who was foaled in 1967 and lived to the remarkable age of thirty-eight! His dam, Ayle Glory (Ire 2616), travelled from Ireland to England as a two-year-old, and also lived to the good age of thirty-one. As a weanling, Erinmore was bought from his breeder by Mrs Piercey, the owner of his sire. She began showing him as a yearling, and he did very well in-hand including winning youngstock champion and reserve supreme champion at the BCPS Breed Show as a three-year-old. He was then purchased by Valentine Richardson of the Hungry Hall Stud to replace Snowball (UK 2941) who had died, and was never sold on.

Wisbridge Erinmore (Ire 484)

Photo: Anne Rolinson

Tiercel Mystical winning supreme at the 1996 BCPS Breed Show with Benita Sanders.

Lian Shaw. Shawshot

Erinmore proved to be a very useful pony with an excellent temperament. He was used in harness, as well as under saddle, including carrying the coursing judge all day through winter at the East of England Whippet Coursing Club. His successful progeny included his first foal, Wisbridge Golden Virginia (UK 14305), who proved to be an excellent foundation mare for the Tiercel Stud in England,

Chapter 4   Lavalley Rebel Line

Helen Sloane Photography

Barwidgee Storm with Sue Kelly

and Tiercel Mystical (UK 569) who won Olympia in 1991, was champion broodmare and supreme champion at the BCPS Breed Show in 1996, and was a champion working hunter pony. Erinmore won the Parry Perpetual Trophy for three successive years, being the sire of at least two progeny (out of different mares) gaining most points within the performance scheme, and was a triple premium stallion. He also sired five stallions, including Millfields Commodore (69) who was imported to Australia.[8] Erinmore is further represented in Australia by two iiu daughters Kemill Hill Bridgina (1119) and Connemara Park Maureen (1087).

Rory of Millfields (Ire 158) is Inver Rebel's second son for review and was a 13.2hh chestnut roan foaled in 1959. He was bred by Thomas Conroy and very closely related to Wisbridge Golden Rebel, being out of Gold Rose (Ire 1437), a daughter of Wisbridge Golden Rebel's dam Gold Flake. He was purchased by the CPBS but as they had sufficient Inver Rebel colts at the time, he was sold on to Anne Rolinson of the Millfields Stud through Colonel Bellingham, along with Wisbridge Golden Rebel and some mares to start Pat Piercey's Wisbridge Stud. Rory would have been gelded as he was so closely related to Golden Rebel, but Captain Wyatt, owner of Dukes Stud, needed a teaser for his Thoroughbred mares, and this is where Rory spent most of his life.[9] He was used regularly by Anne over her mares, however, and is described by her as being a very sensible, kind pony who was always easy to handle and of true pony type. He sired wonderful family or pony club ponies, who for the most part were not top show ponies, but inherited his wonderful temperament. One gelding son, Millfields Coronach, was exported to Sweden where he became a top performance pony leading to Anne being awarded the Swedish Breeders Award.

Rory is represented in the Australian studbook by his imported stallion son Millfields Viking (41), his two iiu stallion sons Robinhill Sterling Silver (53) and Cundedin Rory Richard (55), and by his iiu daughter Oakdale Fanny Hill (1064). Interestingly, he also sired the first gelding recorded in our studbook, Barwidgee Storm, who was imported in-utero with Easter Strand (1008)

---

8 R5 p22, R7 p42, R29:1, R33:2, R36:2, R45:1
9 R6 p37, R19:1

Chapter 4   Lavalley Rebel Line

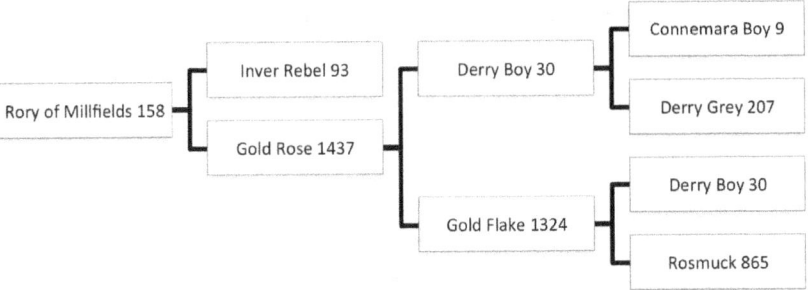

Rebel Wind (Ire 172), Inver Rebel's third son to directly influence the Australian studbook also has an influential family sub-branch. Rebel Wind was a 13hh grey stallion bred by Colman Griffin in 1960 out of his mare Windy (Ire 782). Windy was by the Connemara Boy line stallion Heather Bell (Ire 15) and out of Furnace Lass (Ire 366), a black mare without recorded breeding, owned by Colman's father Martin. Windy won her class at Clifden twice, was a hard working farm pony, and an excellent broodmare who, like Bridge Boy's dam Irene, created a dynasty in Connemara Pony breeding through her eleven registered progeny.[10] Rebel Wind was purchased by the CPBS in 1963 and served them very well, producing three hundred and thirty-four registered progeny before his death from ragwort poisoning in 1978.

Rebel Wind (Ire 172) in his twilight years

Marble (Ire 254)

Rebel Wind was not an outstanding performer in the showring, but he is renowned for his true native pony character, his intelligence and kindness, and for the consistency of his progeny – many of his daughters proving to be excellent broodmares. His most famous son would be Marble (Ire 254), who won the stallion class, was reserve champion of the show and also won the ridden class at Clifden in 1973 before being sold and exported to Denmark where his influence has proven to be quite remarkable.

---

10   R3 p102, R4 p219

Chapter 4 — Lavalley Rebel Line

Rebel Wind is represented directly in the studbook by his imported to New Zealand daughter Windward (1196), and further through his sons Errislannon Sparkler (Ire 210), Island Baron (Ire 327), Roundstone Oscar (Ire 337) and Ocean Minstrel (Ire 420).

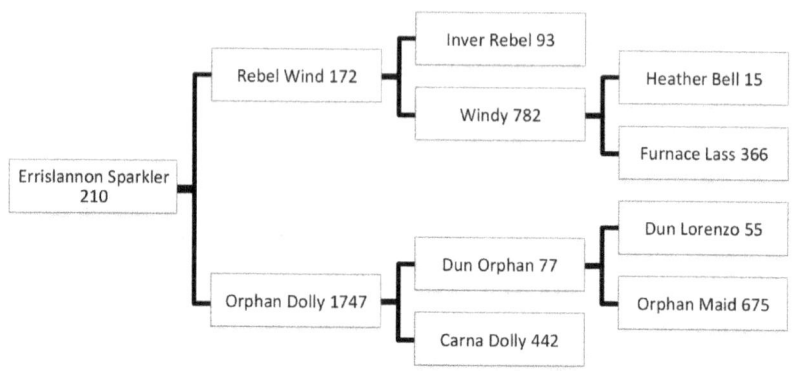

Errislannon Sparkler (Ire 210) was a grey stallion of 13hh foaled in 1965 out of Orphan Dolly (Ire 1747) who shares the same dam as Carna Bobby, Carna Dolly. Errislannon Sparkler was bred by the Mulkerrin family and taken to Maam Cross Fair, where he was spotted by Stephanie Brooks of Errislannan Manor. After some reassurance from her friend Pam Forman, one of the original English breeders, that he indeed had stallion potential, Stephanie purchased the colt. He was taken home to Errislannan on Guy Fawkes Day. On his arrival the children showed their sparklers to the new colt through the gate of his yard – hence his name 'Sparkler'. Stephanie describes Sparkler as having been "very nice and easy". The Brooks put him in the furthest field on the property, and neighbours added their mares for a day or two if they wanted a foal by him. Unfortunately he began to jump out into the neighbour's cabbages, so

Errislannon Sparkler (Ire 210)

Errislannon Diamante competing under saddle in England for Millfields Stud

Chapter 4 Lavalley Rebel Line

he was sold, but the Errislannon Stud retained his line through his daughters.

Errislannon Sparkler's most decorated progeny is the mare Errislannon Diamante (Ire 2026). She was winner of the four year old mare class and reserve champion 'Best Pony Bred in Connemara and Exhibited by an Owner Resident in Connemara' at Clifden in 1977. After being sold to Anne Rolinson of Millfields Stud in England, Diamante continued on her winning ways. At the 1984 BCPS Breed Show she won the mature broodmare class, the Fred Unwin Cup for best mare with foal at foot, and her filly foal won the Hindon Cup for best foal.[11]

Sparkler has left quite a mark on our studbook through his imported son Errislannon Spartan (30) (a full-brother to Errislannon Diamante); his two iiu sons Toorigal Danny Boy (33) and Millfields March Winds (48); and two imported daughters Errislannon Alainn (1027) and Errislannon Cailin (1029).

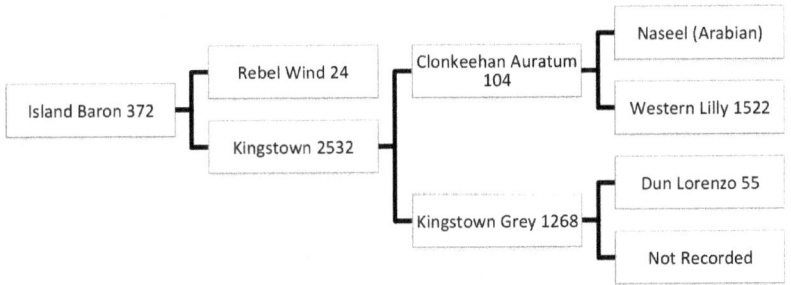

Rebel Wind's second son to directly influence our studbook is **Island Baron (Ire 327)**, a 13.2hh grey stallion bred by Joe Gorham in 1967. Island Baron was out of a buckskin mare named Kingstown (Ire 2532), who is listed in the CPBSA studbook as being by Doon Paddy (Ire 95), but was found by Pat Lyne to be by Clonkeehan Auratum (Ire 104).[12] John Daly purchased him as a yearling, hence his 'Island' prefix and his siring of the imported Irish mare

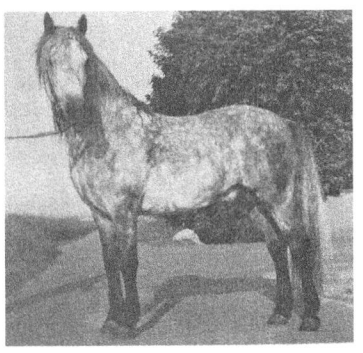

Island Baron (Ire 327)

Photo: Milleder Archive

---

11 R24:2, R45:2
12 R5 p286

Kingstown (Ire 2532)

Roundstone River (Ire 4746) Clifden 1974

Easter Journey (1022). He was subsequently sold as a young pony to Jan-Harald Koelichen, Germany's first Connemara pony breeder.

Roundstone Oscar (Ire 337), Rebel Wind's third son of interest to us, was a cream buckskin foaled in 1968 and standing 13.3hh. His dam, Dancing Spanner (Ire 1750) has no dam recorded in the CPBSA studbook. She was one of ten mares by the Thoroughbred sire Little Heaven that passed classification and were registered as purebred. Roundstone Oscar was on the CPBSA approved stallions list from 1973 to 1977, and produced one registered stallion son, Ballinaboy Barry (Ire 655).

William Diamond showed Oscar at Clifden in 1974 and 1975, and on both occasions he came in second place in the 'Registered Stallion for Service in Connemara' class. Also in 1974, Oscar's full-sister Roundstone River (Ire 4746) won her class and the Clonkeehan Cup for 'Best Connemara Pony Bred in Connemara and Exhibited by Owner', and also the Jan Harald Perpetual Challenge Cup for the best registered pony in the show.

In 1977 Roundstone Oscar was sold to the Bar S Ranch in Canada to improve the owner's Quarter Horses. Three purebred mares followed him and together they have left their mark both in Canada and the United States with progeny being noted for their temperament and trainability.[13] Oscar is represented in the Australian studbook by his iiu son Yarraman Park Toby (94), his imported daughter Diamonds (1146) and his iiu daughter Yarraman Park Sugar (1168).

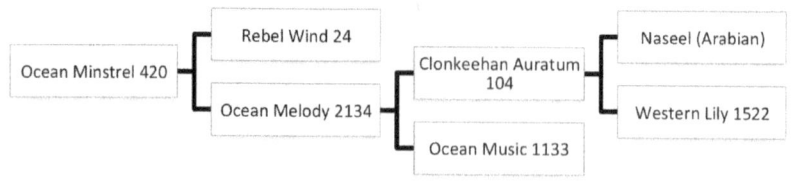

---

13 R3 p169, R4 p188, R5 p134 235 271

Chapter 4 Lavalley Rebel Line

Ocean Minstrel (Ire 420) is the last of Rebel Wind's sons to be represented in Australia. A grey stallion of 13.2hh, he was foaled in 1969 out of Ocean Melody (Ire 2134), winner of the Killanin Cup at the 1962 Clifden Show and the RDS Silver Medal in 1964. At nine years of age, Ocean Minstrel was given to the CPBS by his breeder Graham Tulloch for the 1978 season after they had so tragically lost his sire. One year later, the CPBS exchanged Ocean Minstrel for Thunderbolt (Ire 178), as they wished to regain a representative of the Mountain Lad line. Ocean Minstrel did not produce a large number of progeny, but one daughter, Ballinaboy Mermaid (Ire 6952), won the Carrew Cup as a two-year-old at Clifden in 1978.[14] He sired the imported Australian mare Ashfield Bay Sparrow (1113)

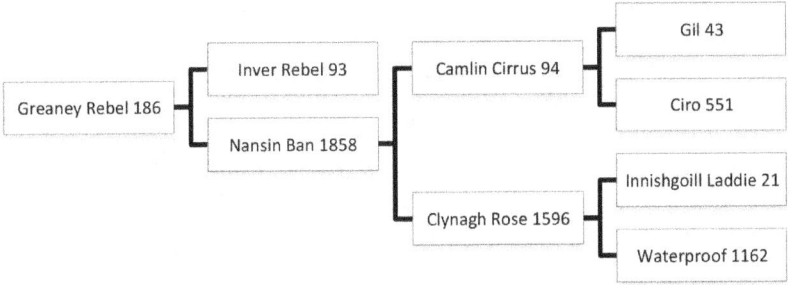

Greaney Rebel (Ire 186), the last of Inver Rebel's sons for review, was a grey stallion of 14hh foaled in 1963. His pedigree shows his dam line tracing back to Waterproof (Ire 1162), who has no dam recorded, but was by the Black Paddy (Ire 8) line stallion, Airgead (Ire 45), who we do not often see in our Connemara pedigrees. Greaney Rebel was registered by Martin Macnamara of Co. Clare and won the stallion class at Clifden in 1968.

Greaney Rebel (Ire 186)

He was then sold to Henry Whyte of Galway with whom he remained and won the confined class at Clifden in 1979 at sixteen years of age.[15] Greaney Rebel is represented in the Australian studbook by his iiu son County Clare Mickey (21), and by his imported daughters Irish Mist (1026) and Derryowen Seagull (1145).

---

14 R3 p131 170, R12 p4
15 R3 p128 170 177 187, R5 Preface, R6 p65

Chapter 4 Lavalley Rebel Line

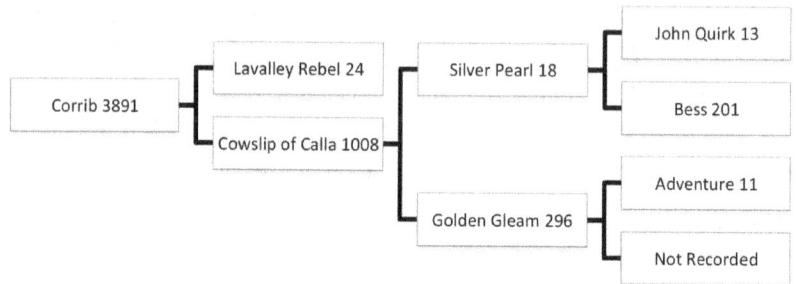

Corrib (UK 3891)

We return now to the second son of Lavalley Rebel to directly influence our studbook. **Corrib (UK 3891)**, a grey from buckskin stallion of 14.1hh, was foaled in 1956 and lived until 1982. He was bred by one of the first Connemara breeders in England, Eileen Thomas of the Calmore Stud. Eileen initially bought her Connemara ponies from Cynthia Spottiswoode, who introduced the breed (as a registered pony rather than an Irish saddle pony or showjumper) to Britain, to be used in Eileen's family's holiday home and riding school for children. One pony, Cowslip of Calla (Ire 1008), was a mare with quality and presence and was very well regarded by both Cynthia and Eileen. When Eileen set up her own farm, Cowslip became her foundation mare.

Cowslip has an interesting pedigree, being out of the mare Golden Gleam (Ire 296), noted previously as producing the stallion Gil (Ire 43). Cowslip was sent to Lavalley Rebel (Ire 24) in 1955, and the resulting foal, Corrib, became Calmore's resident sire. Corrib has been described by Susan Bowen, who lived and worked at Calmore, as having free, straight action, bone, great kindness, a lovely 'pony' head and – so necessary in a running stallion – courage."[16] He was a pony of great character with an affection for the pigs bred by Eileen, and a great reputation for successfully breeding difficult mares, which he always paddock-served. Corrib remained at Calmore until Eileen's health deteriorated when he was sent 'on loan' to Scotland, living there for a couple more years.[17] He is represented in Australia by his iiu son Glenormiston O'Neill Clanaboy (86).

---

16 R1 p53
17 R3 p27, R4 p175, R5 p67, R7 p27, R11, R17:1

Chapter 5

Calla Rebel Line

Cannon Ball (Ire 1)
↳ Rebel (Ire 7)
   ↳ **Calla Rebel (Ire 38)**
      ↳ Strongbow (Ire 90)

The last of Rebel's three sons to have a direct line influence on the Australian studbook was the 13.3hh grey stallion **Calla Rebel (Ire 38)**. He was bred by Val Keaney in 1938 from the mare Calla Roan (Ire 196), who has no dam recorded but was by the second stallion to be entered in the CPBS studbook, Charlie (Ire 2). Calla Rebel was purchased by the CPBS as a foal, and later worked as a farm pony for his custodians, pulling the plough as well as performing stud duties. At seventeen years of age he was sold on to Thomas Fahy, who had cared for him as a custodian from 1941 to 1947 and who kept him for a further ten years before selling him on as a teaser in his last years.[1] Calla Rebel's influence on our studbook is through his son Strongbow (Ire 90).

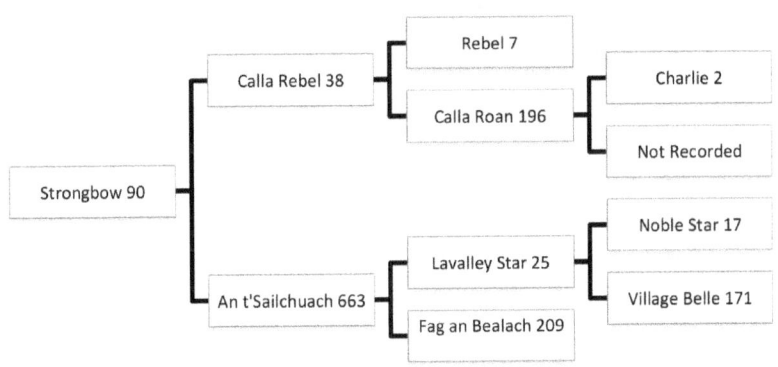

---

1 R4 p154

Chapter 5 — Calla Rebel Line

Atlantic Breeze winning her class at the 1965 Royal Dublin Show

CPBS Studbook Irish Times Photo

Strongbow (Ire 90)

Photo: Milleder Archive

Strongbow (Ire 90) was a 13.3hh black stallion foaled in 1949 from the Black Paddy line mare An t'Sailchuach (Ire 663). An t'Sailchuach produced four registered progeny in total, all by different stallions. One daughter by Carna Bobby was the well-decorated Atlantic Breeze (Ire 2174). Another, by Dun Aengus (Ire 120), was Forest Flower (Ire 2692), dam of the imported stallion Inis O'Hara imp (29).

Strongbow was also bought by the CPBS as a foal, but sold to the Cloghran Stud in Dublin to work as a teaser as a two-year-old after he passed classification.[2] Later in his life, he was purchased by Frances Lee Norman of the Clonkeehan Stud in Slane. His fertility by this time was poor, however, and he left few progeny in Ireland before being exported to Germany in his twentieth year.[3] He also left few progeny in Germany, and his owner subsequently purchased a Strongbow son, Moyglare Samson (Ire 329), who covered a few mares in southern Germany. Interestingly, it was noted by Strongbow and Samson's owner that neither stallion liked to serve grey mares! An additional stallion son of Strongbow is our Australian import, Clonkeehan Archer (15).

---

2 R47:3
3 R3 p79, R4 p161, R5 p165, R23:2

Part 3

Cannon Ball Stallion Families in Australia

Tulira Colman (7) ridden by Sue Kelly

Chapter 6
The Imported Cannon Ball Line Stallions

In the previous chapter we have traced Cannon Ball's stallion line from Cannon Ball himself to the sires from this line imported to Australia. In the following chapters we shall see how our imported and iiu stallions fared in establishing their own family lines in Australia. Twenty-eight stallions in total, including eighteen imported stallions: Island King (1), Tulira Colman (7), Clonkeehan Archer (15), Cregmore Dun (IRE 223), Lydican Dun (22), Garafin Boy (28), Errislannon Spartan (30), Glory Boy (31), Millfields Viking (41), Millfields March Winds (48), Cregmore Galway (62), Millfields Commodore (69), Sydserff Brig-O-Doon (83), Mylerstown Huckleberry Finn (89), Abbeyleix Finbar (93), Millfields Cabin Boy (99), Tiercel Galloping Major (103) and Atlantic Rebel (107); and ten iiu stallions: Connemara Park Seumas (3), County Clare Mickey (21), Toorigal Danny Boy (33), Blandings Bobby (44), Robinhill Sterling Silver (53), Cunderdin Rory Richard (55), Green Hills Rebel (56), Glenormiston O'Neill Clanaboy (86), Yarraman Park Toby (94), and Shelford Downs Berwick Boy (96) originate from this line. Chapter 7 of Part 3 is devoted to our first import, Island King, and the following four chapters are divided into stallion lines as set out in Part 2: Inishgoill Laddie – Gil line; Inishgoill Laddie – Tooreen Laddie line; Lavalley Rebel line and Calla Rebel line.

Island King (1) in Ireland preparing for his voyage to Australia.

Photo: Scorpio

Chapter 7
The Island King Family

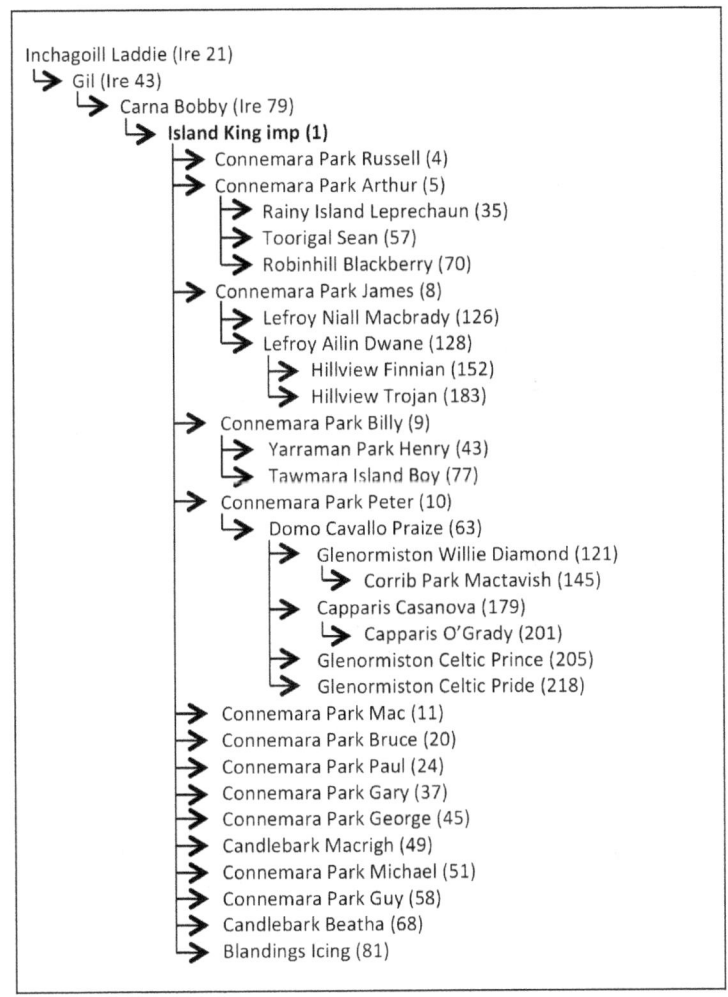

Chapter 7   The Island King Family

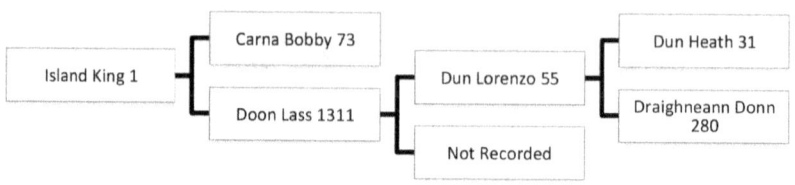

Island King (1)

Photo: Pastoral Review

Australia's first import, **Island King (1)**, was bred in 1958 by Thomas Burke of Doonreaghaun, Ireland. He was a grey stallion, stood 13.3hh and was by the society-owned stallion Carna Bobby (Ire 79). His dam, Doon Lass (Ire 1311), was a small mare kept and used by Thomas in the typical manner of single pony owners in Connemara at the time: she bred a foal to be sold at Maam Cross Fair each year, was regularly used as a pack pony to carry items such as peat, seaweed or hay over the rough terrain of the local mountainside in baskets, as well as being Thomas's only form of transport.[1]

Thomas sold Island King as a weanling, and he was subsequently purchased by John Daly of Lough Mask who bought and sold many Connemara ponies. He registered the stallions with the 'Island' prefix (Island King being the first with the prefix) and the mares with 'Easter'. Each stallion had his own island in the lough and herd of mares. The stallions were swum to islands behind a row boat and the mares were ferried standing in a flat-bottomed turf boat!

In 1963 an Irish-born veterinarian from Victoria, Fred Wiltshire, began searching for suitable ponies for his children to ride. Memories of riding 'do anything, go anywhere' ponies in the west of Ireland while on holidays as a child led Fred to write to an Irish cousin, Hugh O'Donnel, detailing the type of pony he desired. Island King was quickly found, purchased, and imported to Australia.

Island King made this journey as 'deck cargo', confined to a single-stall wooden

---

1 R5 p136

Chapter 7   The Island King Family

box with a door at the front for feeding and watering, and one at the back for removal of manure. On his arrival, Fred, who was by all accounts quite charismatic and had a way with the press, secured a story and photo of the event in The Age newspaper. Island King was the first stallion to be owned by the Wiltshires and became a firm family favourite. Fred's son, Ken Wiltshire, described him as: "Strong without being coarse, a marvelous mover, and above all [having] an excellent temperament. He stamped his progeny unmistakably regardless of the breeding of the mare involved."[2] He became a very popular sire, and attracted visiting mares of all shapes and sizes, despite his stud fee of sixty pounds, when the average charge for a pony stallion at the time was about fifteen pounds.[3] Island King sired fifteen purebred stallions, however ultimately only two of these have left lasting stallion families in Australia as can be viewed in his stallion line chart (p45). He is also represented by thirteen purebred daughters: Connemara Park Ann (105), Connemara Park Sally (1006), Barwidgee Frederika (1025), Connemara Park Mary (1031), Blandings Lamington (1066), Connemara Park Margaret (1077), Connemara Park Trudi (1098), Connemara Park Leonie (1099), Connemara Park Joybelle (1132), San Ed Cara (1134), Candlebark Eamhair (1135), Toorigal Emma (1136) and Blandings Agapanthus (1138).

Of his many exceptional partbred offspring, Macushla, out of a Thoroughbred mare, did particularly well for Helen Marshall, winning many championships in ridden and led show classes and O'Shea was an outstanding pony club and eventing competitor in South Australia. Kildare was initially ridden and competed in dressage with Annie Creighton (nee Wiltshire) before Ken Wiltshire took over the ride, winning the novice section of the Melbourne Three Day Event in 1973. He was sold to Raymond Thomas, becoming an A grade showjumper with national level wins.

Kildare (Island King x TB)

Connemara Park Arthur (5): Island King's first stallion son for review, Connemara Park Arthur, was foaled in 1969 out of Australia's first imported mare, Ardan (1001), and stood 13.0½hh.

Connemara Park Arthur (5) at the Sydney Royal Show

2 R1 p6
3 R1 p5-9, R13, R5 p136, R6 p23 45 90, R3 p113 139

Chapter 7 — The Island King Family

Helen Sloane Photography

Connemara Park Arthur at the Australian Connemara and Native Pony Festival at Bowral.

Arthur was purchased by Di Cumming, who used him as her stud sire for the Robinhill Stud in New South Wales, as well as showing him successfully both in-hand and under saddle. He was particularly successful in preliminary and novice dressage, either winning or placing highly in classes of up to fifty entries.

When Robinhill Stud was dispersed in 1979, Arthur was sold to Rose Rushton of the Chittering Gully Stud in Bargo. Rose wrote of Arthur in the June 1983 Hoofs and Horns magazine: "I remember the first time I saw Arthur trotting out under saddle, with grey dapples, black stockings and his white tail catching the last of the setting sun's rays, as the late Di Cumming rode him at Scone. It was my husband Vic who insisted on buying him. I didn't particularly want a stallion at that time but I had to admit he was beautiful! So began our association with one of the most generous natured horses we have known. Of course we had to show him (he was eleven years at the time) and he took with obvious delight the rugs, hoods and umpteen dozen baths needed before each show. His favourite colour was mud! Yes, he was a great success including royals and nationals, but there is more to him than 'just beauty'. Arthur has a sense of fun that doesn't always match mine! At Castle Hill show we entered him for the Connemara Jump and after a terrific build-up on how Connies jump, we went in. He loves jumping and will take anything – well almost. The first jump was a blue and green pole all of six inches off the ground. He acted as though it was a snake ready to strike and refused to even walk over it. I wished the earth would open up and swallow us and I swear to this day he was grinning from ear to ear as we left the ring. On the other hand Arthur is very gentle. A hen and a dozen new chicks took up residence in his stable, running riot while poor Arthur stayed in one corner. When his feed was put in he would gently nudge chickens away before gingerly walking over to his feed bin. All twelve survived to become adults."

This, interestingly, was not the first time Arthur had shown a gentleness towards baby birds as Di Cumming wrote in a 1977 CPBSA newsletter: "I thought readers might be interested to hear a little story about our Connemara stallion. For the past few years a pair of swallows have built a nest in the rafters in the middle of his box. He usually stands directly underneath it, to the detriment of his rug! He accepts with little interest

Chapter 7   The Island King Family

the comings and goings of the parent birds and the cries of the young for food. His attention is only aroused when a dog or cat dares to venture into his territory – behavior much appreciated by the birds. The other morning, attracted by frantic bird noises in that vicinity, I went to investigate and found a young bird, not yet ready to fly, had fallen from the nest and was flopping about on Arthur's back with its parents swooping distractedly. He, usually so active, remained quite still while I rescued the bird and returned it to its nest and its frantic parents. Then with a look that seemed to say 'that's settled that then' he shook himself and trotted out into his paddock."

Arthur is represented by three stallion sons: Rainy Island Leprechaun (35), Toorigal Sean (57) and Robinhill Blackberry (70), however no breeding stock progeny were produced from any of these stallions. Fortunately, fourteen purebred daughters by Arthur are also recorded, these being Barwidgee Discus (1160), Robinhill Blueberry (1174), Shelford Downs Royal Star (1178), Robinhill Silver Jubilee (1182), Toorigal Melody (1207), Rainy Island Song of Joy (1282), Mitchell Connemara Ma-Ria Park (1290), Chittering Gully Fantasy (1328), Chittering Gully Cameo (1351), Chittering Gully Guinevere (1352), Chittering Gully Windsong (1377), Chittering Gully Sweet Whisper (1454), Bergerrone (1492) and the bred-up mare Robinhill Reverie (2B/020).

Robinhill Lara
(Connemara Park Arthur x TB)

Arthur also sired some exceptional partbreds, including the Thoroughbred cross, Robinhill Lara, and Robinhill Timoshay who was out of an Anglo-Arab mare. Lara won many champion and supreme champion sashes in both in-hand and ridden events, and was also awarded the CPBSA's Partbred Connemara of the Year title in 1984. Timoshay led a very full life as a pony club mount, and competed in showing, eventing and dressage before moving on to Riding for the Disabled in Canberra where he was in high demand as a favourite mount.

Rainy Island Leprechaun (35)

Rainy Island Leprechaun (35), out of Easter Sparkle imp (1007), **Toorigal Sean (57)**, out of Errislannon Columbine imp (1023) and **Robinhill**

Chapter 7 The Island King Family

Tracey Smith sits on Toorigal Sean (57), held by Irene Smith.

Connemara Park James (8) at the 1974 Perth Royal Show

Lefroy Ailin Dwane (128) at the Perth Royal

Blackberry (70), out of Barwidgee Snowberry (1053) were foaled in 1972, 1974 and 1976 respectively. Leprechaun was purchased by the Amergin Stud at Narangba in Queensland and shown successfully both in-hand and under saddle in Connemara, buckskin and open classes by Julie Pratten. Sean, owned by the Smith family of Nullegai Stud in Queensland, was campaigned successfully at low-level showjumping in open competition by eleven year old Kathy Jeffries. Blackberry, the last of Arthur's stallion sons to be registered, stood at the Carnardan Stud in Rolleston, Queensland, where the focus was on breeding partbreds.

Island King's third stallion son, **Connemara Park James (8)**, foaled in 1968, was a full-brother to Arthur. He was purchased by Marie Thompson, and made the long journey to Western Australia where he produced a number of successful partbreds under the Karingal prefix. In his later years James took up residence with the Wade family of Lefroy Stud. Marnie Wade describes him as having been a real character and a delight. Even as an elderly pony he was spritely and full of himself, but always easy to do anything with. He produced two stallion sons out of Shelford Downs Michelle (1117), Lefroy Niall Macbrady (126) and Lefroy Ailin Dwane (128), and four purebred daughters: Lefroy Keara O'Kindelan (1343), Lefroy Una MacGilna (1481), Lefroy Prudence O'Hederman (1538) and Lefroy Abaigeal Mackilveen (1551). He also sired a number of successful partbreds including Karingal Flying High, who won the preliminary dressage and was tied for first in the novice at the 1976 Western Australian Dressage Championships.

Chapter 7   The Island King Family

Lefroy Niall Macbrady (126), foaled in 1980, is described by Marnie as having excellent conformation, with a lovely head and particularly good hindquarter. He was handled and shown in-hand by Marni from the time he was a foal, and always displayed an excellent temperament and manners. Niall was never sold on, and did not produce any breeding stock progeny.

His full-brother **Lefroy Ailin Dwane (128)** foaled in 1981, had a very successful stud career, after being purchased by Helen Colleran and Tena Rowe of the Hillview Stud at Wattle Grove near Perth. Before using Dwane as a breeding stallion, Helen started him under saddle and in harness, and he attended many dressage clinics in his early saddle career, including one with the late Nuno Oliveira from Portugal. With his superb temperament, he proved to be a wonderful family pony and all-rounder, even being trained to do circus tricks by a local girl. Dwane was campaigned very successfully in the showring, winning champion and supreme champion sashes in Connemara and open APSB classes both in-hand and under saddle.

As a sire, Dwane, in partnership with the mare Kemill Hill Tinka (1155), has produced one of the most successful show and performance Connemara families in Australia. The pair produced two stallion sons, Hillview Finnian (152) and Hillview Trojan (183), and five daughters: Hillview Ailin C'Ait (1482), Hillview Ailin Patrice (1518), Hillview Vallen (1610), Hillview Irish Mist (1643) and Hillview Shevalli (1822). Three of these daughters have won the CPBSA's Connemara Pony of the Year award. The only breeding stock progeny of Dwane not from this pairing is the mare Hillview Little Tori (1658).

Hillview Trojan as a young pony at the Perth Royal Show

When Helen closed her breeding activities, Dwane was gelded and continues to lead an active life as a ridden family pony.

Hillview Finnian (152), foaled in 1990, won his colt classes at both the Perth Royal and the APSB shows in 1992. I have been unable to trace his current whereabouts and he has not left any registered breeding stock progeny.

Hillview Trojan (183) relaxing at home.

His brother **Hillview Trojan (183)**, foaled in 1997, was purchased at six months old from Hillview by Lisa Christy, his current owner. Lisa had been interested in the Connemara Pony since she was a child, attracted by their strength, temperament and jumping ability. At the time of Trojan's purchase, she had been planning on purchasing a Warmblood colt but on seeing Trojan advertised decided that a 'trial run' of colt raising and stallion ownership with a pony would be a good idea. The trial run became permanent! From the time Lisa picked Trojan up from Hillview, she was impressed with his temperament and personality. She describes him as sensible, kind, curious and playful – and a real boy! He loves to jump, and will clear a five foot gate with ease. Lisa supplies him with balls and witches hats to keep him actively entertained in his paddock.

Trojan has done very well in-hand in the showring. His most impressive win would probably be at the 2001 Gidgegannup Agricultural Show where he stood grand champion led APSB pony over the other pony breeds. For a number of years Trojan enjoyed life as a paddock pony while Lisa rebuilt her property after a bushfire, and concentrated on family activities. He currently has no adult registered stallion sons or daughters but a purebred mare, Exmoor Caitlin (1596), was purchased by Lisa and it will be interesting to see what this cross produces.

Connemara Park Billy (9)

Connemara Park Billy (9): The fourth stallion son of Island King was Connemara Park Billy, foaled in 1968, out of the imported mare Noreen Ban (IRE 2355). Billy was purchased and campaigned by Frank Tynan of the County Clare Stud in Thornton, New South Wales, and sired two stallion sons in his stud career, Yarraman Park Henry (43) and Tawmara Island Boy (77). He is further represented in the studbook by five purebred daughters: County Clare Superstar (1041), County Clare Rebel (1067), Yarraman Park Henrietta (1191), Jabiru Jo's Pride (1248) and Yarraman Park Polly (1278).

Yarraman Park Henry (43)

Chapter 7   The Island King Family

Yarraman Park Henry (43) was bred in 1972 by the Mitchells of Yarraman Park Stud in Scone, New South Wales, from the imported mare Katie (1014). As a just-broken two-year-old he travelled to Queensland to become the foundation sire of the Conroy's Shelford Downs Stud near Stanthorpe. Jack and June Conroy's interest in the Connemara pony stemmed from their desire to breed large ponies and small horses with the conformation, temperament, constitution and the all-round ability to excel in any discipline their owner wished to pursue. Henry was described to me by Jack as "not a top horse on looks, but very sound, intelligent and quiet, and could jump across twelve foot. He was also an excellent stockhorse, as were his progeny". He was very well-liked by English author and Connemara Pony breeder and judge Pat Lyne on her tour of Australia in 1980. After the Conroys imported Millfields Commodore (69) Henry was sold on to the Burenda Merino Stud at Orgathella where he was used as a station sire for breeding stockhorses.[4]

Yarraman Park Henry ridden in the indoor arena at Shelford Downs by Jack Conroy.

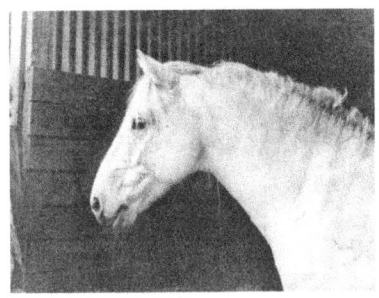

Connemara Park Peter (10)

Henry did not produce any purebred stallion sons, but has four purebred daughters recorded: Shelford Downs Revelation (1141), Shelford Downs Ascension (1175), Shelford Downs Dearliza (1177) and the bred-up mare Moonie Argentina (1225). Two of Henry's memorable partbred daughters were Shelford Downs Sparkle and Shelford Downs Pollyanna. Sparkle won the champion led partbred award at the 1987 Mountain and Moorland Pony Festival held in Brisbane and Shelford Downs Pollyanna was a very successful ridden and led show pony in New South Wales.

Tawmara Island Boy (77), Connemara Park Billy's second stallion son, was foaled in 1974 out of Sweet Sue imp (1012). He was bred by Terry White of the Tawmara Stud in Tasmania and has no breeding stock progeny recorded.

---

4   R5 p146

Chapter 7   The Island King Family

Connemara Park Peter (10) as a young pony.

Domo Cavallo Praize (63)

Domo Cavallo Praize show jumping with John Robertson in the saddle.

Connemara Park Peter (10): Connemara Park Peter stood 14.1½hh and was foaled in 1968 out of Easter Mask imp (1003). He was Island King's fifth stallion son. Peter was purchased by Max Stoliznow of the Domo Cavallo Stud in Crows Nest, New South Wales, who described him in 1983 as having: "proven himself in the showring and, more importantly, through his progeny. A pony of great nature and a beautiful pony to ride, [Peter] has a remarkably quiet temperament and is a pleasure to handle."

Connemara Park Peter is very well-represented in the CPBSA studbook through his one stallion son, Domo Cavallo Praize (63). He is also represented by two purebred daughters, Domo Cavallo Petra (1109) and Toorigal Hannah (1243).

Domo Cavallo Praize (63) was a grey (from buckskin or palomino) stallion of 14.1½hh foaled in 1975 out of Kirtling Haze imp (1028). At eight months of age he was purchased from Max by Dr Barton and Susan Clarke of the Glenormiston Stud and moved to Queensland. Since childhood, Sue had harboured a fascination for Connemara Ponies, and when the Clarkes moved to a property in Brookfield with their young family, they decided that the Connemara was the ideal family pony to breed. During the Clarke's search for foundation mares, however, they happened upon a colt that stole Sue's heart. This was Domo Cavallo Praize, a pony that has made a large impact on the breed, both as a stud stallion, and through his outstanding competitive ability. His contribution to the promotion of the Connemara pony in Australia has been significant.

Chapter 7 The Island King Family

Praize was the first pony to be started under saddle by Sue. He took it in his stride, and an active ridden career followed. He competed successfully in show classes, eventing, dressage, and showjumping. Although his usual partner was John Robertson, Praize also proved to be a well-mannered performer for the Clarke children. In twelve consecutive ODEs he placed in the first three at novice and restricted novice level, winning four of these.

In his in-hand show career, Praize amassed many championships and supremes, and was never beaten at a royal show, competing at Brisbane, Sydney and Melbourne. The 1981 Queensland APSB Show could be seen as his greatest showring success – he won both the supreme champion led stallion of all breeds award, and the supreme champion pony of all breeds under saddle! He also worked well in harness – taking Sue for short trips to the local store and winning harness events.

Domo Cavallo Praize eventing

Sue has described Praize as: "the most wonderful and talented pony that we have ever owned. He loved to jump and would jump anything you aimed him at and his progeny can all jump – he was a superstar! He had a fabulous personality and was totally trustworthy at all times." He remained as part of the Clarke family until thirty years of age when his health began to deteriorate.

Domo Cavallo Praize in harness with Sue and Sophie Clarke

Four stallion sons by Domo Cavallo Praize are recorded in the studbook: Glenormiston Willie Diamond (121), Capparis Casanova (179), Glenormiston Celtic Prince (205) and Glenormiston Celtic Pride (218). He is also represented by thirty-two purebred daughters in the studbook: Glenormiston Katie Corkery (1199), Glenormiston Lillee O'Brien (1233), Glenormiston Birdie O'Loan (1269), Wattle Hills Laurel Wreath (1313), Wattle Hills Primera (1314), Portadown Irish

Glenormiston Patrick with Amelia Hawthorne

Feldale Mouse and Isabel English compete at Quirindi Horse Trials in 2013

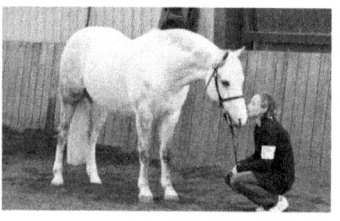

Glenormiston Ciaran shares a quiet moment with Kate Duff at the first Victorian Connemara Pony Showcase.

Glenormiston Clare side saddle

Rose (1412), Glenormiston Diamonds Forever(1420), Wattle Hills Medlar (1434), Wattle Hills Dochas (1435), Wattle Hills Golden Wedding (1436), Glenormiston Laura (1439), Glenormiston Alanna (1440), Glenormiston Abbey Lara (1475), Emerald Valley Revelation (1486), Emerald Valley Pride of Erin(1493), Glenormiston Jessie Diamond (1495), Glenormiston Dolly (1497), Meadowbank Stormgirl (1506), Corrib Park Camilla (1509), Crystal Shannon (1513), Wattle Hills Marde Gras (1524), Carawah Briar Rose (1576), Glenormiston Clonmel (1638), Glenormiston Ballycara (1640), Glenormiston Amelia (1670), Glenormiston Celebration (1672), Glenormiston Ciara (1679), Glenormiston Lauren (1694), Glenormiston Adare (1726), Glenormiston Aislinn (1799), Glenormiston Flashy Diamond (1808) and Glenormiston Rosalie (1809). Praize was a homozygous grey, and as such all of his progeny have been grey.

In addition to his breeding stock progeny, Praize also sired a large number of successful geldings and partbreds. The partbred gelding Kooringa Park Bennelong won many championships in the Galloway hack ring, and competed up to advanced level dressage. Glenormiston Patrick, a purebred gelding of 14.3hh owned and ridden by Amelia Hawthorne, was bought for eventing, but displayed so much bravery and technique that Amelia decided to concentrate on showjumping with him. He competed extensively on the open showjumping circuit up to C grade level and against horses of all sizes. A partbred mare, Michmel Fine Girl, competed successfully in endurance with her owner Teena Cashin, and another partbred mare, Glenormiston Clare, won many championships in the Galloway hack and side-saddle rings.

More recently, Glenormstion Ciaran, a purebred gelding out of Oxenholm Tiffany imp (1268) has taken Victoria by storm with his owner Kate Duff (nee Gardiner). Ciaran attracts attention wherever he is taken, and as well as being an 'all-rounder', has taken home many broad sashes in both led and ridden events up to royal level in open competition. Feldale Mouse, a partbred son out of a Thoroughbred mare, has done exceptionally well in eventing at state and national level with young rider Isabel English.

A number of Praize's progeny have been exported, including three geldings, to the USA and one to Japan. He has one stallion son, Glenormiston Cuchulainn, in the USA, and another, Capparis Casanova, in New Zealand. Four daughters are also in the USA: Glenormiston Amelia, Glenormiston Innisheer, Glenormiston Diamond Lil and Glenormiston Clonmel.[5]

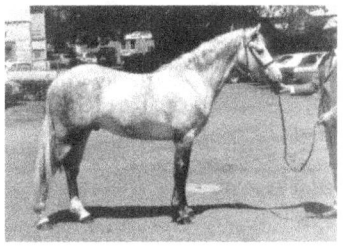

Glenormiston Willie Diamond (121)

Praize's first stallion son, **Glenormiston Willie Diamond (121)**, was foaled in 1982 out of Four of Diamonds imp (1070). He sired one stallion son in 1986, Corrib Park Mactavish (145), but no daughters, and was gelded as a young stallion when his owners moved into the city.

Corrib Park MacTavish (145) was purchased from Sue Clarke as a foal at foot with his dam, Glenormiston Macadamia (1220), by James Crowley of Corrib Park Stud in Biddaddaba, Queensland. Corrib Park was established with the aim of breeding pony club ponies. James believes the Connemara pony, with its all-round ability and temperament, to be ideal in this role. MacTavish passed his classification and was successfully shown, winning the supreme led Connemara Pony award at the 1994 Marburg Show, but was tragically lost to colic a year later without siring any foals.

Corrib Park Mactavish with James Crowley

Capparis Casanova (179) in New Zealand

---

5 R23:5, R25:3, R40:2, R43:4

Chapter 7   The Island King Family

Domo Cavallo Praize's second stallion son, **Capparis Casanova (179)**, was foaled in 1997 out of Glenormiston Rusheen (1620). Wendy and Lloyd Lord of the Capparis Stud at Chinchilla in Queensland purchased Rusheen from Glenormiston Stud in 1996. Before her move to Capparis Rusheen was covered by Praize because Wendy "wanted something special".

Wendy writes of Casanova: "He was sensitive and a little shy to break in, but soon became very, very quiet. When we had beginner riders come to stay, Cas was the obvious choice for them to ride. Matthew started his dressage lessons on him when he was twelve and Cas was four. His instructor, Linda Schmerglatt, was concerned that Matthew was coming to lessons on a stallion – not only for Matthew's safety, but because of the risk of a stallion being loose at a busy equestrian establishment. She soon changed her opinion after Matthew led him past a row of stables and just dropped his reins while he found his halter, then proceeded to take off his bridle and put on the halter in front of a curious line of horse heads poking out of their stables. She laughed and said that her concerns regarding children with stallions obviously didn't apply to this stallion."

Most of Casanova's competition career in Australia was spent in the dressage arena with Wendy's son Matthew, and they gained fifth and sixth place at the 2000 EA state dressage championships in open competition in the pony dressage. As well as this, Casanova was a brilliant and careful jumper, easily jumping 1.2 metres.

Casanova and Matthew had a special bond, and if Matthew whistled, Casanova would gallop across the paddock to him. He often rode Cas in the paddock without saddle or bridle. It was a great wrench for the Lord family when unrelenting drought conditions in south-east Queensland forced the Capparis Stud to reduce numbers. Casanova was too small to be ridden in competition by Matthew at that stage, and the other Lord children were too young to ride him, so rather than have him gelded the Lords put him up for sale, and he was purchased in 2005 by the Casanova Partnership, and exported to his new home in New Zealand.

Capparis O'Grady (201) ridden by Bodesha Robinson

Photo: Chris Ros Photography

Capparis Casanova is represented in the CPBSA studbook by one stallion son, Capparis O'Grady (201), and two purebred daughters, Mungala Anasta (1813) and Aisling Park Tanielle (1841).

Chapter 7 The Island King Family

Capparis O'Grady (201) (Ollie) was foaled in 2005 out of Glengarry Patsy Malone (1536) and purchased as a weanling by Cassie Erceg of Kaycee Stud in Western Australia. When agisting a stallion became difficult and time constraints increased, Ollie was gelded. He has done outstandingly well showing in-hand for Cassie and at his first show under saddle won the ridden mountain and moorland class, and was top five for the supreme ridden which bodes very well for his future under saddle. Ollie produced one purebred foal before he was gelded.

Domo Cavallo Praize's third stallion son is **Glenormiston Celtic Prince (205)**, foaled in 2005 out of Glenormiston Dulcinea (1570). Sue was thrilled to breed a son of Prince's calibre to continue on his sire's line when Praize was thirty years old! He was too closely related to Sue's broodmares to warrant keeping him at Glenormiston and was sold to Annette and Henry Condie of Kahean Stud in Sulky, Victoria.

The last of Praize's sons, foaled after he had been laid to rest, is **Glenormiston Celtic Pride (218)**. Pride is a full-brother to Celtic Prince, and had only recently passed inspection at the time of writing. He has been purchased by the Charles Sturt University for their breeding program, so it will be interesting to see the results of his efforts with them.

Glenormiston Celtic Prince, 4 years old, at Glenormiston.

Island King's eighth son, **Connemara Park Paul (24)**, out of Easter Mask imp (1003) was purchased by Keith Swan for his Noorookoo Stud in North Queensland, and later leased to Hillgrove Station in Charters Towers, and was a very successful sire of safe and useful partbred mounts used as stockhorses and for children. He is represented in the studbook by one daughter, the bred-up mare Noorookoo Spice (2B/036).

Glenormiston Celtic Pride (218) at the 2013 Aonach in Wagga Wagga

Candlebark Beatha (68) with Dorle Harris

Connemara Park Garry (37), out of Easter Peak imp (1004) was foaled in 1972. He was purchased by Terry White of Tasmania, and was used as the Tawmara Stud's resident sire. Garry produced no stallion sons, but has seven daughters registered, all from the Sweet Sue imp (1012) mare line: Tawmara Primrose (1133), Tawmara Angee (1163), Tawmara Suesanna (1197), Tawmara Yolandi (1320), Tawmara Mitzi (1359), Tawmara Katie (1463) and Hattondale Aspen (1516).

While Island King's tenth son left no breeding stock progeny, his eleventh, **Candlebark Macrigh (49)**, foaled in 1973 from Errislannon Asphodel imp (1018), left five daughters. Macrigh remained with his breeders, the Woodwards in Victoria, standing as a stud sire at their Candlebark Stud and producing: Candlebark Eiliah (1180), Candlebark Marsale (1223), Candlebark Lucrais (1245), Candlebark Mairi (1308), Fitzroy Cluan (1318) and the bred-up mare Alannah Kerry (1338).

Connemara Park Michael (51), Island King's twelfth son, was foaled in 1972 out of Ardan imp (1001), and thus was a full-brother to Connemara Park Arthur and Connemara Park James. He was purchased by Mrs Millward of the Leitrim Stud, Tikokino, on the North Island of New Zealand in 1977, and did not leave any breeding stock progeny in Australia before his export. In New Zealand, he sired one stallion son, Lonsdale Moonwind, and two registered mares. Connemara Park Michael was described by Irish breeder Stephanie Brooks, on a visit to New Zealand in the early 1980's, as having "a great deal of bone and a lovely temperament."[6] Unfortunately for Mrs Millward and the breed in New Zealand, Michael died in about 1983.

Island King's fourteenth son was **Candlebark Beatha (68)** foaled in 1975 out of Errislannon Asphodel imp (1018), and thus a full-brother to Candlebark Macrigh. Beatha was purchased from Candlebark by Mrs Dorle Harris of the Ardagh Stud in Tynong, Victoria, and was described by Mrs Heather Storey in a 1984 CPBSA newsletter as having "matured into a very nice true-to-type pony with a most attractive head and beautifully behaved". Beatha's two registered daughters are Ardagh Maire (1310) and Rowenglen Caitlin (1535).

---

6 R23:6

Chapter 7 The Island King Family

Connemara Park Russell (4); Connemara Park Mac (11); Connemara Park Bruce (20); Connemara Park George (45); Connemara Park Guy (58); Blandings Icing (81):

Island King's first stallion son, Connemara Park Russell, was foaled in 1967 out of Renvyle Rebel imp (1002). He has no breeding stock progeny recorded, however a partbred gelding, Islehurst Bornado, won the Tasmanian section of the Connemara of the Year competition in 1995.

Blandings Icing (81)

Photo: Marion Adams

Neither Connemara Park Mac, out of Renvyle Rebel imp (1002), nor Connemara Park Bruce out of Easter Peak imp (1004), Island King's sixth and seventh stallion sons, have purebred breeding stock progeny recorded, although Mac was used for producing large partbreds from Thoroughbred mares.

Island King's tenth son, Connemara Park George, foaled in 1973 out of Fabian's Rebecca imp (1015) was another stallion to have left no registered breeding stock progeny, as was Connemara Park Guy, the full-brother of Connemara Park Russell and Connemara Park Mac.

Blandings Icing, Island King's last stallion son, was foaled in 1976 out of Connemara Park Judy (1024). He was purchased by Mrs Mason of the Gardak Stud in Victoria, where he was used over Arab, Thoroughbred and Pony mares. He was later purchased by the Adams family of Dylanglen Stud in Rand, New South Wales, but did not produce any registered breeding stock progeny.

Chapter 8
The Gil Line in Australia

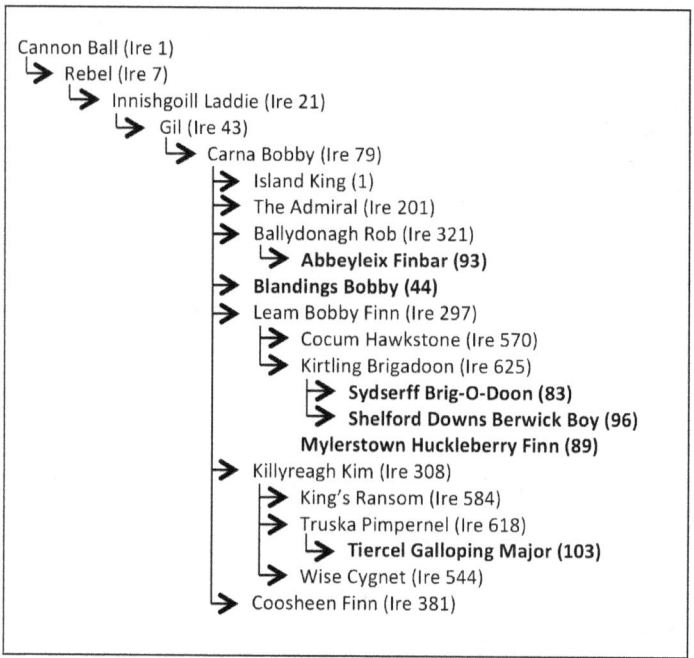

Blandings Bobby iiu (44)

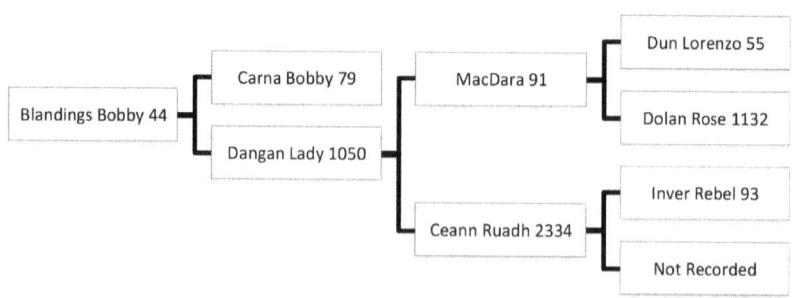

Chapter 8   The Gil Line in Australia

> **Blandings Bobby iiu (44)**
> → Blandings Zircon (92)
> → Blandings Red Fort (100)
> → Blandings John (150)
> → Blandings Ryan (157)
> → Colmaur Kasey (163)
>   → Capparis Champagne Charlie (188)

Blandings Bobby was imported in-utero in 1974. The well-decorated buckskin mare Dangan Lady (1050) had been purchased in Ireland on behalf of the Storeys of Blandings Stud by Fred Wiltshire, who was particularly excited that this daughter of MacDara (Ire 91) was in foal to the popular and successful sire of the time, Carna Bobby (Ire 79). Blandings Bobby was foaled two days after his dam's arrival at Eagle Hill in Victoria and was a grey of 13.1hh at maturity. The Storeys were thrilled with him and he was run on as a stallion prospect, eventually becoming the Storey's first stud stallion.

In a brief competition career Bobby competed successfully in led and saddle classes, ODEs and combined training before being retired to stud. He always ran out with his mares and actively supervised the herd, which kept him very fit throughout his long life. Bobby was also a great babysitter of his foals, caring for and playing with them while his wives grazed.

Kate Storey-Whyte has described Bobby as: "a great stallion for us, very like his sire in appearance (and also in longevity) and what a mover he is! He feels like over fifteen hands to ride, yet is barely over thirteen hands. His foals have been of immense quality without losing type."[1] He remained at Eagle Hill until 2001 when the property was sold, and he moved to Carmel Cassells' Tralee Stud in Tasmania for his final year.

During his lifetime, Blandings Bobby sired five stallion sons: Blandings Zircon (92), Blandings Red Fort (100), Blandings John (150), Blandings Ryan (157) and Colmaur Kasey (163). He is further represented in the CPBSA studbook by twenty-one daughters: Blandings Jubilation (1171), Ridgeway Dream (1173), Blandings Planxty (1181), Bonny Jean of Canningvale (1195), Sandy Park Molly Malone (1203),

Blandings Bobby (44) with Jack Storey.

Photo: Helen Colleran

---
1 R2 p85-86

Chapter 8   The Gil Line in Australia

Blandings John (150)

Blandings John at the 1996 Royal Melbourne Show

Blandings Sylvia (1216), Blandings Ruby (1226), Blandings Jade (1260), Blandings Kimberley (1261), Sandy Park Rosie O'Grady (1350), Blandings Blessington (1388), Blandings Coriander (1389), Blandings Florinda (1391), Blandings Teresa (1398), Blandings Barbados (1534), Blandings Rumba (1544), Blandings Sapphire (1588), Blandings Juby (1652) and Colmaur Colleen (1656).

Blandings Bobby's first stallion son, **Blandings Zircon (92)**, was a grey pony of 13hh foaled in 1977 out of Boffin Heron imp (1051). He did not produce a stallion son, but is represented by two daughters, Blandings Finola (1390) and Blandings Juniper (1393). Zircon was gelded early in his stud career, as the Storeys thought his progeny were a little "too pretty" to be typical Connemara Ponies.[2] He proved to be a very useful pony as a gelding however, being well educated under saddle, and an excellent pony on which to teach children to ride. He was enjoyed and appreciated in this role for many years.

Blandings Red Fort (100) was a chestnut, foaled in 1978 out Lisavalla Rose imp (1049). He did not produce any breeding stock progeny before being gelded.

Blandings Bobby's third stallion son, **Blandings John (150)**, has been more successful in making his mark on the studbook. John is a grey (from chestnut) stallion of 13.1hh, foaled in 1989 out of the imported mare Eaden Calypso (1150). He was purchased in 1990 by Lisa Blazsanyik of Bimini Stud in Broadford, Victoria, Lisa having a high regard for his bay full-brother Blandings Kingston, who had been sold to Western Australia. Although only lightly shown due to his finding showing very boring – he would not "show himself off" – John did win the led Connemara stallion classes at the 1992 Burrumbeet and Geelong Agricultural

---

2 R2 p86

Shows. He also flew the Connemara flag in superb style at the 1994 Melbourne Horse Expo, when he was used in a breaking-in demonstration before a large and knowledgeable audience. Lisa describes John as a very quiet stallion, who seems to reproduce that quietness in his progeny. She also notes his good points as being a lovely head and neck and a good shoulder, with good straight movement.

Blandings John is represented in the studbook by five purebred daughters: Blandings Red Gum (1654), Bimini Cedar (1663), Bimini Aster (1664), Bimini Elsbeth (1812) and the bred-up mare Cootehill Cream Puff (1683).

Blandings Ryan (157), a grey stallion of 13.1hh foaled in 1990 out of Connemara Park Judy (1024), was purchased from Blandings Stud by Vi Gunn and Melissa Smith of Strickland Park Stud in North Creswick, Victoria, and remains there today. Ryan was only lightly shown as a young pony, but won the led-in class for Connemara colts at the 1994 Victorian Summer Royal show. He has been described by Kate Storey-Whyte as being "one of our best", and Vi and Mellissa note that he passes on his bone, depth and wonderful placid nature to his progeny, "many [of whom] have been sold to disabled children" as steady mounts.[3]

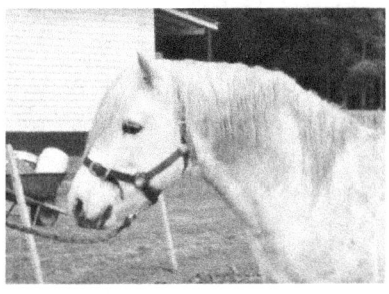

Blandings Ryan (157)

Blandings Ryan has not yet produced a stallion son, but is currently represented by five daughters: Strickland Park Lucy (1665), Strickland Park Carousel (1703), Strickland Park Irish Dancer (1708), Strickland Park Irish Mist (1829) and Strickland Park Diamond Lil (1832).

Blandings Bobby's last stallion son, **Colmaur Kasey (163)** is a grey (from buckskin) pony of 13.3hh. He was foaled in 1992 out of the imported mare Chiltern Martina (1128) and bred by Pam Bertoncello of the Colmaur Stud in

Colmaur Kasey (163) and Jackie Mellett at the 2008 Victorian Connemara Showcase.

---

3 R2 p79

Chapter 8 — The Gil Line in Australia

Colmaur Kasey admires himself in the mirror of Juravon Park's indoor arena
Photo: Tearna Goldston

Smack the Pony and Katie Ryman
Photo: Berni Saunders

Clyde North, Victoria. He was shown regularly in-hand by Pamela, winning the best foal award at the Victorian APSB show and the best yearling award the following year. He followed up this early success with champion led mountain and moorland pony at the Dandenong and Red Hill agricultural shows, reserve champion led Connemara at the National APSB Stud Pony Show in New South Wales and champion led Connemara at the 1996 Melbourne Summer Royal Show, with the judge at this show remarking on his good movement.

In 1995, the Colmaur Stud was dispersed due to a family illness and Kasey was purchased by Lloyd Beasley of the Riverdell Park Stud in Queensland. He was used at stud by both Lloyd and his sister Wendy Lord of the Capparis Stud, producing one stallion son, Capparis Champagne Charlie (188), and four mares: Capparis Patsy's Luck (1688), Capparis Rachelle (1689), Capparis Solitaire (1719) and Capparis Enya (1720).

Colmaur Kasey was sold again in 2001 due to the devastating drought and consequent lack of available feed for the ponies. He was purchased by Jackie Mellett of Dun Manus Stud, and thus returned to Victoria. Jackie and her husband Pat describe Kasey as the perfect stallion for first-time stallion owners and quite a character. He is a "proper gentleman" with his mares, and Jackie notes that if he was a person he would be "all chocolates and flowers" for the ladies!

Kasey is excellent to ride, giving the feeling of riding a horse rather than a pony, and is very reliable both ridden out alone or with mares and geldings. Jackie and Pat started Kasey in harness and he took to it particularly well.

Chapter 8   The Gil Line in Australia

Kasey has been used at Dun Manus to produce both pure and partbred ponies passing on his temperament, movement and athletic ability to his progeny. One of Kasey's outstanding partbred gelding sons, out of a Welsh/Arabian mare, is the top Australian dressage pony, Smack the Pony. Owned and trained by young rider Katie Ryman since he was a three-year-old, and she a nine-year-old beginner rider, Smack has now competed up to Intermediare II level and is training Grand Prix movements. With Katie outgrowing Smack, the difficult decision was made to sell him to another keen young dressage rider, and he was purchased by Australian international dressage representative and competitor Rachael Sanna for her daughter Romany.

Capparis Champagne Charlie (188) with his dam, Shelford Downs Rana (1307)

Photo: Wendy Lord

Colmaur Kasey's stallion son, **Capparis Champagne Charlie (188)**, was foaled in 1999 out of Shelford Downs Rana (1307). He is a grey (from buckskin) standing 14hh. He was purchased as a foal by Carmel Cassells of Tralee Stud and after only a couple of weeks of weaning and handling made the long trip by horse transport to Tasmania, arriving completely unperturbed! 'Charles' has been described by Carmel as having a "special appeal", and she notes that his progeny "are showing excellent bone, type and temperament." He is currently represented by one purebred daughter in the CPBSA studbook, Tralee Ethereal Star (1874).

Sydserff Brig-O-Doon imp (83)

Sydserff Brig-O-Doon was a grey stallion of 13.3hh, bred by Eileen Simpson of the Sydserff Stud in East Lothian, Scotland, in 1977. The Conroys of Shelford Downs Stud imported him as a foal at foot with his dam Belle Heather (1106). He was subsequently purchased by the Wades of Lefroy Stud in Collie, Western Australia to introduce some new bloodlines to the state but was a great disappointment to them, having a difficult temperament and also proving to be infertile. Attempts to improve his fertility were unsuccessful and he was gelded. He is a full-brother to Shelford Downs Berwick Boy (96).

Chapter 8 The Gil Line in Australia

Mylerstown Huckleberry Finn imp (89)

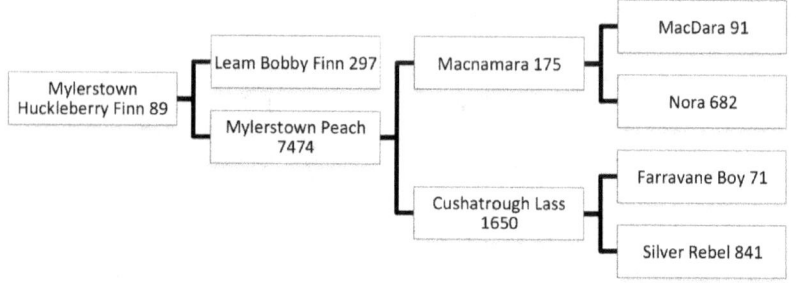

Mylerstown Huckleberry Finn imp (89)
- ➤ Barwidgee Samite (112)
  - ↳ ➤ Rupari Ronan (143)
- ➤ Barwidgee Tom Sawyer (120)
- ➤ Celtic Tipperary Fling (134)
- ➤ Lagoonside Barnabas (142)
- ➤ Celtic Silver Finn (147)

Mylerstown Huckleberry Finn (89) was a grey stallion of 13.3hh foaled in 1975. He was bred by Hugh and Anne Dunsterville, two of the earliest members of the BCPS, out of their homebred mare Mylerstown Peach (Ire 7474). Her dam, Cushatrough Lass (Ire 1650), had been imported to England from Ireland by Hugh and Anne in 1957 after a very successful show career which included class wins at Clifden show as a two and three-year-old and the Killanin Cup for best young mare in 1956. Her show career continued in England with a win in her class at the Royal Windsor Show in 1958 and champion Connemara at the Hindon Show in 1960.

Mylerstown Huckleberry Finn (89) at the Melbourne Royal Show

Cushatrough Lass is listed in the studbook as being by Farravane Boy (Ire 71), but this has been disputed by some who believe she was actually by Carna Dun (Ire 89). Her dam, Silver Rebel (Ire 841), was by the Cannon Ball line stallion Clough Rebel (Ire 33) and the only foal of Silver Bridle (Ire 394), a roan mare registered in 1937 at sixteen years of age and the head of

Chapter 8 — The Gil Line in Australia

this successful mare family.[4] The showring success of Cushatrough Lass, and of her sister Flash Girl (Ire 1771), prompted John and Phyllis Meade of the Leam Stud to purchase Silver Rebel. Initially agisted in Ireland to be bred to MacDara, Silver Rebel had the annoying habit of escaping and walking back to her previous home when her foals were due before she was relocated to Britain.

Mylerstown Huckleberry Finn was shown successfully in Britain where he stood two seasons at stud before his export to Australia in 1979. He won the two and three year old stallion class at the 1977 BCPS breed show and was reserve champion stallion to Cocum Hawkstone. In his short time breeding in Britain, Huckleberry Finn produced eleven registered progeny including Finchampstead Fascinatin' Rhythm (UK 216), who was reserve best foal at the 1980 BCPS Breed Show and did one better in 1981 winning best yearling. One of his colt foals, Rosenaharley Rowley (Ire 775), won the colt foal class at the BCPS breed show in 1979 before being sold to Michael Clancy as a prospective stud stallion. In Ireland, he subsequently won the two-year-old colt class at the 1981 Clifden Show. Rowley has only been lightly used at stud by Irish standards, but produced a Clifden supreme champion and 2012 European champion in his son Curraghmore Cashel (Ire 1128).

Cushatrough Lass (Ire 650)

Photo: Connemara Chronicle Vol IX

Margaret (M) Kelly of Barwidgee Stud in Victoria purchased and imported Huck as she needed a smaller stallion to use over her up-to-height purebred mares by Tulira Colman (7). She stood him for a couple of seasons before he was sold, eventually settling with Penny Brown of the Celtic stud in Ararat, Victoria, where he spent the remainder of his days running with his mares. Penny affectionately remembers

Joe Burke with Curraghmore Cashel winning Clifden Supreme Champion in 2009

Photo: Rozpravka Photography

---

4 R7 p30 39, R47:13

Chapter 8   The Gil Line in Australia

him as dispelling her father's and husband's concerns about having a stallion on the property, noting that he had a wonderful temperament and loved being with people. Once when Penny's daughter Susie was six years old, she took herself off to the horses' paddock. She sat down among the daisies and Huck wandered over to keep her company, happily eating her daisy chain as she made him another.

Huck left a good number of sons and daughters to continue his line in the studbook, however it has not been a lasting stallion line in Australia. Five stallion sons represent him, these being: Barwidgee Samite (112), Barwidgee Tom Sawyer (120), Celtic Tipperary Fling (134), Lagoonside Barnabas (142) and Celtic Silver Finn (147). His ten purebred daughters are: Ben Dhui Cavatina (1265), Glenormiston Maisie McInealy (1267), Barwidgee Fern (1270), Salette Inis Bo Finne (1368), Celtic Silver Thread (1372), Ballantrae Treacle (1429), Galway Park Finness (1441), Celtic Driftwood (1465), Celtic Touch and Go (1469) and Celtic Storm Cloud (1510).

John Tennant with 'Sammy' at Rupari

Photo: Tennant Archive

The first stallion son of Mylerstown Huckleberry Finn, **Barwidgee Samite (112)**, was a brown/bay pony of 13.3hh foaled in 1979 out of Aylesland Silver Velvet imp (1011). He was purchased from Barwidgee at two years of age by John and Pat Tennant who were in the process of setting up their Rupari Stud near Gawler, South Australia. Their intention was to breed both purebred and partbred ponies and horses for pony club and eventing. John had previously bred racehorses, been in charge of the South Australian Mounted Police for ten years and had a continuing involvement in a number of equestrian societies and events. One of these was the Gawler Three Day Event where Connemaras had come to his attention via the partbreds, O'Shea and Oakdale Aran Isle, who starred at advance level.

Barwidgee Samite (112) as a youngster

Photo: John Tennant

Chapter 8   The Gil Line in Australia

As a youngster at Barwidgee, Samite had been disliked by one of the male staff and arrived at Rupari with a distrust of men. However, it did not take long for him to appreciate his change in circumstances and he became, according to John, "gentle, trustworthy, loving and happy in the company of humans".

Sammy was only lightly shown, but picked up a couple of good wins in his lifetime including champion at the South Australian Pony Breeders and Fanciers' Show from a class of four good stallions in 1982. He was never 'officially' broken to saddle, but was a gentleman when ridden. He also realized the aims of Rupari, producing a number of successful riding school and pony club ponies, showring winners and much loved family members with, John acknowledges, Samite's "nature, strength and correctness".[5]

Only one purebred stallion son, Rupari Ronan (143), and two purebred daughters, Rupari Meemani (1558) and Templewood Rose of Tralee (1608), are included in the studbook. Samite produced numerous geldings and partbred progeny, a few of note being the partbred mares Rupari Sumar, Rupari Bridie and Caballero La Casa Lagrimar. Rupari Sumar was campaigned by Joyce Robertson and later Sue Kelly in open and buckskin classes, amassing many championships and supremes. Rupari Bridie was campaigned by Bronwyn Willoughby in South Australia, attaining the CPBSA's South Australian Partbred Connemara of the Year and the National Partbred of the Year awards. Bridie was purchased by Christina Sutherland of the Jamabi Stud in Queensland who describes her as a "brilliant mare under saddle and perfect for children". Caballero La Casa Lagrimar, out of an Arabian Pony mare, was nicknamed Tears as she rapidly deteriorated after birth and was given a 25% chance

Rupari Sumar with Joyce Robertson and some of her awards.

Caballero La Casa Lagrimar with Darren Phillis

---

5 R2 p50-51, R48 2002 2005

Chapter 8   The Gil Line in Australia

Rupari Ronan (143) at the 1997 Adelaide Royal Show

Rupari Ronan (143)

of survival. Despite the odds, she not only pulled through but thrived, maturing into a lovely pony and a multi-champion show winner in pony hack, Connemara, APSB, ASSP and ARP classes with her owner Darren Phillis.

Rupari Ronan (143), by Samite and out of Aran Vasari (1321), was a bay/brown stallion of 14.1½hh foaled in 1987. He was retained by the Tennants, lightly and successfully shown in-hand and under saddle and used at stud. His most notable success under saddle was second place in his class and then reserve champion ridden galloway stallion at the 1997 Adelaide Royal Show.

When the Rupari Stud dispersed in 2005, Ronan moved to the Rowes of Newlands Stud in Victoria, where he was used over the Newlands mares and a number of outside mares. Claire Rowe describes Ronan as having been "a complete gentleman" and he was much appreciated in his new home and resided with the Rowes for the remainder of his life. At the time of writing, Ronan is represented by three purebred mares: Rupari Storm Girl (1657), Rupari Baronia (1696) and Rupari Candy Tuft (1765), and produced a number of foals in Victoria so there will hopefully be additions in the adult register in the future.[6]

Lagoonside Barnabas (142): A grey stallion of 13.3hh, Barnabas was out of Ben Dhui Elphin (1289). He was bred by Mary-Ruth Dowd of Lagoonside Stud at Drysdale, the Dowds having first become interested in the Connemara breed through two geldings, the purebred, Salette Honeycombe, and a three-quarter bred, Aran Vicenzo who partnered the Dowd children as well as being used in their riding school. Ben Dhui Elphin (1780) was purchased and Mylerstown Huckleberry Huckleberry Finn was the stallion chosen to send her to. Barnabas, foaled in 1986, was

---

6 R48 2002, June 2005, R37:1, R2 p50-51

described by Mary as big and beautiful and very, very kind just like his mum".[7] At weaning he was sold to Cassy Shelley of Corio who eventually used him over her Quarter Horse mares. Cassy described him in 1990 as "a proven show sire of quality stock, having an excellent temperament, type and movement". Barnabas is represented by one purebred daughter, Lagoonside Alleluia (1540).

Barwidgee Tom Sawyer (120); Celtic Tipperary Fling (134); Celtic Silver Finn (147):

The second stallion son of Mylerstown Huckleberry Finn was Barwidgee Tom Sawyer. A grey pony of 13.3hh, he was a full-brother to Samite. M Kelly described him as "a very nice pony", and he was sold to Senga Bissett who lived near Wagga Wagga. He is not represented by any breeding stock progeny in the studbook.

Celtic Tipperary Fling is the third of Huckleberry Finn's sons, and the last of his union with Aylesland Silver Velvet imp (1011). Another brown, he was foaled in 1986 and stood about 14.2hh. He was sold to John and Rosemary Hermanns at Moyston, and they showed him in-hand successfully as well as breaking him to both saddle and harness. He was always willing to please and once when Rosemary had been working him he suddenly halted. She insisted he go forward, which he did, and both fell down an old mine shaft! Fortunately, he managed to struggle out without injury to either of them.

Barwidgee Tom Sawyer (120)

Celtic Tipperary Fling (134) with the Hermanns family in 1990.

Tipperary Fling was sold on to the Adams of Dylanglen Stud in New South Wales in

---

7 R2 82

1994, and from there was sold to a property in Queensland for breeding stockhorses. He also has no breeding stock progeny recorded in the studbook.

Huckleberry Finn's last foal was the stallion Celtic Silver Finn. Described by Penny Brown in 1990 as "an attractive, intelligent, quality pony", Silver Finn was foaled in 1988 out of Barwidgee Snowdrift (1058). Most unfortunately, he died soon after classification and left no breeding stock progeny.

Abbeyleix Finbar imp (93)

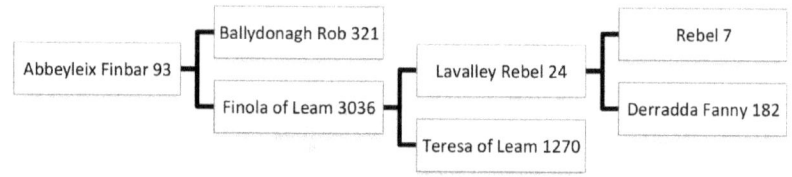

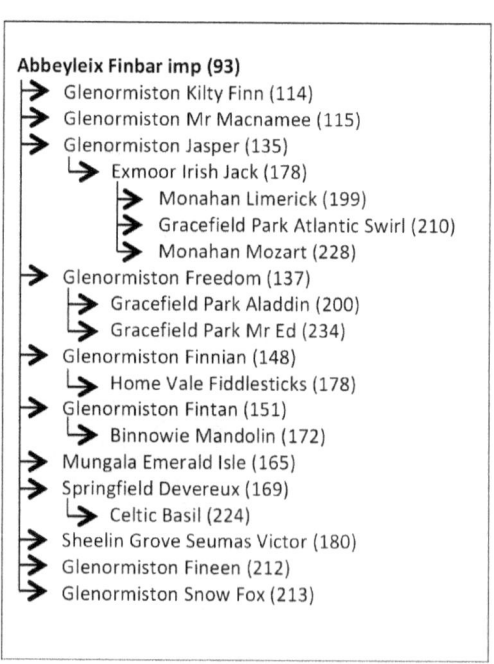

Chapter 8   The Gil Line in Australia

A grey (from black) 13.2hh stallion, Abbeyleix Finbar was bred by Lady Susan de Vesci of the Abbeyleix Stud in Co. Laois, Ireland, in 1978. His dam, Finola of Leam, has been mentioned previously as the dam of Leam Bobby Finn and Coosheen Finn, and shall be discussed further in the next volume of this series as dam of the imported mare Abbeyleix Fiona (1151).

Abbeyleix Finbar (93) with Dr Barton Clarke

In 1979, the Clarkes of Glenormiston Stud in Queensland were searching for a colt to use over their Domo Cavallo Praize fillies. They toured England and Ireland inspecting colts and although they had heard about 'Viscountess de Vesci's lovely colt', they had not managed to see him. They put a deposit on a colt in England but decided that the colt was not quite what they were looking for, so it seemed that they would return to Australia empty-handed. However, at

Abbeyleix Finbar eventing

the English breed show, Sue was asked by Michael Clancy and Jimmy Jones if she had seen the colt belonging to Lady de Vesci – a bit small and a bit Welshy, but a top yearling and one of the best bred in Ireland – that they had told her about. This conversation took place on a Thursday, and Sue was due to fly home to Australia on the Saturday, so she rang Lady de Vesci who said that she had sold him to a keen young breeder, Padraic Hynes, who didn't have a phone line but that she would try to track him down. This was in the days of the non-automated telephone exchanges, where the operator put you through, or in the case of Padraic she sent a message via a neighbour with a phone. Sue caught a flight back to Ireland, headed to Abbeyleix and then drove to Galway to meet Padraic, who really didn't want to sell Finbar. After some negotiations a deal was made, with Finbar to stay with Padraic until after the Clifden Show. Sue rushed back to England to catch her flight and Finbar competed in the yearling colt class where he was placed second to the bay Earl of Doon (DEN 33) who had been purchased by Bent Nielsen of Oxenholm Stud in Denmark.

Finbar settled into his new home in Brookfield with the Clarkes and was well used by them as a stud stallion, under saddle and in harness. In led classes, he won many championships and supremes up to Royal level, and he carried both adults and the Clarke children in pony jumping and eventing.

Chapter 8 The Gil Line in Australia

In his 28 years Abbeyleix Finbar made a great impact on the Connemara breed in Australia, providing the studbook with twelve stallion sons: Glenormiston Kilty Finn (114), Glenormiston Mr Macnamee (115), Glenormiston Jasper (135), Glenormiston Freedom (137), Glenormiston Finnian (148), Glenormiston Fintan (151), Glenormiston Slipper (164), Mungala Emerald Isle (165), Springfield Devereux (169), Sheelin Grove Seumas Victor (180), Glenormiston Fineen (212) and Glenormiston Snow Fox (213). He is also represented by thirty-eight daughters: Glenormiston Mary Murphy (1292), Glenormiston Mavourneen (1347), Wattle Hills Question (1354), Wattle Hills Liberty (1375), Glenormiston Macroom (1409), Glenormiston Finola Grey (1410), Glenormiston Mallow (1415), Glenormiston Araminta (1424), Glenormiston Theresa Diamond (1438), Glenormiston Fenella (1447), Glenormiston Catriona (1496), Corrib Park Micaela (1507), Glenormiston Clementine (1520), Glengarry Patsy Malone (1536), Glenormiston Dulcinea (1570), Glenormiston Lizzie Diamond (1571), Mungala Fenella (1597), Glenormiston Fintona (1606), Mungala Pocheen (1629), Glenormiston Flora (1639), Glenormiston Fionnuala (1641), Glenormiston Rosaleen (1673), Clairvale Cenedra (1685), Dylanglen Diamond Tiara (1695), Glenormiston Cornamona (1698), Glenormiston Fiona (1699), Glenormiston Roskeen (1700), Glenormiston Cloonlara (1710), Glenormiston Cloonshee (1742), Glenormiston Cashel (1747), Glenormiston Fionnabhair (1770), Glenormiston Tess (1776), Glenormiston Clonakilty (1780), Glenormiston Kinsale (1785), Glenormiston Aedin (1803), Glenormiston Treasa (1804), Glenormiston Fintra (1806) and Glenormiston Firenne (1846).

Abbeyleix Finbar

Photo: Jo Heard

Finbar also sired a large number of successful geldings and partbreds. Glenormiston Mellerick, a partbred gelding out of a Thoroughbred mare, is owned by Tracey James and together they do dressage and pony club. Tracey's brother Dan, now famous for 'Double Dan Horsemanship', gained tremendous enjoyment mustering, eventing and showjumping him and they competed in the Stockman's Challenge at Beaudesert in Queensland. In this event, the horse and rider team complete various activities including "trimming a horse's hooves, cutting out a calf, roping and throwing it, riding a cross country course in a stock saddle with a stockwhip in your hand, catching and saddling your horse and then riding a course around obstacles, unsaddling and a bareback ride over obstacles".[8] They won this event against very experienced stockmen and stockhorses - an excellent example of the all-roundability of the Connemara.

Beginning our review of Finbar's stallion sons with those having registered breeding stock progeny, we start with **Glenormiston Mr Macnamee** (115). 'Mac' was foaled in 1981, a grey (from palomino) stallion of 13hh. His dam, Macaroon of Calmore imp (1079) died when he was six weeks old and Mac was purchased by David and Tricia Deakin of Kilkieran Stud at Rosewood in Queensland when he was twelve weeks old. He refused to take a bottle, so received his milk powder in his hard feed.

Glenormiston Mr Macnamee (115)

Mac as a Unicorn and Dave as a leprechaun for the Warana parade in Brisbane

Tricia remembers Mr Macnamee as "a real character" and the aspect the Deakins loved most about him was his attitude. A testament to his temperament was his enjoyment of being taken out to events, at which times he was always on his best behavior. One of these events was the Brisbane Warana Parade, in which he was festooned with flowers and a horn to make him the unicorn of the Connemara group parading.

Mac developed a special bond with a stable cat named Emily. As a young pony, he would walk down to a fence post and Emily would climb up the post and onto his back. He would then take her for a ride before returning her to the post to dismount! The Deakins moved to a new property, and Emily decided to live with Mac, curling up on top of his feed bin and playing with his forelock while he ate. If he lay down she would curl up in between his legs for warmth and company. They were inseparable during Emily's lifetime and Mac mourned for months after she died.

---

8 R2 p35-36

Mr Macnamee did not leave a stallion son to continue this family, however he is represented by four daughters: Kilkieran Rinamee (1449), Kilkieran Michael's Miss (1498), Kilkieran Kirsten McNeill (1574) and Mungala Siobhan (1575). He was also well supported as a stud stallion by local farmers who found his partbred progeny to be excellent working horses.

Abbeyleix Finbar's third stallion son, **Glenormiston Jasper (135)**, was a grey (from black/buckskin) pony of 14.1hh foaled in 1985 out of Oxenholm Dulcinea imp (1232). He was purchased as a yearling by Sally Withers of Exmoor Stud in Naracoorte, South Australia, as an outcross to use over her Glenormiston Macinnerney Muskerry (95) fillies and visiting mares.

Jasper did well in the showring, winning championships both in-hand and under saddle at the Adelaide and Melboune Royal shows, and was also named the South Australian Connemara of the Year in 1994. He was ridden by Sally at her dressage club and jumping, and she described him as "one of the nicest stallions, [having] a lovely temperament. He moves beautifully and is a lovely ride". She sold him to Bruce Sturgeon of New Zealand in 1996 and it was a sad sale for the Withers as he had become part of the family. It was Sally's intention to keep some of Jasper's daughters, introducing new bloodlines by using some older stallions in the region. She felt that Jasper's qualities would be better utilized in a new stud situation.

During his time at the Exmoor Stud, Jasper produced one stallion son, Exmoor Irish Jack (178) and four registered daughters: Exmoor Sinead (1595), Exmoor Caitlin (1596), Exmoor Grania (1609) and Exmoor Jamaica (1613).

One well performed son of Jasper is the purebred gelding Exmoor Silver Finn, out of Silver Mill imp (1038). Silver Finn was purchased as a two-year-old by Sue Fitzpatrick, and they made quite a team, gaining championships in led and ridden Connemara, open APSB and saddle pony classes. The pair also competed in dressage, showjumping and eventing, as well as enjoying pleasure rides in the forests around their home. Silver

Glenormiston Jasper (135)

Photo: Jo Heard

Chapter 8 The Gil Line in Australia

Finn was the South Australian Purebred Connemara Pony of the Year in 1999 and is described by Sue as having versatility, a good nature, intelligence, being true to type and a great ambassador for the breed.[9]

Another noteworthy son is the partbred gelding Just Lately, or Chook. Chook's dam was a Thoroughbred mare of over 17hh and he grew to 16.2hh himself. Kirsty Withers started him in introductory horse trials as a four-year-old and then Sally worked on his dressage training for eighteen months. It was decided that a new home where his outstanding potential could be realized would be found for him. Sally Withers writes: "Seoul Olympian, Scott Keach, came down to check him out and started by popping him over a single jump – something he hadn't done for well over a year. Scott kept asking me to raise the jump up and up and up. Obviously impressed with his natural jump Scott loaded the grey onto his float and took him straight home!"[10] At the time of writing, Chook had been campaigned by Scott up to novice level eventing and was competing successfully at A and B level showjumping.

Exmoor Irish Jack (178), Jasper's Australian stallion son, is a buckskin pony of 13.3hh foaled in 1996 out of Blandings Barbados (1534). Sally described him as "an outstanding type of pony, showing true breed characteristics with lots of quality. His conformation and movement are excellent [and] he has a lovely nature". She sold him in 2000 to Christa and Trevor Jones of Monahan Stud who had seen him advertised in a CPBSA newsletter and fell in love with him as soon as they saw him.

Exmoor Irish Jack (178)

Monahan Mozart (228)

Irish Jack has done well for Monahan Stud, competing successfully in-hand achieving supreme Connemara exhibit at the 2001 and 2004 Victorian APSB Stud Shows. He has so far produced three stallion

---

9   R2 p41, R39
10 R48 Summer 2006 p16

sons, Monahan Limerick (199), Gracefield Park Atlantic Swirl (210) and Monahan Mozart (228), and six adult registered daughters, Monahan Keely (1744), Monahan Odele (1831), Monahan Oaks (1833), Exmoor Molly Malone (1839), Monahan Quickstep (1866), and Monahan Pistacio (1867). He also has a number of youngstock in the wings and a daughter, New Song Autumn, and gelding son, Wildwych Judas Hascarrots, in the USA, the results of Glenormiston Rossleague (1725) and Glenormiston Clemma (1724) visiting him before their export.

Monahan Limerick (199) is a buckskin pony of 14hh foaled in 2003 out of Green Hills Final Fling (1660). He was purchased in 2006 by Naomi Holmes of Holmwood Stud in Serpentine, Western Australia, to be used for breeding partbreds. A 'keen to please' character he was unfortunately found to be infertile and subsequently gelded without leaving any progeny. He enjoys being worked and is headed for a saddle career.

Gracefield Park Atlantic Swirl (210) is a bay stallion of 14hh foaled in 2004 and a full-brother to Monahan Limerick. He is currently owned by Dylan Glen Stud in New South Wales, so is in a good position to breed on but is not yet represented by any breeding stock progeny in the studbook.

The last stallion currently representing Exmoor Irish Jack in the studbook is **Monahan Mozart (228)**. Mozart is a 14.2hh bay stallion out of Ballina Melody (1633) and foaled in 2004. He is owned by Belinda Dicker who writes: "I actually spent some five years looking for Mozart [and he] has proven to be everything I was looking for. I wanted an older style, more traditional type of pony. He was only a foal when I looked at him but carried far greater bone than any other pony I had previously seen. He also presented a nice head, moved beautifully and had a temperament second to none, which he passes on to his progeny."

Glenormiston Freedom (137)

Photo: CPBSA Archive

Belinda leased Mozart to Clare Downs Stud in Western Australia where he was used to breed both purebred ponies and sporthorses, and was also shown in-hand and started under saddle. At his first outing in-hand, he won the Connemara stallion class at the 2009 Perth Royal Show. He has now returned to Victoria and continues in his role as a stud stallion with Belinda planning to breed both purebred ponies and sporthorses to carefully selected Warmblood mares.

Glenormiston Freedom (137) is the fourth stallion son of Abbeyleix Finbar, and is a full-brother to Glenormiston Jasper. A grey pony of 13.3hh, Freedom was foaled in 1987 and purchased at weaning by the Wilsons of Gracefield Park Stud in Victoria as a stallion prospect. He was shown extensively and with outstanding success, both in-hand and under saddle by Jayne. Freedom's greatest achievements, according to Jayne, are his pure and partbred progeny that have gone on to be successful children's ponies in a wide range of activities – from endurance to dressage and showjumping. Jayne also notes that he has an outstanding temperament and can be handled and ridden by children – this trait being passed on to his progeny. At the time of writing Freedom was represented by two stallion sons, Gracefield Park Aladdin (200) and Gracefield Park Mr Ed (234), and by one adult-registered daughter, Lagoonside Trinity (1690).

Somerville Park Pollyanna with Lucinda Doodt competing at the 2012 Victorian Connemara Showcase.

Gracefield Park Aladdin in 2013

Freedom has also produced exceptional partbred progeny, including Gracefield Park Majestic Dancer, a multi-champion both in-hand and under saddle who won the Victorian Connemara Performance Award in 2012. Another daughter, Somerville Park Pollyanna out of a Thoroughbred mare has been doing exceptionally well in pony club eventing with owner Lucinda Doodt.

Gracefield Park Aladdin (200) is a grey (from black) 13.3hh stallion, foaled in 2004 out of Boonahburra Carousel (1635). As a four-year-old he was purchased by Kathy Roberts of South Australia who describes him as having a "typically 'pony' temperament - very laid back and accepting of everything asked of him" and noting that he is quite a smoocher and loves a good cuddle and scratch. At the time of writing he had a number

Gracefield Park Mr Ed (234) in 2013
Photo: Sharyn Callander

Glenormiston Finnian (148)
Photo: CPBSA Archive

Home Vale Fiddlesticks (176) on Flinders Island
Photo: Karen Holloway

of partbred sporthorse progeny on the ground with plans to also breed some purebred foals from him.

Gracefield Park Mr Ed (234) is a grey full-brother to Aladdin foaled in 2009 standing 13.3hh. Mr Ed is owned by Sharyn Callander in Victoria, who describes him as being easy-going with a loveable and cheeky nature, and having a great temperament. He was shown regularly in-hand in 2012, winning supreme led Connemara Pony at the Victorian APSB Stud Show and the Royal Geelong Show, and was 2012 APSB Victorian Junior Led Connemara Pony of the Year.

Glenormiston Finnian (148): The fifth stallion son of Abbeyleix Finbar, Finnian, was a grey stallion of 14¼hh foaled in 1989 out of Kirtling Haze imp (1028), dam of the Clarke's successful foundation stallion Domo Cavallo Praize (63). As a weanling, Finnian was purchased by John and Lyn Ibbott of Springfield Stud in Tasmania as they were hoping to introduce another bloodline into the Tasmanian gene pool.

John and Lyn first became interested in the Connemara Pony through the purchase of the partbred Home Vale Lindy for their daughter, Wendy. The pair was very successful in saddle events. Finnian himself became a regular winner in the showring in-hand, with probably his most notable result being the champion led Connemara Pony and champion led stallion of all breeds at the 1994 Tasmanian APSB Show.

Finnian left one stallion son to continue his line, Home Vale Fiddlesticks (176) and nine purebred daughters: Springfield Abbigail

Chapter 8 — The Gil Line in Australia

(1592), Home Vale Diamond (1593), Home Vale Emerald (1599), Springfield Darina (1634), Springfield Eryleen (1646), Springfield Grace (1675), Springfield Gemmagh (1676), Biwmares Madonna (1681) and Springfield Irinagh (1686).

Home Vale Fiddlesticks (176) was a grey stallion of 13.3hh foaled in 1994, and bred by Lyn Ibbott's good friend Ann Patterson from her multi-champion home-bred mare Home Vale Perfection (1219). As a youngster, Fiddlesticks, known as Jasper, was found to be quite a handful and changed hands numerous times. He eventually found a home with a lady who loved him and had him started under saddle, but when she became ill he was sent to her father's farm in north-eastern Tasmania where there were no other horses.

Lyn tracked him down and persuaded his owners to have him inspected. He finally settled on Flinders Island with Karen Holloway of the Caragh Glen Stud in 2002. He stayed with Karen for the remainder of his life, producing some gelding sons but unfortunately no breeding stock progeny.

Glenormiston Fintan (151): Glenormiston Fintan (151), the sixth stallion son of Abbeyleix Finbar (93), was a grey (from buckskin) pony of 13.2hh foaled in 1990 and a full-brother to Jasper and Freedom. He was purchased as a foal by Margaret Campbell of Binnowie Stud in Wowan, Central Queensland, as a stallion prospect to use over her Inis O'Hara (29) daughters.

Glenormiston Fintan (151) with Margaret Campbell

Fintan proved to be very successful in the showring, being awarded supreme champion Connemara at the Brisbane Royal Show five times, supreme champion colt of all breeds at the Queensland APSB Show, and many times supreme champion led of all breeds at agricultural shows.

Fintan (151)

Chapter 8 The Gil Line in Australia

Binnowie Mandolin and Jessica Weiss winning EQ Reserve Champion Novice Pony 2010

Glenormiston Slipper (164) in 2012

Margaret describes Fintan as a lovely pony with a 'look at me' attitude. He was lovely to ride, had enormous jumping talent and was ridden by both adults and children. In addition to Binnowie's purebred mares, he was a popular sire to a wide range of outside mares, with the Arabian cross proving to be particularly successful. Fintan is represented by one stallion son, Binnowie Mandolin (172) and by three adult-registered daughters: Binnowie Spotlight (1607), Binnowie Gemmagh (1746) and Binnowie Katie Clare (1748).

Binnowie Mandolin (172) is a 14.1½hh grey pony foaled in 1996 out of Binnowie Eileen (1476). He was bought in 1998 by Tom Lambert of Kingaroy, Queensland, for his Nargun Tarn Stud. Tom had wanted to own a Connemara stallion since listening to Fred Wiltshire talk about them at a Lighthorse Breeders seminar in the early 1970's. Mandolin didn't let him down, impressing Tom with the ease with which he was started under saddle and in harness. He was used extensively mustering cattle in steep, rocky and overgrown terrain where he demonstrated his excellent temperament, agility and toughness.

Work commitments led to breeding operations at Nargun Tarn being ceased, and when another breeding home could not be found for him, Mandolin was gelded. He did not leave any purebred progeny, but has a number of useful partbreds from Thoroughbred and appaloosa mares. He was sold on, eventually finding a home with Jessica Weiss who writes of him: We bought him as a project pony, and had heard great things about the Connemara breed. Within a month he was a different horse, he really took to dressage training (at 12!!!), and with some basic training under his belt (with a lot of help from my instructors) he turned into a really fun and enjoyable horse to ride, and much to the surprise of his old owners (and myself!), turned into a very competitive dressage pony. One competition, a women came up to me and asked who I bought this pony from,

Chapter 8 The Gil Line in Australia

and said "It cannot be Binnowie Mandolin, he can't do dressage!" despite winning my prelim and novice class! Every ride, he would try his heart out, and every competition he seemed to really concentrate and put in that little extra effort than he would at home. He really seemed to thrive under the pressure, and was a much happier horse when being treated as a performance horse rather than a child's pony, and was always happiest once he had finished his tests (probably due to his favorite competition treat of a salad roll with tomato sauce from the canteen, after stealing enough food from everyone we gave up and bought his own!). Despite being a touch on the lazy side, he was very responsive, intelligent, and very, very, very, calm and quiet. My sister jumped him at a few interschool competitions however his height limit was about 90cm and he certainly wasn't fast. She also taught him a few tricks like how to bow."

Mungala Emerald Isle relaxing at home

Mungala Emerald Isle and Pauline Munn

Glenormiston Slipper (164): Glenormiston Slipper is a grey (from bay) pony of 13.3hh foaled in 1994 from Oxenholm Tiffany imp (1268). He takes his name from the book *The Diary of an Irish RM*, as does his older full-brother Glenormiston Flurry Knox.

Slipper was purchased in 1995 by Wendy Lord of Chinchilla in Queensland as the foundation stallion for the Capparis Stud and although only used lightly, did sire a number of foal-recorded foals. A lease by Asham Stud in the Hunter Valley, New South Wales, produced his only adult-recorded breeding stock progeny so far, the mare Asham Madonna (1850). More recently he has relocated to Penny Brown's Celtic Stud, so is sure to be well-represented in the future.

Mungala Emerald Isle (165): Mungala Emerald Isle (Smudge) was a 14hh grey, foaled in 1994 from Glenormiston Bridie O'Loan (1269). He was extensively and successfully campaigned in both led and ridden classes by his owner and breeder Pauline Munn, with whom he remained for all of his life apart from one breeding season when he was leased to Michelle Vasseur and Jamie King of Ballyshannon Lodge near Warwick in Queensland.

Pauline describes Smudge as having been honest and faithful, and protective of his family – particularly of Pauline and her daughter Stephanie. He was a wonderful pony to ride, needing no working down before classes, and performing exceptionally well in both ridden and led classes, both in breed rings and open competition. Smudge was champion pony under saddle at the Queensland APSB Show after having been under saddle for only six weeks. He never scored lower than a third in dressage competition and won at royal level under saddle. He was also sashed supreme champion Connemara Pony at the Brisbane Royal Show three times.

When Stephanie was first learning to rise to the trot on Smudge, Pauline would lead the pair up and down the road. Stephanie would laugh all the way and if it seemed that she was about to fall off, Smudge would stop. He was ridden out on trail rides and in pairs with mares beside him, and was never a problem. Unfortunately, in 2006 Smudge suffered a paddock accident to his hock that left him unsound and he retired from his ridden career. Pauline lost Smudge in 2011, and although he did not produce a stallion son, he is represented by three daughters in the studbook: Mungala Ceitein (1650), Mungala Aisling (1651) and Mungala Lacey (1702).

Springfield Devereux (169) at Celtic Stud

Celtic Basil (224) ridden by Kayla Lenehan in SA

Springfield Devereux (169): Springfield Devereux, a grey (from black/buckskin) stallion of 13.3h, was foaled in 1995 from Emerald Valley Revelation (1486). He was bred by Lyn Ibbott of Springfield Stud in Longord, Tasmania, and run on as a stallion prospect with the intention of his being an eventual replacement for her original Finbar stallion, Finnian. After he was classified in 1998 though, he was leased by, and later transferred to Penny Brown of Celtic Stud in Victoria, who had been without a stallion for two years after the loss of Cregmore Colm (84). Penny describes Devereux as having been a dominant herd stallion who kept his mares well in line but was good with them too. She states that he had "a lovely classical head, good body, lovely legs and movement… he moves as if on air [and is also] a very sensible, quiet pony".[11] Devereux was never started under saddle, but spent his life running with his mares – proving his worth through his progeny. Devereux has one stallion son registered, Celtic Basil (224), and thirteen adult registered daughters: Celtic Sweet Ashrinn (1692), Celtic Rosemary (1706), Celtic Seadrift (1707), Celtic Santolina (1711), Celtic Fiddlesticks (1732), Celtic Spice (1733), Celtic Cymbal (1737), Clairvale Cuiliuir (1755), Celtic Sweet Katie (1761), Celtic Marjoram (1782), Celtic Sweet Candy (1783), Celtic Kathy O'Hara (1793) and Wychwood Blue Wren (1854).

Celtic Basil (224) is a grey stallion of 14.2hh and was bred by Penny out of Celtic Thyme (1587) in 2005. He was purchased as a youngster by Cheryl Heynemann who, impressed with his type and temperament, ran him on as a stallion prospect. On maturity he was leased to Charles Sturt University for two breeding seasons, working as the university's stud stallion and teaching the students about breeding management and stallion handling. He was then returned to Cheryl and at the time of writing was the regular mount of Cheryl's twelve year old daughter Kayla, proving to be a wonderful ride which is a great testament to his temperament after two years of being used solely as a breeding stallion! With only youngstock on the ground at the time of writing, Basil is not yet represented in the studbook.

Celtic Basil and Kayla

Glenormiston Kilty Finn (114); Sheelin Grove Seumas Victor (180); Glenormiston Fineen (212); Glenormiston Snow Fox (213):

Finbar's first registered stallion son, Glenormiston Kilty Finn, was a grey pony of 14.2hh foaled in 1981 out of Tulira Fuchsia imp (1131). Described by Sue Clarke as "a very attractive pony with tons of bone, presence and good looks, [and] a magnificent, unflappable temperament", Kilty was left entire and sold. When he again came on the market and a stud home could not be found, he was gelded and purchased by Pauline Munn of Cedar Vale in Queensland.

Glenormiston Fineen (212) enjoying life in New Zealand.

---

11 R2 p88

Chapter 8 The Gil Line in Australia

Glenormiston Snow Fox (213) at the 2013 Aonach at Wagga Wagga

Photo: Michaela Adams

Pauline had become interested in the Connemara Pony as a child, and Kilty was her first horse. He took Pauline from being a novice rider to winning in led and ridden Connemara, saddle pony, Galloway hack, bridlepath hack, hunter hack, dressage and showjumping classes. He won the supreme champion gelding of all breeds at the 1993 and 1994 Queensland Stud Pony Shows, was never beaten in ridden Connemara classes at the Brisbane Royal Show during his career and won the Brisbane Region Connemara Action Group's high point gelding of the year every year he entered – ten years in a row. He was such a stand-out pony that judges would even offer to buy him! Owning Kilty whetted Pauline's appetite for more Connemaras, and she formed the Mungala Stud in 1990. Kilty lived with Pauline for the remainder of his life.[12]

Abbeyleix Finbar's tenth stallion son is Sheelin Grove Seumas Victor. Seumas Victor is a grey pony of 13.2hh, foaled in 1993 out of Chittering Gully Fantasy (1328). He was bred by C Salkeld of Gladstone in New South Wales and at the time of writing was owned by Melanie and Graham Lakiseumas. Victor does not have any breeding stock progeny recorded in the studbook.

Glenormiston Fineen, foaled in 2006 and 13.3hh, was the last foal of Glenormiston Stud's very successful Finbar/Oxenholm Tiffany (1268) cross. As soon as he passed inspection he was sold by Glenormiston to Paula Reed in New Zealand. He therefore has no progeny recorded in the CPBSA studbook, but he will be well-used in his new home.

Finbar's last CPBSA recorded stallion son, Glenormiston Snow Fox, also foaled in 2006, is a grey (from chestnut) stallion out of Glenormiston Celebration (1672). He is not yet represented in the studbook, but was purchased by the Dylanglen Stud in New South Wales, so we are sure to see him represented within the next few years.

---

12 R2 p26

Another stallion son of Abbeyleix Finbar who is worthy of further mention but does not appear in the studbook is **Glenormiston Flurry Knox**. This grey (from chestnut) stallion was foaled in 1993, another son of Oxenholm Tiffany (1268). As a stud stallion for Wildwych Stud in the USA, Flurry has produced four stallion sons and twenty-nine purebred daughters. His owner, Mary Prewitt, notes that his best traits are his prepotence – she could pick out his offspring from a herd of Connemara foals, even if she had never seen them before – his amazing athleticism, which he passes on to nearly every foal, and his temperament. She describes him as just "such a lovely person". One of his sons, Wildwych Eclipse, out of the iiu to the USA mare Wildwych Dreamtime (Aran Milano (101) x Glenormiston Roscrea (153)) is owned and produced by Redbud Ranch, and is a great ambassador for the breed through his exceptional performances in open dressage and combined training events.

Glenormiston Flurry Knox at home in Colorado, USA

Wildwych Eclipse

Shelford Downs Berwick Boy iiu (96)

Shelford Downs Berwick Boy was a bay/brown stallion foaled in 1978 and standing 13.2hh. He was by the British stallion Kirtling Brigadoon (UK 6347) and imported in-utero by the Conroys of Shelford Downs Stud in Queensland.

Berwick Boy was taken by the Conroys to the Connemara and Native Pony Festival in Bowral in 1980 where he won his class of seven for colts three years and under. The judge, Pat Lyne of Chiltern Stud in

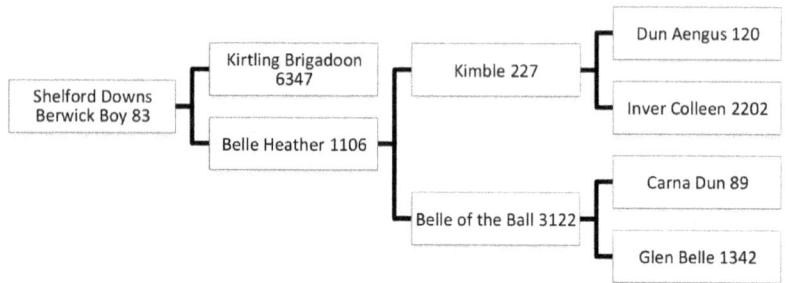

Shelford Downs Berwick Boy (96)
- Tylani Artel (146)
- Corrib Park Kelly (159)
- Corrib Park Ballymac (162)
  - Garnet Phineas (206)
  - Garnet Phoenix (208)
  - Garnet Quicksilver (211)
    - Clairvale Padraic (240)

Britain, appreciated him for his "pony character and charm".[13] The Conroys showed him in led and harness classes until Shelford Downs Stud dispersed. Berwick Boy was purchased by June Woolett who continued to show him in these classes and under saddle, as well as using him at stud. June described him in 1990 as being "a multi-supreme champion with a pony head, excellent length of rein, a good wither, strong quarters, and outstanding movement. Overall [he is] a quality pony throwing top progeny".

June lost Berwick Boy at only fourteen years of age, but he fortunately left three stallion sons: Tylani Artell (146), Corrib Park Kelly (159) and Corrib Park Ballymac (162), and three purebred daughters: Shelford Downs Pegeen (1302), Corrib Park Katie Clare (1508) and Corrib Park Macushla (1568) to continue his line.

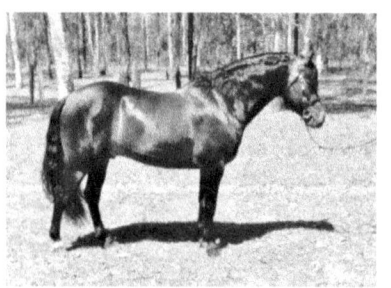

Shelford Downs Berwick Boy (96)

Photo: Eileen Simpson

Tylani Artell (146): Tylani Artell, was a bay/brown pony of 13.2hh foaled in 1987 out of Robinhill Blueberry (1174) and bred by David Nettleton of Tylani Stud at Park Ridge in Queensland. He was purchased by Annette Hodda, who succumbed to the difficulties of owning a stallion and had him gelded in 1992. He did not leave any breeding stock progeny.

---

13 R5 p140, R20

Corrib Park Kelly (159): Corrib Park Kelly was a black stallion of 13hh foaled in 1991 out of San Ed Petrini (1179). He was retained as a stallion prospect by his breeder James Crowley who considered him to be "very stylish, with excellent Connemara characteristics and with a good temperament and conformation". Kelly did well in the showring as a youngster and was only newly classified and with a promising stud career ahead of him when he died in a paddock accident. He did not leave a stallion son, however he has two registered daughters, Corrib Park Cherub (1627) and Corrib Park Clarissa (1628).

Shelford Downs Berwick Boy in harness.

Corrib Park Kelly (159)

Corrib Park Ballymac (162): The third and last stallion son of Berwick Boy was Corrib Park Ballymac. He was a dark brown/black stallion of 14hh foaled in 1992 out of Glenormiston Macroom (1409). He was raised as a stallion prospect by James who appreciated him for his lovely pony head, good length of rein, strong hindquarters and ample back. He was exhibited at a number of shows, winning champion two-year-old Connemara at the 1994 Brisbane Royal Show and champion led Connemara at a number of agricultural shows. James notes that he also showed talent in dressage and showjumping but he did not receive a great deal of training due to time restraints and the lack of a rider. James considered Ballymac to have a strong and determined character and a variable temperament.

Corrib Park Ballymac (162) with James Crowley.

In 2000 he was sold to Gary and Annette Johnston of the Garnet Stud at Helidon in Queensland where he settled in well, running with mares. This

Chapter 8   The Gil Line in Australia

Garnet Phineas (206)

Garnet Phoenix at two years old

Garnet Quicksilver (211) two years old

lifestyle suited him better than the solitary life he had previously led. He produced a number of quality stock for Garnet and was well used until his death, thought to be from snakebite, in 2007.

Ballymac is represented by three stallion sons in the studbook: Garnet Phineas (206), Garnet Phoenix (208) and Garnet Quicksilver (211), and by eleven purebred daughters: Garnet Lovely Lyric (1718), Garnet Morin (1750), Garnet Oseille (1792), Garnet Prelude (1810), Garnet Portrait (1814), Garnet Quantum Leap (1815), Garnet Quelle (1824), Garnet Panache (1834), Glenrose Roisin (1838), Wattle Hills Christmas Eve (1844) and Garnet Penny (1852).

Garnet Phineas (206) is a 13.3hh black stallion, foaled in 2005, out of Garnet's top-producing mare, Kilkieran Kirsten MacNeill (1574). He has been retained by Garnet Stud where he is appreciated for his type, colour and wonderful temperament. He was started under saddle, and after passing classification Phineas commenced stud duties. He now has a couple of seasons' foals on the ground.

Garnet Phoenix (208) is Ballymac's second stallion son. He is a chestnut of 13.3hh, out of Garnet Helena (1669), and was also from the 2005 season. He has been sold by Garnet to a stud with the focus on breeding partbred palomino all-rounders.

Garnet Quicksilver (210) is a full-brother to Phineas. A grey from palomino, Quicksilver was foaled in 2006 and is 13.3hh. Gary Johnston believes that he is one of the 'typiest' ponies he has bred, with wonderful movement, a lot of jumping talent and a wonderful easy-going temperament. Having been started under saddle, Quicksilver spent a couple of seasons standing at stud at Garnet, but was used very lightly producing only two foals, including his stallion son Clairvale Padraic (240), as he was closely related to many of the Garnet ponies. He was then sold in 2012 to Stephanie Ivatts in Western Australia before being gelded.

Clairvale Padraic (240): With my young mare Clairvale Eibhlin (1837) agisted at Glenormiston Stud while we were living in Darwin, and a return service of one of the nearby Garnet Stud stallions available to use, I chose Garnet Quicksilver to be her first 'husband'. I had liked Quicksilver's typical pony type and character since he was a foal, and also liked the overall pedigree that would result from the cross. As such, Padraic (Paddy) was foaled on St Patrick's Day in 2011, a liver chestnut to turn grey, with a bold and friendly personality. I liked him so much I ran him on as a stallion prospect, but he is only just beginning his story. It will be a great pleasure for me to follow his journey.

Photo: TearnaGoldston

Clairvale Padraic (240) in 2013

Tiercel Galloping Major imp (103):

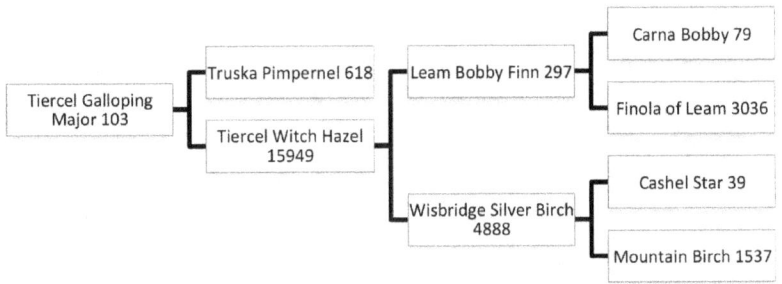

Tiercel Galloping Major, a grey pony of 13.3hh, was bred by Benita Sanders of the Tiercel Stud in Huntingdonshire, England in 1978. His dam Tiercel Witch Hazel (UK 15949) was the first Connemara Pony bred by Tiercel Stud and was an outstanding show mare winning many supreme championships in Connemara and open Mountain and Moorland classes and qualifying for Olympia after having been started under saddle for only eight weeks.

Tiercel Galloping Major (103) as a yearling before leaving England
Photo: Benita Sanders

Tiercel Witch Hazel (UK 15949) with Benita at the 1984 Ponies of Britain Show
Anthony Reynolds LMPA

Wisbridge Silver Birch (UK 4888)
Photo: Sanders Archive

After Witch Hazel's death in 1996 from Cushing's disease, Benita wrote: "Without her, the stud would never have achieved so much unforeseen success and excitement – she was soft and cuddly, but also wild, naughty and full of jokes.... She was what Connemaras should be and, if you are lucky, you will be privileged to know one like her in a life time."[14]

Not shown on Galloping Major's pedigree chart are his great-granddam, Mountain Birch's (Ire 1537) sire Lavalley Rebel (Ire 24) and dam Glentrasna Grey (Ire 1154), who was, in turn, by Derry Boy (Ire 30) and out of Rosmuck (Ire 865). Rosmuck has previously been viewed in Wisbridge Golden Rebel's (Ire 130) dam line.

Tiercel Galloping Major was imported by Roger and Lindy Salkeld of Garland Stud in New South Wales as a weanling. He was classified and sired one purebred daughter, Garland Silver Willow (1366). In 1980, however, the stud was partly dispersed due to an illness in the family and the Salkelds moving to South Australia. Galloping Major, described by Lindy as "a great children's pony" was gelded and used as a pony club mount by the Salkeld children.

---

14 R36:5

Chapter 9
The Tooreen Laddie Line in Australia

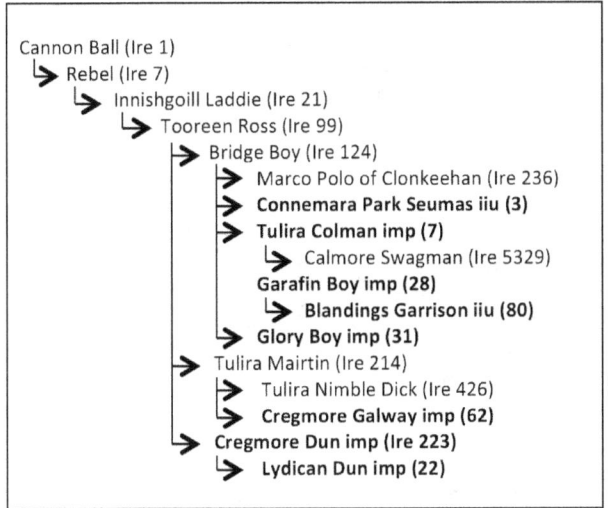

Connemara Park Seumas iiu (3)

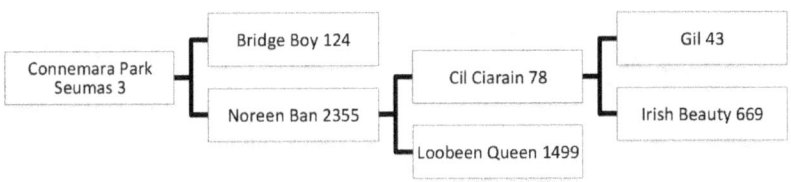

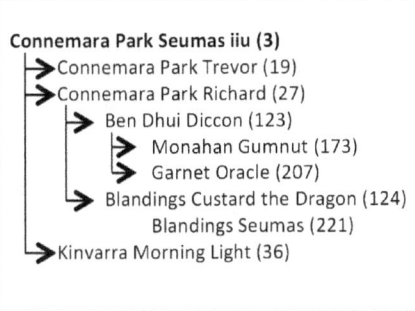

Connemara Park Seumas was foaled in 1967 at Connemara Park, Lancefield, Victoria, having been imported in-utero with his dam. Seumas, a grey stallion of 13.1hh was retained for a number of years by Connemara Park and produced three stallion sons: Connemara Park Trevor (19), Connemara Park Richard (27) and

Connemara Park Seumas (3)

Connemara Park Richard (27)

Blandings Cean Ruadh
with Rosemary Glaisher

Kinvara Morning Light (36). He is also represented by seven purebred daughters: Connemara Park Judy (1024), Connemara Park June (1030), Galway Park Clare (1042), Connemara Park Bonnie (1059), Connemara Park Hilda (1062), Connemara Park Kathleen (1082) and the bred-up mare Candlebark Sharon (2B/009).

Connemara Park Trevor (19): The first of Connemara Park Seumas's stallion sons, Trevor, was foaled in 1970 out of Connemara Park Ann (1005). He did not produce a stallion son, however three purebred daughters are registered in the studbook. These are Candlebark Mudlark (1120) and the bred-up mares Aran Medea (1184) and Tintagel Guinevere (2B/003).

Connemara Park Richard (27): Connemara Park Richard's bloodlines show perhaps the strongest influence of any stallion in this family on the Australian studbook. He was a grey stallion of 13.2hh, foaled in 1971 out of Ardan imp (1001). Richard was purchased from Connemara Park and stood at stud for a time with Dorothy Ross of the Tintagel Stud in Holbrook, New South Wales.

When the Storeys of Eagle Hill in Victoria found him again on the market, they quickly purchased him for their Blandings Stud. Kate Storey-Whyte had recently had an unproductive search in England for a stallion suitable to use over Blandings Bobby's (44) daughters. Richard was of particular interest to the Storeys, being a full-brother to their much loved foundation mare Connemara Park Judy (1024) and having no Carna Bobby (Ire 79) – the sire of Blandings Bobby – in his pedigree. Also attractive to the Storey's were his bone, substance and delightful temperament, traits that were passed on to his progeny.

Chapter 9   The Tooreen Laddie Line in Australia

Connemara Park Richard sired two registered stallion sons, Ben Dhui Diccon (123) and Blandings Custard the Dragon (124). Seventeen purebred daughters are also registered: Tintagel Kathleen (1221), Blandings Ambrosia (1235), Blandings Holly (1237), Blandings Marmalade (1238), Blandings Emerald (1329), Blandings Bluebell (1341), Blandings Millfleurs (1342), Sandy Park Peggy O'Neil (1349), Blandings Tiger Lily (1367), Blandings Amaranthus (1386), Blandings Amethyst (1387), Blandings Frangipani (1392), Blandings Millais (1394), Blandins Nutmeg (1395), Blandings Rusheenamarna (1396), Blandings Sandlewood (1397) and Blandings Kashmir (1427).

Richard also sired a number of wonderful geldings and partbreds. One outstanding purebred gelding was Blandings Cean Ruadh, who was owned by Sharon Seymour for a time and proved to be the catalyst for her to start breeding Connemaras with the Roscommon prefix. Sharon writes: "I had always had a soft spot for ponies and decided when I had children, to look for something that both the children and I could ride. I saw an advertisement for Blandings Stud in the paper and went off to look at their ponies. Kate Storey took me around and showed me Connemara Park Richard and various youngstock by him and Blandings Bobby. Rosemary was selling a lovely chestnut gelding called Blandings Cean Ruadh. He was out of Dangan Lady, so a half-brother to Blandings Bobby. He was a lovely, lovely pony – very honest, with a bushy blond mane and tail, and very eye-catching with the most beautiful movement courtesy of Richard. I bought him and had him for a couple of years at Ben Dhui Stud. I loved the Connemaras so much I decided that I really wanted a mare to breed from so I did a trade with Kate and Rosemary and ended up with Blandings Millais. Rosemary loved Rudi and they went on to be extremely successful in combined training."

Ben Dhui Diccon (123) with Christa Jones

Monahan Harrison and Clarissa Bailey

Ben Dhui Diccon (123), the first of Connemara Park Richard's stallion sons, is a 13.3hh grey (from chestnut) pony foaled in 1982. He was bred by Shirley Aird of the Ben Dhui Stud in Drysdale, Victoria, out of her foundation mare Blandings Sylvia (1216). During his early years, Diccon

Chapter 9　　　The Tooreen Laddie Line in Australia

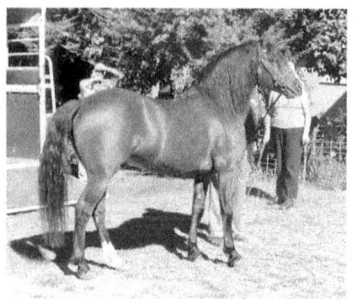

Monahan Gumnut (173)

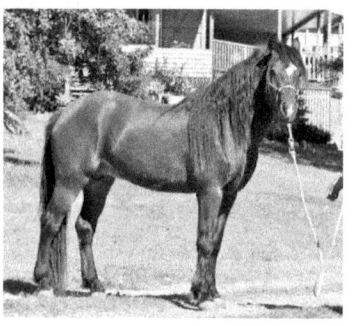

Garnet Oracle (207)

remained at Ben Dhui where he was regarded as one of the most outstanding ponies the stud produced.[1] He was appreciated for both his looks and his great sense of humour, often entertaining his human family with acrobatic displays performed with his paddock buddy, PC (Prince Charles), a 10hh Irish donkey.[2]

In 1990 Shirley met Christa Jones at the Connemara Jubilee Show in Victoria and agreed to lease and then sell Diccon to her. This was the beginning of the Monahan Stud at Gnarwarre in Victoria and Diccon has proven to be a very successful sire for the stud. He is currently represented by one stallion son, Monahan Gumnut (173), and eleven daughters: Monahan Bridie (1539), Monahan Ballad (1542), Monahan Deanna (1590), Monahan Encore (1602), Monahan Gypsy (1655), Monahan Hullabaloo (1697), Kiahma Susi (1730), Monahan Jessie Belle (1735), Monahan Irish Melody (1736), Monahan Nightingale (1789) and Springfield Kylemore (1858).[3]

Monahan Gumnut (173) is a 13.3hh bay stallion foaled in 1997 out of Yarraman Park Sarah (1231). He was purchased by Linda and Colin Guldbrandson of the Emerald Valley stud in Tasmania in 1999, and Linda has described him as having "a wonderful temperament, being very easy to handle, and having beautiful conformation and movement". After passing classification and siring a few foals for Emerald Valley, he was purchased by the Wattle Hills Stud in 2001, and made the big move from Tasmania to Mudgeeraba in Queensland.

The Wattle Hills Stud was originally established by Ursula and Archie Bury who bred Connemaras for their riding school and trail riding business. Their children Peter and Jenny, with their partners, purchased Gumnut as an outcross to use over their Wattle Hills mares, but unfortunately they discontinued breeding soon

---

1　R2 p81
2　R2 p81
3　R48 June 2006

Chapter 9 The Tooreen Laddie Line in Australia

after he took up stud duties there. He was subsequently purchased by Robyn Wallace of Mollys Stud at Thulimbah, where he sired one partbred gelding, and was then sold to his owners at the time of writing, Michelle Vasseur and Jamie King at Ballyshannon Lodge, near Warwick. Ballyshannon Lodge is well known for its Irish sport Horse breeding, and the stud's aim is to use Connemaras to produce ideal children's performance ponies.

Gumnut is currently represented by one stallion son, Garnet Oracle (207), and by two daughters, Emerald Valley Lilly Pilly (1709) and Emerald Valley Monsoon (1713). A number of other progeny have been foal recorded but have not yet been adult registered. One foal-recorded filly by Gumnut, Glenormiston Kitty O'Day, was sold to Fiona Comer in New Zealand where she will be an invaluable introduction of new bloodlines.

Gumnut's son, **Garnet Oracle (207)**, is a bay stallion of 14.1hh foaled in 2004 out of Corrib Park Macushla (1568). He was foaled in the midst of Australia's worst recorded drought and was a fairly rangy weanling colt when I first saw him. Nevertheless I found his pedigree quite interesting. At the time I was looking for a solid-coloured colt as an eventual partner for my grey dilute filly Clairvale Cuiliuir, so I purchased Oracle to see how he would turn out. As a two-year-old he won the colt class at the Queensland stud APSB Show – the only time he has been shown. He had been started under saddle and was due to come to me to continue with his education when my husband received a posting to Darwin where we would not have the facilities to keep a colt. His breeder, Gary Johnston, purchased him back and he has since produced a number of foals for Garnet Stud.

Blandings Custard the Dragon (124) was Connemara Park Richard's second son. He was a palomino stallion of 13hh, foaled in 1981 out of Blandings Buttercup (1096). He has one stallion son registered, Blandings Seumas (221), as well as two daughters, Blandings Sorbet (1543) and Blandings Jaipur (1616). He is described by Kate Storey-Whyte as having had an exceptional hindquarter and hock action and also being quite a character. He loved going to shows and receiving all the attention that these events entail!

Blandings Custard the Dragon with Kate Storey-Whyte in 1991

Photo: Jo Heard

Blandings Seumas (221), foaled in 1995 from Blandings Planxty (1181), was purchased by Jan Rockman of the Itsa Shamrock Stud in Western Australia as a genetic outcross

Chapter 9   The Tooreen Laddie Line in Australia

Blandings Seumas (221) at Itsa Shamrock Stud

for her breeding program. A grey from chestnut of 13hh, he is described by Jan as being "very pony and old-fashioned in type, and having a very quiet and sweet temperament.

Kinvara Morning Light (36): The last of Connemara Park Seuman's sons, Kinvara Morning Light, was a grey stallion of 13.3hh foaled in 1972 out of Connemara Park Ann (1005). Initially retained by his breeder, Dr Helen Davies, he was sold in 1974 when Helen dispersed her ponies and returned to live in the UK. He has no recorded breeding stock progeny.

Tulira Colman imp (7)

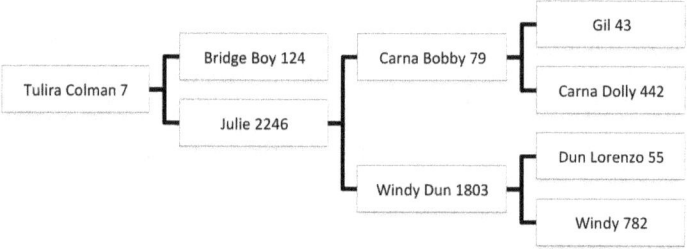

Tulira Colman was a grey stallion of 14hh foaled in 1965. He was bred, as were his dam Julie (Ire 2246) and previous generations of her mare line, by Colman Griffin of Maam Cross in Ireland. Julie, winner of the class for dry mares seven years old and over at Clifden show in 1969 was a big mare of good quality, according to Lady Hemphill. She was a granddaughter of Windy (Ire 782) who has been previously discussed as the dam of influential Irish stallion Rebel Wind (Ire 127). Julie was also the dam of Tulira

Tulira Colman (7) at the Melbourne Royal Show

Chapter 9   The Tooreen Laddie Line in Australia

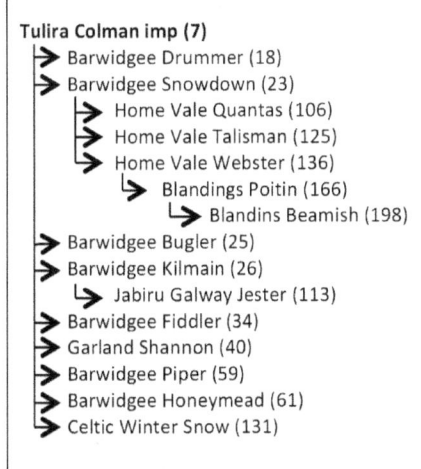

Tulira Colman imp (7)
- Barwidgee Drummer (18)
- Barwidgee Snowdown (23)
  - Home Vale Quantas (106)
  - Home Vale Talisman (125)
  - Home Vale Webster (136)
    - Blandings Poitin (166)
      - Blandins Beamish (198)
- Barwidgee Bugler (25)
- Barwidgee Kilmain (26)
  - Jabiru Galway Jester (113)
- Barwidgee Fiddler (34)
- Garland Shannon (40)
- Barwidgee Piper (59)
- Barwidgee Honeymead (61)
- Celtic Winter Snow (131)

Highball (Ire 750) who was exported from Ireland to Sweden where he produced exceptional performance progeny.[4]

As a young colt, Colman was purchased by Lady Hemphill for thirty pounds when her mother spotted him and told her that she had to buy him as he was going to be sold at the fair. Lady Hemphill describes him as a very well made, very typical Connemara. She presented him at the 1967 Clifden Show where he won the two year old colt class and at the Oughterard Show where he came second, before he was sold to the British partnership of Blanche and Ruth Miller of the Rosenaharley Stud and Thalia Gordon-Watson to use as an outcross for their mares.

Colman remained at Rosenaharley for only one season as he proved to be quite a handful for his new owners, both at stud and at the Ponies of Britain Show. While at stud there he sired several fillies, including the 1973 winner of the Leam Cup at the Ponies of Britain Show, Shipton Nadir (out of another import to Australia, Macaroon of Calmore imp 1079), and one stallion son, Calmore Swagman (Ire 5329), sire of the imported mare Eaden Calypso (1150).

M Kelly of the Barwidgee Stud had become interested in breeding partbred Connemara sporthorses, after watching a partbred carry its inexperienced rider around Badminton in 1952, and having been impressed with the success of Connemara crosses of that era such as Dundrum. She was particularly interested in purchasing mares with a strong performance pedigree, or ones that had proved themselves as performers, to cross with Thoroughbred stallions. She visited the Misses Miller at Rosenaharley Stud to look at a mare while Colman was in residence and he galloped up the paddock to greet

Julie (Ire 2246)

4 R47:12

Chapter 9   The Tooreen Laddie Line in Australia

Shoogle ridden by M Kelly

Faro competing with
Vicki Roycroft

her. She was impressed with him at first sight and made an offer to purchase him that day. So in 1969 'Mr C' became the third Connemara stallion to be imported to Australia. M has described Colman as being her favourite person as a horse, and "probably the most endearing, annoying, evil, but marvellous" of all the horses and ponies she has owned.[5]

He was a gifted stock pony and was well used in this role at Barwidgee. He evented, showjumped, and even competed in novelty events, winning the junior novelties at the Ararat Show one year with Lisa Kelly, who 'borrowed' him for the event without the knowledge of her parents, and without officials realising that he was a stallion! Lisa cared for Colman in his final years and he ran with a number of mares, producing partbred progeny and remaining fertile until his death at twenty-eight years of age. He is represented by nine purebred stallion sons: Barwidgee Drummer (18), Barwidgee Snowdown (23), Barwidgee Bugler (25), Barwidgee Kilmain (26), Barwidgee Fiddler (34), Garland Shannon (40), Barwidgee Piper (59), Barwidgee Honeymead (61) and Celtic Winter Snow (131). He also sired eight registered daughters: Galway Park Maura (1108), Barwidgee Snowberry (1053), Barwidgee Nandina (1057), Barwidgee Mizen (1094), Aran Kilkenny (1185), Glenormiston Maggie Macnamara (1234), Ben Dhui Fanfare (1344) and Barwidgee Sonata (1362).

Colman was particularly noted for producing exceptional performance partbreds. A favourite of M's was the half-Thoroughbred gelding Shoogle who was by all accounts a marvellous character. M competed with him up to FEI level dressage and he was later lent to eighty-five year old Noel Mason, Master of the Findon Harriers, who vowed that Shoogle was the best hunter he had ever ridden. Faro, a quarter-bred out of a mare by Colman, was selected for the Los Angeles Olympics. Sadly he became unsound and was unable to compete, but it did raise the profile of Connemaras and their jumping and performance ability in Australia.

Another partbred by Colman, the mare Ballantrae Acushla, was integral in

---

5 R2 p45

Chapter 9   The Tooreen Laddie Line in Australia

leading her owners to form a Connemara stud. Cushy, bred by the late Jo Heard from her children's pony, so impressed the Heards with her willingness to please and delightful nature that a purebred breeding program was begun. After leaving the Heards, Cushy became a wonderful RDA mount for the Hamilton RDA – a testament to her nature.

Barwidgee Snowdown (23)

Barwidgee Snowdown (23): From a studbook perspective, the most successful of Tulira Colman's stallion sons was his second, Barwidgee Snowdown. Kelly as he was known, was foaled in 1971 out of Aylesland Silver Velvet imp (1011). As a weanling he was purchased by Ann Paterson as the foundation stallion for her Home Vale Stud in Tasmania, to breed top class pony club and performance ponies from Thoroughbred and pony mares. This partbred breeding

Barwidgee Snowdown (23) under saddle

program proved to be highly successful, with the Home Vale prefix gracing the names of champion pony club, show and eventing horses and ponies. Two partbreds of note are Home Vale Nicholas, out of a pony mare, and Home Vale Sinbad, out of a Thoroughbred mare.

Kaye Young wrote in a 1984 CPBSA newsletter: "Home Vale Nicholas, a partbred gelding, was announced overall APSB Pony for 1983 – three hundred points ahead of his nearest competitor. He is the only heavyweight pony in this state to perform consistently well, winning or gaining champion and reserve sashes and has never been unplaced at an EFA show, which is quite an achievement in itself. Nicki is a true ambassador of his breed, showing tractability, reliability and versatility. He has wins and placings in dressage, showjumping, one day events, saddle classes, fancy dress classes for the children and activity classes. He has taught many children to ride and obtain confidence and is at present ridden by a thirteen-year-old lass who has been completely won over and is now an avid Connie lover. He is a delightful character, is well known around the show circuit, and is well respected by fellow competitors for his faultless disposition and impeccable manners."

Chapter 9 The Tooreen Laddie Line in Australia

Home Vale Sinbad excelled in pony club eventing, showjumping and dressage, and amassed countless wins and placings in these fields. He was described as a very happy and easy to handle horse, but quite mischievous, by his first partner Johanna Hughes, who began his education under the tutelage of Andrew and Manuela McLean. His successes with Johanna culminated in gaining the Junior NTEC Horse of the Year in 1989. He then moved on to Johanna's younger sister Sarah. Together they won the Tasmanian state pony club horse trials and were selected for the Tasmanian pony club team to compete at Naracoorte young riders TDE, where they placed second overall and were part of the winning team in 1992. The pair also won the state Pony Club Dressage Championships 13-17 years. He also repeated his state trials win in 1998 with a new rider, Alick Weber!

As a result of the success of the partbreds, Ann decided to incorporate a purebred breeding program into the stud and imported three purebred mares from England for this purpose. Barwidgee Snowdown is therefore well represented in the studbook by three stallion sons: Home Vale Quantas (106), Home Vale Talisman (125) and Home Vale Webster (136); and by ten registered daughters: Home Vale Perfection (1219), Huon Valley Lady in the Snow (1239), Home Vale Serenade (1370), Home Vale Samantha (1371), Home Vale Tracey (1402), Home Vale Velvet (1411), Home Vale Yeltor (1501) and Home Vale Zadia (1512). Ann notes that Kelly grew well up to height and produced ponies with a good temperament, excellent conformation and outstanding free-flowing movement. The only thing about him with which she could find fault was that his head was a little plain!

Homevale Quantas (106) 4 years old
Photo: Doug Jervis

David and Anne Moore riding Tinderry Clancy and Tinderry Linton, full-brothers by Home Vale Quantas and out of Robinhill Silver Jubilee.
Photo: Su Moore.

Home Vale Quantas (106), Kelly's first son, was a grey pony of 14hh foaled in 1979 out of Chiltern Gemini (1074), the first purebred mare to be imported by Ann. Quantas was purchased as a weanling from Home Vale in 1980 by Su and John Moore of the Tinderry Stud after losing their foundation sire Tyn-Y-Rhos Erin (71). They had been particularly interested in obtaining a stallion from Tulira Colman's line, after having viewed him at Barwidgee and being very impressed with him.

Quantas duly arrived at Tinderry, near Captains Flat in New South Wales where, after maturing and passing classification, he performed stud duties – running out with his mares, standing guard while mares gave birth and playing with his colt foals. He was regularly used by the Moores as a stock pony, in fact if cattle were being moved through his paddock he would come over and help. Su recalls that no matter where on the property he was working stock, his ears always pointed in the direction of his mares! He fulfilled all expectations the Moores had of him, displaying an excellent temperament and work-ethic, and siring ponies with all-round ability suitable for both children and adults. He had a very limited showring career due to time, distance and the lack of local classes, but won the led Connemara colt class at the 1981 National Stud Horse and Pony Show, and supreme led Connemara exhibit at the 1984 Canberra Royal.

Home Vale Quantas left no stallion sons. He is, however, represented by seven purebred daughters: Tinderry Donna (1379), Curra Melody (1484), Tinderry Norah (1522), Argenta Megan (1533), Tinderry Jinden (1605), Tinderry Enya (1642) and Curraglen Whisper (1749).

Home Vale Quantas

Home Vale Talisman (125), Tulira Colman's second stallion son, was a grey pony foaled in 1982 and a full-brother to Home Vale Quantas. He was purchased as a yearling by Bengt and Katrina Kindblad of the Sycamore Stud in New Norfolk, Tasmania and won the filly or colt class for them at the 1983 Tasmanian Connemara Field Day, judged by Irish breeder and author Lib Petch of the Coosheen Stud. For the event, the Kindblads donated a coffee table handcrafted by Bengt for the supreme exhibit. At the end of the day, this special trophy was won by Talisman's full-sister Home Vale Perfection (1219).

Home Vale Talisman (125) as a two years old

Chapter 9 The Tooreen Laddie Line in Australia

Talisman remained at Sycamore until his eighth year, siring three purebred mares: Sycamore Antarctica (1451), Sycamore Blossom (1491) and Sycamore Delight (1531).

Talisman was then gelded and sold to the Betts family of Hobart for their son Stewart. After he won the CPBSA's Connemara of the Year award and the Jo Heard Trophy, Suzanne Betts wrote a tribute in a 1999 CPBSA newsletter which reads as follows: "Our son Stewart was only seven when Tally came to us and the combination has been together for seven years now. It is rare in the horse world for a partnership to endure so long. Their jumping career started with a pole on the ground and they now pop over three foot something. Stewart is now moving on to a larger horse so it's over to me who now has a chance to ride him. I've already competed at showjumping days and ODEs. This weekend we are going to an adult pony camp. And I thought I'd retire!! Harness – his steady temperament encouraged me to break him to harness which has been a lot of fun and was quite easy to do. Although we mainly go on bush drives he has successfully competed at agricultural shows and the Royal Hobart show. He is not fazed by the razzle dazzle of a busy show which is comforting to his novice driver. Showing – Home Vale Talisman has also competed in breed classes and was champion Connemara at the 1997 Royal Hobart Show. General – Tally is always the perfect patient gentleman at the school fair and provides many hours of 'pony rides'. Similarly he often gives pony rides at home for visiting friends or my young nieces from interstate. He has mastered the art of the slow walk where small children are involved. Finally, he earns his keep around the farm and is used to round up the cattle. He seems to really enjoy trotting back and forwards behind the herd picking up any stragglers."

Home Vale Webster (136) in 1991

Photo: Jo Heard

Home Vale Webster (136), a full-brother to Quantas and Talisman, was foaled in 1985. The third and last of Barwidgee Snowdown's stallion sons was a grey pony of 13.3hh. Kate Storey-Whyte, who had selected Gemini in England for Ann Patterson, bought Webster for her family's Blandings Stud in Victoria to use over their Blandings Bobby and Connemara Park Richard daughters. Hooley, as he was nick-named, proved to be quite a handful as a youngster, but the Storeys were reassured by Ann who told them that he would settle down as he matured, which he did sooner than anticipated and became a delight according to Kate.

Home Vale Webster remained at Blandings Stud until his death in 1999, siring one stallion son, Blandings Poitin (166), and nine purebred daughters: Killarney Park Spinifex (1537), Blandings Ingrid (1541), Blandings Mufty (1545), Blandings Amalfi (1546), Blandings Tiger Lily (1547), Blandings Folly (1611), Blandings Columbine (1630), Blandings Sally (1644) and Blandings Colleen (1653).

Blandings Poitin (166) in Tasmania

Webster's son, **Blandings Poitin (166)**, is a buckskin pony of 13.3hh foaled in 1995 out of the iiu mare Blandings Coinneac (1127). Poitin (pronounced potcheen) produced one stallion son, Blandings Beamish (198), and one registered daughter, Ballina Cleopatra (1738), while residing in Victoria as a young stallion. He has remained in the ownership of the Storeys, but was leased to the Nicholas family of the Athabascan Stud in Tasmania from 2004 to 2007, and at the time of writing is leased by the Condon family in Gympie, Queensland.

Blandings Beamish at the 2008 Victorian Connemara Showcase

Whilst in Tasmania Poitin sired a number of purebred foals, however these were not foal recorded. In Queenland Poitin will have further opportunity to continue his line as the Condons have purchased some purebred mares. He is also used as a stock pony by Brendan, who finds he has brilliant ability in this area – a trait often repeated in this line.

Poitin's son, **Blandings Beamish (198)**, is a grey (dilute) stallion of 14.1½hh foaled in 2000 out of Blandings Amaranthus (1386). He, too, has remained in the ownership of Blandings Stud and spent most of his earlier years under the management of Cheryl Ellis of the Lachernleigh New Forest Pony Stud in Victoria. There, Beamish was started under saddle and classified before being leased to Annette Gardiner of the Kahean Stud at Sulky.

Annette notes that Beamish was initially standoffish, but once settled in he loved being involved in activities with people, seeking out attention

Barwidgee Bugler (25) with
Lindy Salkeld and M Kelly's JRT

and enjoying his work. She describes him as being very gentle and easy to do anything with. He was used as a stud stallion at Kahean for a season and produced two purebreds, a filly, Kahean Snowblossom, and a gelding, Blandings Foxtrot. In 2008 Blandings Beamish was leased to the Dylanglen Stud at Rand in New South Wales, and more recently to Icarus Park Irish Sporthorses at Lancefield in Victoria.

Barwidgee Bugler (25): Tulira Colman's third stallion son, Barwidgee Bugler, was a grey (dilute) pony of 14.1hh foaled in 1971 out of the imported mare September Song of Millfields (1010). He was purchased by Roger and Lindy Salkeld and stood at their Garland Stud in New South Wales until 1979 when he was sold to a Thoroughbred stud as a teaser. Lindy described Bugler as "a brilliant looking horse who did well in the showring". She also noted that as newcomers to stallion ownership they found he could be quite difficult to handle and ride. Bugler did not produce any stallion sons, however he is represented by six purebred daughters: Toorigal Robyn (1137), Toorigal Purdie (1164), Garland Celebration (1187), Yarraman Park Four Bells (1210), Garland of Blossom (1217) and Glenormiston Molly Malone (1244).

Bugler also produced some outstanding partbred progeny. Garland Marele, a buckskin of 15.2hh out of a Thoroughbred mare, did exceptionally well for teenage rider Liane Gorham in the early eighties. In an article written by Roger for a CPBSA newsletter in 1981, he lists some of Marele's achievements that year: second place at the National Capital Two Day Horse Trials Championships, overall winner of C Grade level at the local pony club showjumping and dressage day, second at preliminary level at the southern Highlands ODE, third in the restricted novice at the NSW ODE and winner of the Junior Novice ODE at Bowral. All this as a five-year-old who was also regularly used as a stockhorse. The next year the pair won the NSW state junior championship ODE. Another competitive partbred by Bugler, Spare Time, ridden by fourteen-year-old Elsie Richards, won the Tasmanian Showjumping Association's horse of the year in 2001.[6]

---

6 R48 December 2001

Chapter 9   The Tooreen Laddie Line in Australia

Tinderry Merlin, the first pony bred by Su Moore, was a gelding by Bugler and out of an Australian Pony mare. Merlin partnered Su's brother-in-law on many treks including a 350 kilometre ride from Bathurst to Lyons Creek near Cooma. Merlin was used regularly for mustering cattle in the high country and was an experienced and reliable pack horse.[7]

Barwidgee Kilmain (26) ridden by Grant Woolett

Barwidgee Kilmain (26): Barwidgee Kilmain was Tulira Colman's fouth stallion son and was a grey (dilute) pony of 13.2hh foaled in 1971. He was purchased as a foal-at-foot with his dam, the imported mare Easter Strand (1008), by the Salkelds of Garland Stud and later sold on to June Woolett of Barkala Stud at Jimboomba in Queensland. As a two-year-old the Wooletts decided that he needed some education, but he was too young to start under saddle. They couldn't find anyone suitable to start him in harness, so purchased a book, gathered together some harness and started him themselves. It took only four hours! Kilmain won many events in-hand, under saddle and in harness. He produced one stallion son, Jabiru Galway Jester (113), and one purebred daughter, Jabiru Jennifer Clare (1405).

Kilmain as an older pony with Michael Deakin

One partbred by Kilmain, named Silver, was very successful at pony club events with his very young rider, Kathy Tyler. The pair won the champion sash and trophy for the child ten years and under at the Ipswich Show in both 1980 and 1981. Kilmain was gelded when the Wooletts purchased another stallion, Shelford Downs Berwick Boy (96), but he continued to be well used as a ridden pony by their son Grant. He was leased to the Deakins of Kilkieran Stud as a twenty-three year old and they describe him as having been "really old-fashioned and plain, but the most adorable, beautiful pony who would do anything and go anywhere for anybody!" He proved to be an excellent ambassador for the breed as an aged pony, being used by the Deakin's daughter Katie for pony club, and for RDA, and

---

7 R1 p81-83

Barwidgee Fiddler (34) and Carol Paine

Harknow ridden by Andrew Clarke

for teaching beginners at the local riding centre. Kilmain also retained his excellent health and native pony hardiness and was over thirty years old when he was euthanased after injuring his hip.

Jabiru Galway Jester (113), Kilmain's son out of County Clare Celtic Song (1073), did not produce any breeding stock progeny before he was gelded.

Barwidgee Fiddler (34): Barwidgee Fiddler, a full-brother to Drummer and Bugler, was foaled in 1972. He is recorded in the studbook as standing 14.1hh, but is known to have grown over height. Fiddler was bought as a weanling stallion prospect by Mrs Carol Paine of East Gippsland, Victoria, who bred a number of partbreds by him. He and Carol were a successful campdrafting partnership and he introduced her to eventing. Carol wrote about Fiddler in the June Hoofs and Horns of 1983: "Ten years ago I was wondering what I was going to do for horse entertainment when my daughter finished at pony club. Thinking my riding days must be coming to an end, I thought I would join the ranks of those energetic people who run about leading ponies at shows and spend a lot of time polishing and pampering them – possibly boring but at least still involved in the horse scene. I enquired from Margaret Kelly if she had anything suitable. The price of a purebred filly being out of the question, she suggested a colt. I didn't think I wanted a colt. 'Oh! Connemaras are different – no trouble at all!' – so I went to Barwidgee and a tiny little seven month old colt and I inspected each other. I liked his bright-eyed intelligent look and I seemed to pass his careful examination of smell (and taste), so into the float and a very long trip to Gippsland. Because he was so young the colt spent the next two years in the company of an old gelding, and apart from chewing the ears off several sheep, he proved to be 'No trouble at all!' In spite of almost continuous lack of grass, due to either drought or flood, Barwidgee Fiddler grew into a very strong two-year-old of 15hh. He broke in easily and well, was only away for a week. He never put a foot wrong and I rode him everywhere. Stock work he loved – but of course I was only going

Chapter 9   The Tooreen Laddie Line in Australia

to lead him! So we went to Melbourne Show and as a three-year-old Barwidgee Fiddler won the reserve champion stallion in spite of a few raised eyebrows at his rather obvious over-height. That year (1976) he was never unplaced, led or ridden, at all the local shows, finishing champion at the Bairnsdale Show. I was then talked into competing at a combined training event – first taste of dressage for us both, and to everyone's surprise we won! Fired by success we then competed in everything possible for the rest of our time together; my retirement was over, the led ring forgotten and I enjoyed six years of safe, active and fun riding. Barwidgee Fiddler show jumped with flair and style with a pony club rider; I campdrafted, did trail riding, dressage schools, one day events, novelties – he thoroughly enjoyed being out and about and, apart from moments in the dressage arena, I felt we had a real understanding. Barwidgee Fiddler has now retired to stud at Barwidgee, and I hope he leaves a lot of foals with his personality, charm and ability. Good luck Fiddler! Connemaras are different!"

An exceptional partbred by Fiddler was the mare Harknow, out of a Thoroughbred mare. This 16.1hh mare was bred by Mrs Joan Pearson, and bought by the Clarkes of Glenormiston Stud in Queensland for their son Andrew when he grew too tall for the ponies. Andrew and Harknow competed successfully in pony club eventing up to international level, as well as enjoying led-in events, show rider classes, campdrafting and polocross.[8]

Although used by his owners to breed partbreds, the Woodwards of Candlebark Stud sent a couple of their purebred mares to Fiddler. This resulted in two purebred daughters, Candlebark Leitis (1190) and Candlebark Lili (1192).

Tulira Colman's eighth stallion son, **Barwidgee Honeymead (61)**, was a grey stallion of 13.2hh foaled in 1974. Honeymead was initially named Corrib by M, but his name was changed by the Bayards who purchased him from her. He is the sole registered progeny of the imported mare, Clonterna Honeysuckle (1017), and is himself represented by only one purebred daughter, Blandings Ardrahan (1281). Honeymead also sired the successful gelding, Salette Honeycombe, out of Barwidgee Snowdrift (1058), who was much appreciated by the Dowd family of Drysdale, Victoria. He was outstandingly successful at pony club and in pony dressage (trained up to medium level), as well as being a wonderful family and riding school pony.

---

8 R6 p112, R18, R25, R28

Barwidgee Drummer (18) in Western Australia

Garland Shannon (40)

Celtic Winter Snow (131): The ninth and last of Tulira Colman's stallion sons, Celtic Winter Snow, was a grey stallion of 14hh foaled in 1984 and, being out of Aylesland Silver Velvet (1011), a full-brother to Barwidgee Snowdown (23). Penny Brown of Celtic Stud bought Silver Velvet from Barwidgee with Winter Snow in-utero and he was sold as a youngster. Penny describes him as having been well up-to-height and much like his sire. He did not produce any stallion sons and has one purebred daughter Celtic Fairytale (1855).

Barwidgee Drummer (18); Garland Shannon (40); Barwidgee Piper (59):

Drummer was Tulira Colman's first stallion son. He was a grey (as are all of Colman's progeny) 14.2hh pony foaled in 1970 out of the imported mare September Song of Millfields (1010). He was one of the very few colts at Barwidgee that was not sold as a foal and was started under saddle and used as a stockhorse before being sold. M describes him as such a quick stock pony that you needed a stock saddle to keep you on the pony! She is also of the opinion that he is one of the best ponies that she bred. After he was bought by Margaret and Lindsay Kenney of the Marglyn Stud, Drummer made the long journey to Western Australia along with Conterna Honeysuckle (1017) and the partbred mare Connemara Park Sheba. Unfortunately, Drummer's testicles were damaged in a paddock accident and he was gelded, leaving no purebred breeding stock progeny. He did produce one Thoroughbred cross, Kettledrum, who proved to be an excellent eventer and performance mare.

What Barwidgee Drummer missed in stud breeding he more than made up for in promotion of the Connemara Pony in Western Australia. Under the ownership of Helen Colleran he competed in led and ridden show classes and in sporting events, winning both ribbons and admirers well

Chapter 9   The Tooreen Laddie Line in Australia

into his twenties. At twenty-three, his successes when ridden by Amy Barnard led to him being awarded the CPBSA Connemara Pony of the Year title.

Tulira Colman's sixth stallion son, Garland Shannon, was a grey pony of 13.3hh. He was foaled in 1972, with his dam, the imported mare Easter Strand (1008), carrying Shannon when she was purchased from Barwidgee by the Salkelds. He is a full-brother to Barwidgee Kilmain.

The Whittington family of Hill N' Dale Stud in Westbury, Tasmania, purchased Shannon as a yearling and he remained with them for his thirty-one year lifetime. He was successfully shown both in-hand and in ridden events as a young stallion and continued to be ridden into his old age by the Wittington children and grandchildren. He took part in St Patrick's Day parades until his 26th year. He did not produce any purebred breeding stock, but produced some outstanding partbreds. His first foal, Dancing Queen, had a very successful show career in the 1980's. Dark Warrior was a state representative in eventing and a successful showjumper, and Daddy Cool was Tasmanian Junior Showjumper of the Year.

Garland Shannon's last foal, Riverdance, was named the Northern Tasmanian Eventing Club's Horse of the Year (preliminary, training and freshman's grades) in 2000 with Mrs Whittington's daughter Phylliss Pyke and proved to be a wonderful all-rounder with a sensible and reliable temperament. She also competed in pony club games, polocrosse, as well as general riding for fun at home. In recognition of her all-round ability and promotion of the Connemara in Tasmania she was awarded the CPBSA's Jo Heard Trophy in 2000.

Barwidgee Piper, another Tulira Colman/September Song of Millfields cross, was a grey stallion of 14.2hh, foaled in 1973. He was purchased from Barwidgee by Di Cumming of Robinhill Stud and competed successfully in well supported combined training events in open company. Piper was sold on to the Carpenter family of Sydney and did not produce any breeding stock progeny before being gelded.

Barwidgee Piper (59)

Photo: Sue Clarke

Chapter 9   The Tooreen Laddie Line in Australia

Cregmore Dun imp (Ire 223)

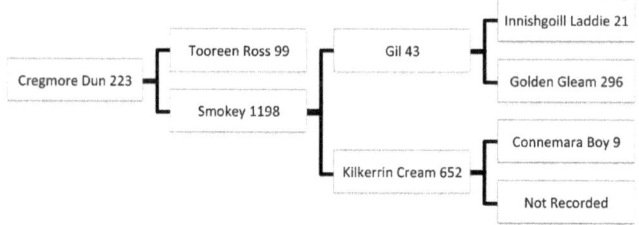

Cregmore Dun (Ire 223)
↳ Lydican Dun imp (22)
  ↳ Tyn-Y-Rhos Sir Anthony (74)

Cregmore Dun (Ire 223) in Ireland

Smokey (Ire 1198)

Cregmore Dun was a dappled buckskin stallion of 14hh foaled in 1965. He was bred by Michael Carr of Moycullen in Ireland. His dam, Smokey, was the foundation mare of Murty McGrath's breeding program and was described by Lady Hemphill as "a top, top mare". She produced the Hemphill family's outstanding performance pony gelding Patsy Fagan (Ire G58), and also produced the mare Our Smokey (Ire 2969), dam of another Australian import, Cregmore Colm (84).[9]

Cregmore Dun sired fifteen ponies in Ireland between 1968 and 1971, and was presented at the parade of stallions at Tulira Castle in 1970. He caught the eye of Penny Galbraith of the Barolin Australian Pony Stud, when she was on a tour of Europe with her parents looking at stud cattle. Penny's first experience with Connemara Ponies had been in 1964 when she went to Ireland to ride hunters. She recalls: "To watch [the Connemara Ponies] threading their way through mountain defiles, dodging peat bogs and other pitfalls while cantering down some rocky slope is to realise why

---

9 R3 p199 236 239

Chapter 9 The Tooreen Laddie Line in Australia

they have attained a sure footedness which has become proverbial." At the time of her visit, she was hoping to find an up-to-height stallion to add height and bone and an outcross of bloodlines to her Australian Pony breeding program.

Patsy Fagan ridden by Angela Hemphill

Penny describes Cregmore Dun as being "a large pony with presence, a lovely front, wither and shoulder, and a beautiful head". He was purchased and imported to Australia, but was tragically lost six months later, having sired no purebred foals. One of his partbreds, a 15hh mare named Melanita, was owned by June Woolett of the Barkala Stud in Queensland, and she competed very succesfully under saddle with her.

Lydican Dun (22)

Lydican Dun imp (22): A son of Cregmore Dun, Lydican Dun was purchased sight-unseen by Penny in 1971 from his breeder, Tom Noone of Oranmore, Ireland, to replace his sire. He was imported as a foal-at-foot with his dam Ice Blue (1016). It was a little disappointing for Penny that he threw to his dam's height, and reached only 13.1hh. However he was, "a great pony. He had a lovely temperament, was very game, and was just a nice pony to own". He moved to Penny's sister Jennifer Cribb of the Barncleuth Stud in Bundaberg, Queensland, in 1983 to replace his half-brother Barolin Aer-Lingus (32) who had been sold. Lydican Dun produced some exceptional partbreds for Jennifer before he was gelded. She described him in 1984 as a pony with "excellent conformation, a rhythmic springy stride, and superb presence" as well as "quiet and hardy". He competed successfully with Jennifer in ridden stallion classes and showjumping.

Lydican Dun produced one stallion son out of Connemara Park Ann (1005), **Tyn-Y-Rhos Sir Anthony (74)**, who did not produce any breeding stock progeny, and three registered daughters: Galway Park Theresa (1149), Tyn-Y-Rhos Ria (1154) and Tyn-Y-Rhos Ele (1205). A gelding son, Chittering Gully Shadow, was purchased by the McClements of Hillville, New South Wales, for their young daughter Anne to ride at pony club. The pair earned outstanding success, with ribbons, trophies and rugs won in showjumping, sporting events and agricultural shows. He was then leased to a succession of happy young riders who enjoyed the same results with him, leading to him being awarded the CPBSA's Jo Heard Trophy in 2000. He so impressed the McClements family that they formed the Kaledon Stud in 2001, hoping to breed ponies just like 'Shady'.

Introducing another family to the joy of owning a Connemara Pony was the mare Glenormiston Kerima, nicknamed Prickles. Another partbred by Lydican Dun, this mare, foaled in 1974, was the first Connemara foal for the Clarkes of Glenormiston Stud in Queensland – there followed thirty-eight years of Connemara Pony breeding!

Garafin Boy imp (28)

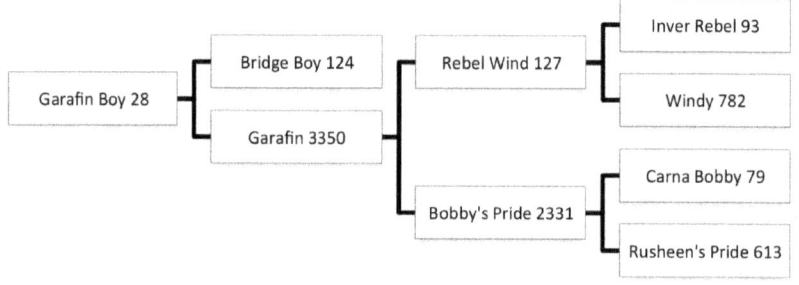

Garafin Boy was a grey stallion of 14.1hh, foaled in 1967. He was bred by Mrs M Conroy of Galway, Ireland. His dam, Garafin (Ire 3350), came from the very successful Sliabh na mBan (Ire 227) mare family. The founding mare of this line was owned and used as a broodmare by Festy Folan of Carna as well as competing successfully with her in the showring. She was placed second at the CPBS's society show as a two-year-old in 1935, and won the young mare class and RDS Silver Medal the following year.[10]

Garafin Boy passed classification in Ireland and produced three daughters between 1972 and 1974, before being purchased and imported to Australia by Richard and Helen Mussared of the Cunderdin Stud in Cunderdin, Western Australia. He stood at stud for a number of years, being used over the

---

10 R4 p211, R47:4

Chapter 9   The Tooreen Laddie Line in Australia

Mussared's purebred mare Oakleigh Mermaid (1036) as well as producing a number of crossbreds. Unfortunately, to the great disappointment of the Mussareds, some of the foals he sired displayed incorrect hoof conformation, so he was gelded and Cunderdin closed its Connemara breeding program.

Garafin Boy (28)

Garafin Boy was used as a 'Clerk of the Course' pony at Harness racing meets by Richard who describes him as having a marvellous temperament and being a very useful pony. After he was gelded he was sold to Rose Bowen as a child's pony and he remained with her for the rest of his life. Garafin Boy is represented by one stallion son, Blandings Garrison iiu (80), and three daughters: Yarraman Park Sophie (1081), Cunderdin Ann Oakleigh (1085) and Cunderdin Dolphin (1183).

Two partbreds by Garafin Boy bred at Cunderdin Stud named Despatch and Boa were employed as police horses by the Western Australian Police Department. Another, Leisafryn (out of a Standardbred mare), did exceptionally well in harness classes in the early 1980's.

Blandings Garrison iiu (80): Blandings Garrison was a grey pony imported in-utero by the Storeys of Blandings Stud with his dam, Lisavalla Rose (1049), and foaled in 1974. Described by the Storeys as having excellent bone and a good temperament, he was sold to a stud breeding stockhorses and did not produce any purebred progeny.

Glory Boy imp (31)

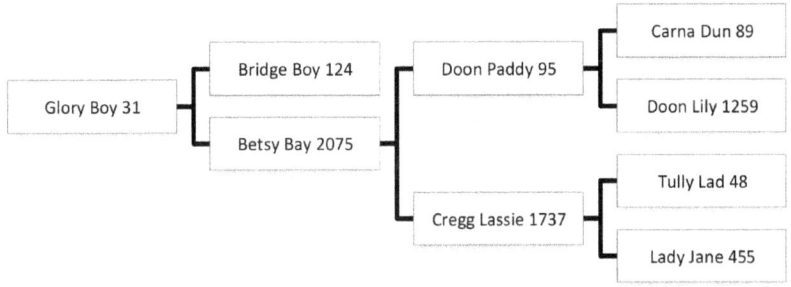

Chapter 9   The Tooreen Laddie Line in Australia

Glory Boy (31) with Joe Scanlon
Photo: Scanlon Archive

Glory Boy was a grey stallion of 14hh bred by T Dixon of Galway, Ireland, in 1967. He was also by Bridge Boy (Ire 124) and out of Betsy Bay (Ire 2075). Betsy Bay's dam, Cregg Lassie (Ire 1737), bred a regular foal for her owner Jim Walsh, and was worked n harness and shown both in-hand and in harness classes.

Glory Boy was imported to Australia by Joe Scanlon and stood at his property at Biloela in Central Queensland where he was used to produce hardy stockhorses. In the late 1970's, Margaret Campbell of Wowan in Central Queensland inspected Glory Boy at Joe's property. Although believing him to be somewhat plain, she sent a Thoroughbred mare to him to be bred. This was the beginning of the Binnowie Stud. The resulting filly impressed her greatly and she notes that all the ponies she had with Glory Boy in their breeding had long and successful careers as showjumpers and eventers. When Joe dispersed his ponies, Margaret bought a partbred mare named Marric Cortina, by Silver Sultan (6) in-foal to Glory Boy. The resultant filly, Binnowie Gemini, became one of the best performed ponies in Central Queensland in the 1980's, winning many ODEs, combined taining, dressage and showjumping competitions. She was also awarded champion working hunter by Anne Rolinson at the Mountain and Moorland Pony Festival held in Brisbane in 1987, in addition to winning two dressage tests and placing in the led and saddle classes! She was also used extensively for stockwork by Margaret, proving her versatility.

Cregmore Galway imp (62)

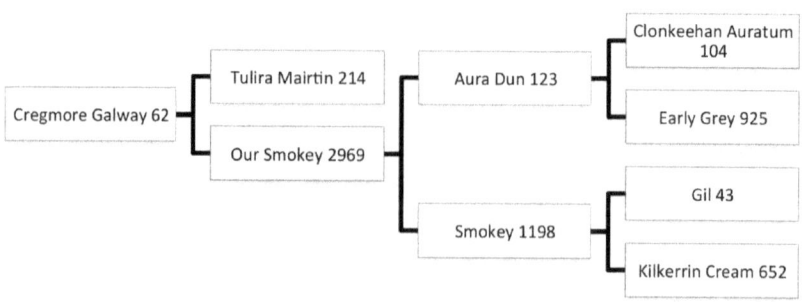

Chapter 9   The Tooreen Laddie Line in Australia

Cregmore Galway was a grey stallion of 14.2hh by Tulira Mairtin (Ire 214). Foaled in 1975, he was bred by Murty McGrath of Claregalway, Ireland. His dam Our Smokey (Ire 2969) was also dam of the imported stallion Cregmore Colm (84) and the mare Smokey Jane Grey (Ire 7477), dam of Clifden supreme winner Smokey Duncan (Ire 871). Cregmore Galway's grand dam, Smokey (Ire 1198), has been discussed previously in this chapter as the dam of Cregmore Dun (Ire 223).

A young Cregmore Galway (62)

Cregmore Galway, or Murty to those who knew him, was imported as a young pony by M Kelly who intended using him over the Barwidgee mares. However, he grew right up to height which made him unsuitable for the Barwidgee purebred breeding program which was at the time experiencing some over-height problems. He was sold to the McGowans of Yarrandoo Stud in Barnawartha,

Our Smokey (Ire 2969)

Victoria, where he was very much appreciated by the three McGowen girls for his outstanding temperament and used as a regular mount for riding around the farm. From there, he moved on to Pam Jeffery of Keyneton in South Australia.

As well as siring many partbreds who went on to be successful pony club mounts, Murty was used by Pam to teach beginner riders, including Gill Beaton's (Clifden Stud) youngest son James. Two of Pam's young grandsons, Travis and Charles, rode Murty regularly in lessons and at competitions.

As stallions were excluded from pony club, he was gelded at thirteen years of age and then continued in his role as child educator and companion. John Tennant of Rupari Stud noted in 1990 that "we can't say that being gelded has made him more tractable, he has always been a delight to ride and have around!"

Cregmore Galway did not leave any stallion sons, but is represented by six registered daughters: Barwidgee Velour (1201), Barwidgee Silver Dollar (1222), Barwidgee Lusitanica (1240), Yarrandoo Eily (1241), Exmoor Silver Swallow (1249) and Green Hills Shannon (1271). One of his partbred daughters of note was Glenormiston Carrilon (out of the partbred mare Kettledrum), a very successful pony club and inter-school competition mount in Queensland for her owner Tanya Adams.

Chapter 10
The Lavalley-Rebel Line in Australia

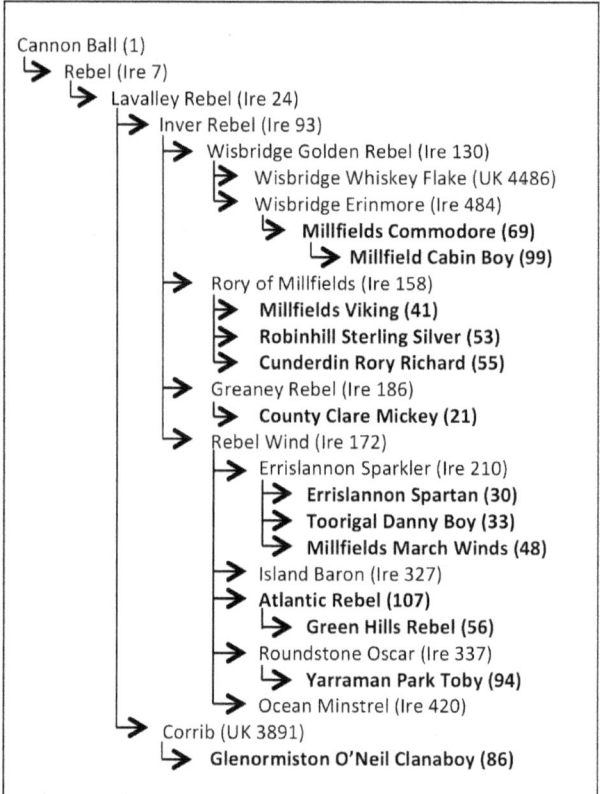

County Clare Mickey iiu (21)

County Clare Mickey iiu (21)

County Clare Mickey was a grey stallion of 14.1½hh (13.2hh in the studbook) imported in-utero by Frank Tynan of New South Wales, and foaled in 1971. He was shown successfully in-hand by the Tynans, winning champion Connemara stallion at the 1973 Melbourne Royal Show and champion Connemara pony at the 1974

Chapter 10   The Lavalley Rebel Line in Australia

National Horse and Pony Show. Mickey was started under saddle – and described as being "a pleasure to ride with good jumping potential" – before being sold on to the Garveys for their Corrib Stud, also in New South Wales. Of interest in Mickey's pedigree is that he shares the same dam line as the imported mare Ardan (1001), who shall be reviewed in the second volume of this series.

County Clare Mickey did not leave a stallion son, but is represented by six daughters: Yarraman Park Amy (1086), Shelford Downs Michelle (1117), Hunter Lodge Blixen (1126), Phylmar Sophie (1220), Toorigal Sarah (1124), and Corrib Bridget (1340). He also produced a number of partbreds. Margaret Baggott of the Bagoolie Stud in Hall, Australian Capital Territory, bought one of these - a bay mare named Phylmar Tammy as a foal-at-foot with her dam, Phylmar Annette (by Connemara Park Justin (17) and out of a station mare). Margaret describes Tammy and her purebred half-sister Phylmar Sophie as her "pride and joy". Tammy was used for most of her life as a pleasure riding and stock pony, but also produced a few partbred foals.

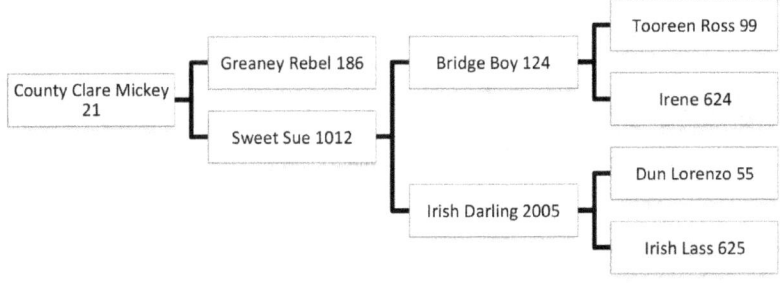

Errislannon Spartan imp (30)

Errislannon Spartan was a 14hh grey stallion bred in 1972 by Stephanie Brooks of Errislannan in Ireland. Spartan's grand dam, Drimeen Dun (Ire 1449), had been bought by Stephanie and her husband Donal as a riding pony for their children after purchasing Errislannan Manor in 1957. This was the start of a long and successful relationship with Connemara Ponies for the Brooks. As well as breeding a line of successful ponies, Stephanie formed a Connemara Branch of the pony club and in 1967 began the Errislannan Trekking and Riding Centre, which continues to be a popular and successful business today. Drimeen Dun was, according to Stephanie, "a great goer and a

Chapter 10   The Lavalley Rebel Line in Australia

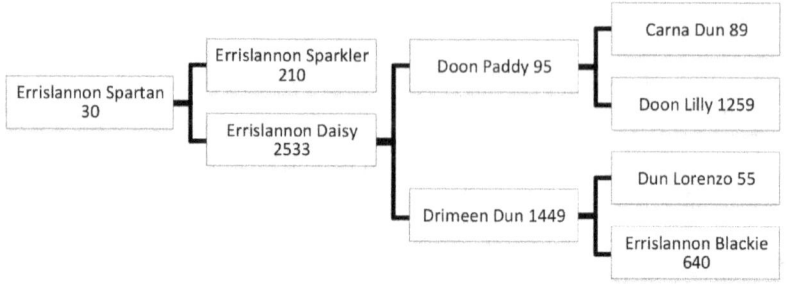

great breeder". This tough little 13.2hh mare proved to be quite a character, and difficult to catch if she felt disinclined! She was purchased by the Brooks in foal to MacDara (Ire 91) and the resulting foal, Errislannon Coltsfoot (Ire 115), won his colt class at Clifden in 1960.

Drimeen Dun's 1962 foal, Spartan's dam Errislannon Daisy (Ire 2533), was described in her 1990 eulogy by Stephanie as: "a very lively lady, having had sixteen foals and a lot of riding years. She was never a 'beginner' ride, even at twenty-seven; everyone had to be ready before you mounted her as she was away at once leading the trek, no time wasted. Nonetheless, she had a lovely mouth and was very biddable."[1] Daisy won reserve champion in the Archbishop's Cup and also the O'Sullivan Plaque at the 1970 Clifden Show, but it was as a broodmare that she really shined.

Errislannon Spartan (30) in 1982

Errislannon Spartan relaxing in his paddock at Kemill Hill

Two full sisters to Spartan were Errislannon Dana (Ire 4769) and Errislannon Diamante (Ire 6026). Dana, purchased by Sarah Hodgkins of the Spinway Stud in England, was a very successful performance pony and dam of Spinway Cailin (Ire 6311), who in turn produced the successful son of Thunderbolt (Ire 178), Spinway Comet (Ire 935). Errislannon Diamante was purchased by

1 R30

Chapter 10   The Lavalley Rebel Line in Australia

the Millfields Stud in England. Diamante had won the four year old mare class and the Archbishop's Cup for the Brooks and was also reserve confined champion to Belle of the Ball (Ire 3122) at the 1977 Clifden Show. Diamante continued her in-hand success in Britain, winning champion broodmare at the BCPS breed show in 1984, with her filly foal, Millfields Sapphire (UK M00483), being champion foal. She was also campaigned successfully under saddle, qualifying for and competing at Olympia with Susan Wicks in 1980.[2]

Errislannon Daisy with Spartan at foot

Drimeen Dun (Ire 1449) at 29 years old

In 1973, Alan Longman from Western Australia became interested in breeding Connemara ponies for his five children to ride in pony club and to sell to others wanting a larger, versatile pony. Margaret Campbell, a prominent Welsh Pony breeder of the Balmoral Stud in Western Australia, was going on a buying expedition to England that year and Alan asked her to find a Connemara colt for him. She found Errislannon Spartan who had been bought as a weanling from Errislannon by Anne Rolinson. Spartan was purchased and transported to Perth on a container ship.

Alan describes Spartan as having had "versatility, ability, agility, a big helping of trainablility and a wonderful temperament". As well as his stud duties, Spartan was used extensively for stock work, droving, mustering and trail riding on the farm. His ridden show career was limited but successful, as was his led-in career. At the Perth Royal Show, Spartan won supreme Connemara exhibit six times. He also proved to be a great promoter of the Connemara Pony as a stud stallion. In the 1980s and 90s he had more progeny being used for Riding for the Disabled classes in Australia than any other stallion of any breed.

Spartan is the sire of three stallion sons: Kemill Hill Spinnaker (91), Kemill Hill O'Reilly (138) and Kemill Hill Halligan (156). He is also represented by eight

---

2 R17:5, R24:2, R30:4, R1 p49, R45:2, R6 p21, R3 p99

Partbred mare by Spartan, Rio Irish Rose with foal Itsa Shamrock Summer Storm at foot

Kemill Hill Spinnaker as a young stallion

Kemill Hill Spinnaker (91) performing piaffe in-hand

daughters: Kemill Hill Tinka (1155), Kemill Hill Siobhan (1224), Kemill Hill Doon (1322), Kemill Hill Rosheen (1323), Kemill Hill Stephanie (1324) and Kemill Hill Amie (1479), and the two bred-up mares Kemill Hill Alicia (1413) and Ballybrack Tullimore (1490). He also produced a number of partbreds. One of these, a mare named Rio Irish Rose is described by Jan Rockman of Itsa Shamrock Stud in Western Australia: "[She] was a super all-rounder who did lots of pony club and tricks. She could turn on a pin and was extremely responsive to all aids. She could jump like the wind and nothing was too much to ask. Rio Irish Rose was a super pony with a super heart. When out on a bush ride, which she absolutely loved, she would deliberately choose the path with a log in it if possible – she loved to jump!"

Errislannon Spartan lived until eighteen years of age when, in 1990, he was laid to rest after developing a large melanoma.

Kemill Hill Spinnaker (91): Kemill Hill Spinnaker, Spartan's first stallion son, was a grey (from chestnut) pony foaled in 1977 out of Knock Ina (1039). As a weanling, he was bought by the Shepherds of the Rio Stud in Woorooloo, Western Australia. He was classified at three, and at five he was sold to Senor Ramon Guerrero, a Spanish haute ecole rider and trainer, and moved initially to South Australia and then to The Palms at Coomera on the Gold Coast in Queensland. There he became an integral part of the display of 'dancing stallions', made up mainly of Iberian bred stallions, performing for many years.

Mary Dowd of the Lagoonside Stud viewed one of the shows and wrote an article about it for the CPBSA newsletter in 1985: "[He was a] beautiful

Chapter 10   The Lavalley Rebel Line in Australia

white/grey pony, about 14hh, with the longest mane and forelock imaginable. A big green plume was on his head and a decorated saddle cloth and tassels adorned him. He looked a picture standing there. But when he began to move, I couldn't believe my eyes. I sat there enthralled! Spinnaker was the pony's name and the elevation and suspension of his passage and piaffes was superior to any of the others, as was the evenness of pace."

Mary spoke with Ramon after the show, and was treated to a special display of Spinnaker's training, showing his Spanish walk, collected and extended trot, passage, piaffe, courbette, capriole, five metre canter circles, pirouettes and changes of lead every stride. At the time, he held the record at The Palms for thirteen courbettes in a row carrying a rider. He was stabled twenty-four hours a day and trained mainly from the ground rather than under saddle and displayed exceptional manners. After the main performance he was often taken outside the equestrian complex for visitors to sit on and have their photograph taken. As a young girl I remember seeing Spinnaker and thought he was a magic pony. I am sure he sparked dreams of riding or owning a dancing white pony for many children in the 1980s!

Spinnaker unfortunately did not stand at stud while performing. Consequently his only recorded progeny is the three-quarter bred mare, Rio Shirhl, sired when he was young, and whose dam, Karingal Patrice, was by Connemara Park James and out of a pony mare. Shirhl had a number of owners during her lifetime and was remembered in her eulogy for her "hundreds of wins" and as having a kind, easy personality to which was added "grace and charisma".

Kemill Hill O'Reilly (138): Kemill Hill O'Reilly, foaled in 1986, was a full-brother to Spinnaker. A grey stallion of 14hh, O'Reilly was bought as a yearling by Hannie Byrne of the Eloura Stud in Wattle Grove. He was shown in-hand by Hannie, winning reserve champion Connemara stallion at the 1987 and 1988 Perth Royal Show and champion in 1989. He also stood supreme champion led Connemara at the 1989 APSB Show. Hannie described him in 1990 as being "an outstanding young stallion, with an excellent temperament, expressive movement, and very true-to-type". That year he was sold to the Malaysian government and took up residence in Kuala Lumpur, having bred some partbreds for the Eloura Stud and one purebred daughter, Whitecrofts Bridie (1585). It is understood that he was purchased to breed pony club mounts for Malaysian children to ride in the South West Pacific Games, and that he proved to be a successful sire there.

One of O'Reilly's partbred gelding sons, Eloura Mickey Finn (out of a Thoroughbred mare), was an outstanding pony club horse, firstly for Naomi Heath, and then for her younger sister Rebecca. His results culminated in winning

Chapter 10   The Lavalley Rebel Line in Australia

Kemill Hill Halligan (156) at the 1994 Perth Royal Show

Halligan steps out in harness with Alan and Jo Longman

Halligan relaxing at Kemill Hill in 2003

the CPBSA's National Pony Club Pony of the Year in 1996 with Naomi; and then both the CPBSA's National Pony Club Pony of the Year and National Partbred Connemara of the Year in 1999 with Rebecca. Mickey was also quite a character, being well known for his squeals, grunts and groans during hack workouts in protest at the boring work he was being asked to perform!

Kemill Hill Halligan (156): Kemill Hill Halligan, the third son of Errislannon Spartan, is again from that very successful cross with Knock Ina imp (1039). Halligan was foaled in 1989 and is a grey (dilute) pony of 13.2hh. He was retained by Kemill Hill as the resident stud stallion and followed in the successful footsteps of his siblings both in-hand and through competitive performance. This includes having been judged supreme Connemara exhibit twice, and supreme champion ridden APSB stallion three times at the Perth Royal Show. He has also shown great talent in harness, claiming the open harness dressage state championship as his own. As well as competing, Halligan and the Longmans enjoyed regular 'bush drives' in their local area.

Halligan was described to me by Alan as having "an excellent temperament, being very pony in type, with excellent movement, and his performance both under saddle and in harness competing against all breeds shows his versatility and trainability. He loves human company and thrives on work and training". Halligan continues to stand at Kemill Hill Stud, and has so far produced one stallion son, Kemill Hill Dermot (189), and two adult registered daughters, Kemill Hill Niamh (1768) and Kemill Hill Neuala (1875). He has also produced some well-performed gelding and partbred progeny. The purebred gelding Kemill Hill Veracious (G291), out of Lefroy Prudence O'Hederman, won the Western Australian Preliminary Dressage Champion in harness in 2003 as well as numerous other awards.

Chapter 10   The Lavalley Rebel Line in Australia

Kemill Hill Dermot (189) is a bay pony of 13.3hh foaled in 2001 out of Lefroy Prudence O'Hederman (1538). He was shown very lightly but successfully as a youngster. At the 2002 Northam Agricultural Show he won the supreme APSB pony exhibit. Dermot, "a reliable, trustworthy pony with free, easy movement, plenty of bone, substance and pony character", passed classification, but the Longmans did not have the facilities to run two stallions so the decision was made to geld him, leaving no progeny. He was sold to the Strickland family who appreciate him as their pony club mount.

Kemill Hill Dermot (189) at two years old, chatting to the author

Toorigal Danny Boy iiu (33)

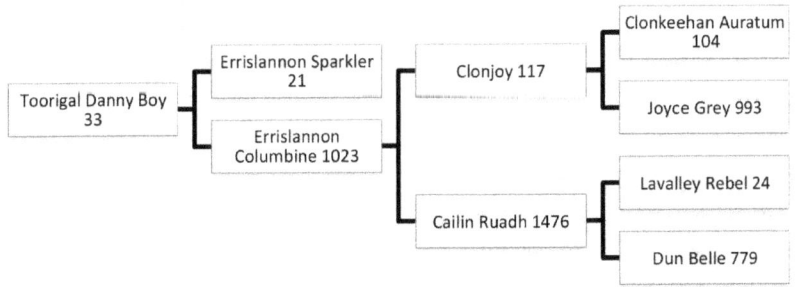

Toorigal Danny Boy iiu (33)
➡ Ballantrae Golden Syrup (144)
➡ Ballantrae Granite (158)

Toorigal Danny Boy was a buckskin stallion by Errislannon Sparkler (Ire 21) and thus a half-brother to Errislannon Spartan. He was imported in-utero by Harold and Judy Baldwin of the Toorigal Stud in Gosford (and later Merriwa) in New South Wales and foaled in 1972. Danny Boy won champion Connemara colt at the Sydney Royal Show before he was purchased by the Brooks family in northern New South Wales. There he gained great experience in stock work until 1977 when he was purchased by Jocelyn (Jo) Heard of Glenthompson in Victoria, after being recommended by M Kelly as a suitable foundation stud sire for the Ballantrae Stud. Jo had always had an interest in the

Chapter 10   The Lavalley Rebel Line in Australia

Toorigal Danny Boy mustering sheep with Janna Heard

Toorigal Danny Boy (33)

Toorigal Danny Boy with Janna, Bindi and Penny Heard

Mountain and Moorland breeds, and thought that a pony "needed to be a friend to the family, able to do the stock work, go to pony club, compete (with credit) and then go swimming in the dam, or act as the diving board".[3] She believed that the Connemara epitomised this 'do everything' family pony. Jo was a valued member of the CPBSA committee for many years and, after Jo's passing, the Jo Heard Memorial Trophy was created in 1996, with members sending in their nominations for the all-rounder pony that has made a special contribution as a Connemara in Australia.

Jo described Danny Boy as "a delightful dun chap with a great personality and superb movement. His stock have not disappointed us, being extremely versatile and useful".[4] He has shown only lightly by the Heards, his greatest achievement being at the 1993 APSB stud show where four of Danny Boy's progeny won the champion led Connemara stallion or colt class, the led dry mare class, the filly class, champion led mare and supreme champion led Connemara!

During his lifetime, Toorigal Danny Boy sired two stallion sons to continue his line, Ballantrae Golden Syrup (144) and Ballantrae Granite (158). He also has sixteen registered daughters: Blandings Buttercup (1096), Ballantrae Erica (1428), Ballantrae Gilliflower (1455), Ballantrae Humbug (1456), Ballantrae Heather (1457), Ballantrae Candy (1458), Ballantrae Gazania (1525), Ballantrae Jaffa (1527), Ballantrae Fiesta (1554), Ballantrae Gemma (1555), Ballantrae Toffee (1582), Ballantrae Ripple (1583), Ballantrae Riff Raff (1589), Ballantrae Flame (1662),

3 R2 p4-5
4 R1 p20

Ballantrae Flora (1677) and Ballantrae Sparkle (1684). Two gelding full brothers by Danny Boy and out of Barwidgee Mallow (1186), Ballantrae Briar and Ballantrae Bracken, have had enormous success in pony club circles in Victoria. Briar was named the CPBSA's National Pony club Pony of the Year in 1999 and the National Connemara of the Year the following year, partnered by Meaghan Ryan.

Ballantrae Golden Syrup (144)

Ballantrae Golden Syrup (144), Danny Boy's first stallion son, was a bay pony of 14hh foaled in 1986 out of Yarraman Park Sugar (1168). Jo described him as being "the best foal I have bred". He had a limited show career, but won the open led pony stallion class and champion pony stallion or colt at the Hamilton Agricultural Show in 1990 and was champion led Connemara stallion at the 1992 Victorian APSB Stud Show.

Ballantrae Golden Syrup (144)

It was, however, for his temperament rather than show awards that Jo appreciated him. In 1995 Jo recalled a day when she was moving horses around the property: "Perhaps the most surprising event was the fact that I led the stallion Ballantrae Golden Syrup half a mile down the road away from his favourite wife with only a piece of bailing twine around his neck. He had not been handled for twelve months – such is the nature of these ponies!"

Ballantrae Granite at the 1993 APSB Stud Show

After Jo passed away, Golden Syrup was transferred to a man who, most unfortunately, soon sold him to an abattoir. He did not leave any stallion sons in his lifetime, but is

Granite at Ballantrae in 2012

represented by three purebred daughters, Ballantrae Gidgee (1612), Exmoor Polly Waffle (1648) and Ballantrae Black Sallee (1795).

Ballantrae Granite (158): Ballantrae Granite is Toorigal Danny Boy's second stallion son. He is a grey (from buckskin) of 13.1hh and was foaled in 1991 out of Abbeyleix Grey Pearl imp (1159). Shown lightly as a youngster, Granite won champion led Connemara stallion or colt at the 1993 Victorian APSB Show as a two-year-old, and reserve champion led stallion or colt at the same show in 1995. Janna Heard has described him as "a very quiet and easy pony who is quiet to ride and moves well". He does not have any registered breeding stock progeny, however he is still living with Janna and may yet continue his line in the studbook.

Millfields Viking imp (41)

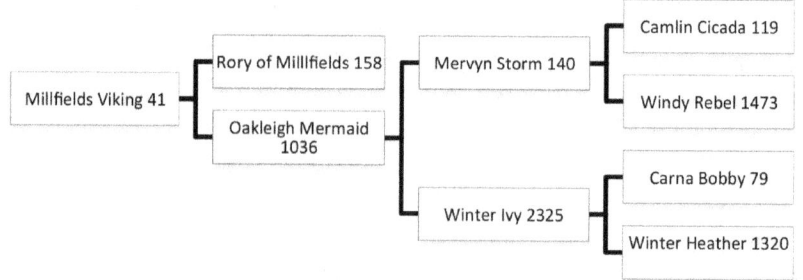

Millfields Viking (41)

Photo: Helen Colleran

Millfields Viking was a chestnut stallion of 13.3hh by Rory of Millfields (UK 158). He was imported by the Mussareds of Cunderdin Stud in 1973 as a foal at foot. Viking was mainly used to produce partbreds in his stud career and did not leave a stallion son. He sired one purebred daughter, Equus Blondie (1283), before he was gelded. After his stud career, Viking was used by the Mussareds' daughter Heather at pony club.

Chapter 10   The Lavalley Rebel Line in Australia

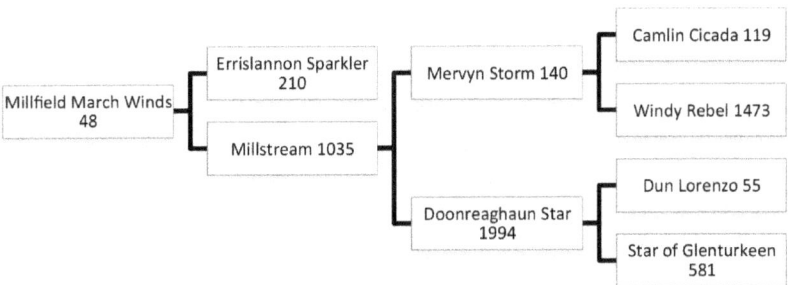

Millfields March Winds (48)

Millfields March Winds was a buckskin stallion of 13.1hh foaled in 1973 and imported as a foal at foot by Jenny Pither, the last of Errislannon Sparkler's sons to be imported to Australia. Jenny's parents, John and Hazel Pither of the Oakdale Stud in Borden, Western Australia, first became interested in the Connemara Pony when their children started riding and Hazel became heavily involved in pony club. She realised at that time how unsuitable most of the pony club mounts were for their young riders and she became very interested in the Connemaras, being impressed with the temperament and versatility displayed by the progeny of the original stallion to reside in Western Australia, Connemara Park James (8). When the wool market slumped the Pithers turned to horse breeding and purchased the stallion Connemara Park Kenneth (2).

Millfields March Winds remained with the Pithers until 1981 when the Oakdale Stud was dispersed and he was sold to Judy Turriff of Dowerin. He did not leave any stallion sons, but is represented by twelve daughters, all from the bred-up mare Connemara Park Rita's (2B/001) line: Oakdale Millhara (1218), Oakdale Iniskillen (1228), Oakdale Clonkilty (1229), Oakdale Tara (1277), Tallamara Misty Lady (1337), Benad Katana (1480), Miravale Star Gazer (1485), Seacliffe Camille (1489), Seacliffe Lady Kate (1517), Benad Lady Sarah (1532), Seacliffe Summer Winds (1565) and Mirravale Firefly (1566).

Chapter 10   The Lavalley Rebel Line in Australia

Robinhill Sterling Silver iiu (53)

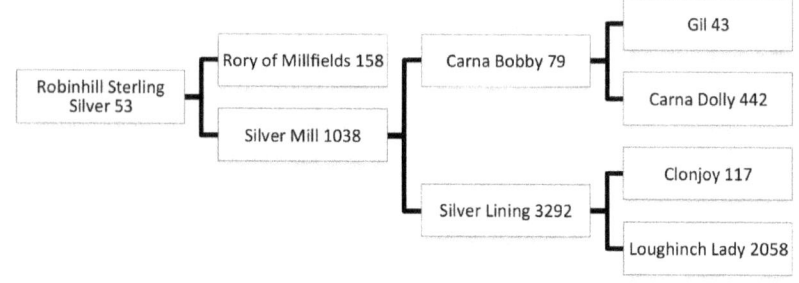

Robinhill Sterling Silver (53)

Photo: Sue Clarke

Robinhill Sterling Silver, a grey stallion of 13.2hh, was imported in-utero with his dam Silver Mill (1038) by Di Cumming of the Robinhill Stud in Armidale, New South Wales. He was purchased by the Salkelds of Garland Stud in Scone as a stud stallion, but they lost him not long after. He did not leave a stallion son, but is represented by two daughters, Garland Grey Feather (1209) and Garland Bayleaf (1247).

Millfields Commodore imp (69)

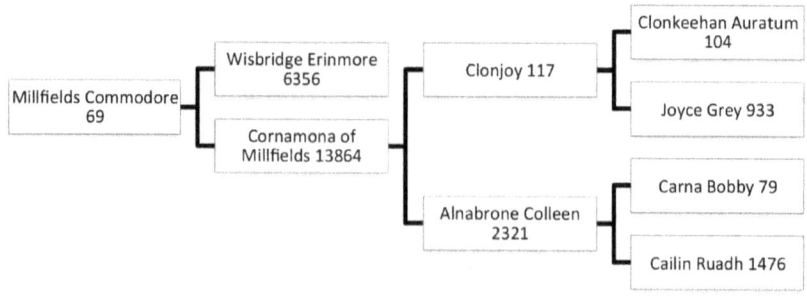

132

Chapter 10 The Lavalley Rebel Line in Australia

Millfields Commodore imp (69)
➤ Millfield Cabin Boy imp (99)
➤ Connemara Park Andrew (104)
    ➤ Achill Fiddler (196)
➤ Shelford Downs Captain Curragh (105)
➤ Portadown Encore (133)

Millfields Commodore was a bay stallion of 14.1½hh bred by Anne Rolinson of the Millfields Stud in Suffolk, England. He was foaled in 1973 out of Cornamona of Millfields, a chocolate buckskin mare who Anne bought as a foal at Maam Cross Fair. Anne had been attracted by Cornamona's "lovely head and large, dark eye"[5] and by her pedigree, as Alnabrone Colleen was a half-sister, through Cailin Ruadh, of Anne's foundation mare Gentle Breeze of Millfields (Ire 2684). According to Anne, Cornamona matured into "a grand type of brood mare, staying under 14hh, with great depth and heart room, rather too long in her back for a top show mare, but strong over her loins. Not as placid as Breeze but with great presence and a good disposition."[6] Anne named her from a signpost in Connemara that she though was lovely, but was later told by John Daly that it meant 'Black Bog'! Cornamona became a BCPS super premium award winner in 1985 through her competitive progeny. Among her successful offspring was Millfields Coronet (UK 17254), a full-sister to Commodore, who competed successfully in-hand and also under saddle in Britain. Her achievements included a Mountain and Moorland working hunter class win at the Royal International Show. Cornamona's dam line is headed by Dun Belle (Ire 779) who was by the Connemara Boy stallion Heather Bell (Ire 15).[7]

Millfields Commodore (69) with Jack Conroy

As a yearling, Commodore was taken to the BCPS Breed Show, winning his colt class over Chiltern Curlew and Kirtling Brigadoon (both later became very well-decorated stallions in the UK). He was awarded best yearling and reserve champion young pony. The next year he was second in his class to Chiltern Curlew. In 1976, as a three-year-old classified stallion,

Cornamona of Millfields (UK 13864)

---
5 R45:2
6 R45:2
7 R27:2, R32:2, R45:2

Chapter 10   The Lavalley Rebel Line in Australia

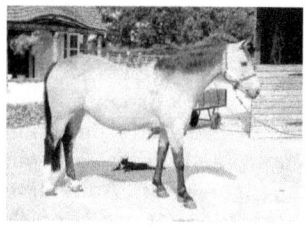

Millfields Coronet, a full-sister to Commodore, at home at Millfields Stud

Millfields Commodore in England with Anne Rolinson, Gentle Breeze of Millfields, Sue Wicks and foal, Millfields Cadet.

Commodore again won his class and his filly foal Millfield Seaspray imp (1130) won best foal. Pam Forman described him at this age as a "young stallion [showing] great promise, with a nice head and bold eye. He has quality with substance, 8.5 inches of bone and a very kind temperament... I feel we shall hear a good deal more of this likeable animal in the future".[8]

Commodore's successes caught the attention of Jack and June Conroy of the Shelford Downs Stud in Dalveen, Queensland, who were expanding their stud at that time. The Conroys inspected many ponies for sale in Britain and Ireland and eventually purchased and imported fourteen ponies. Jack believes that the Connemara is a wonderful pony, with ability in all fields limited only by their owner's ability. His criteria for the ponies they bought were: soundness in wind and limb, excellent conformation, intelligence and a good temperament, ability and quality. He saw all of these qualities and more in Commodore, believing him to be the best stallion in Britain if not all of Europe, and managed to convince Anne to part with him.

Before flying to Australia, Commodore left two season's worth of progeny in the UK, including Millfield Cabin Boy (99), Millfield Seaspray (1130) and Vale Southern Cross (1093), who also made the trip to Australia; Millfield Festival, who won champion foal at the 1976 BCPS breed show; and Cheviot White Clover who won the two year old filly class, best yearling and champion young pony at the 1978 BCPS breed show. He also left two stallion sons, Coleby Horatio (UK S12) and Cottenham Sailor (UK S15). Through his progeny, Commodore held the junior stallion record in the BCPS award points scheme, and was only a few points behind the senior stallion record at only four years of age!

Commodore, or Charlie (nicknamed for his regular handler, Charlie Game), flew to Australia in 1977 while his future wives travelled by container ship. He settled in well to stud duties at Shelford Downs, and was campaigned by Jack in the showring. His notable successes in-hand included being champion led stallion

---

8 R15:9

Chapter 10   The Lavalley Rebel Line in Australia

at the 1980 Bowral Connemara and Native Pony Festival judged by Pat Lyne and winning supreme of supremes at the Clifton Show in Queensland over all other breeds. Jack remembers Charlie as being completely trustworthy. One swelteringly hot day at the Warwick Show Jack decided to utilise the only shade available by sitting underneath Charlie and leaning up against his legs. This caused the other exhibitors great amusement and amazement! Commodore also proved to be a successful stud stallion, siring eighty-five progeny in the four years he stood at Shelford Downs.

Jack illustrates by example his story from the Warwick Show.

When Shelford Downs dispersed, Charlie was purchased by Dr Ron and Velyian Todd of Portadown Stud in Ipswich, Queensland. Velyian had heard that the Shelford Downs Stud was dispersing and went to view some mares to purchase. She hadn't considered buying a stallion but as soon as Velyian saw Charlie she fell in love with him and had to have him! He was heavily campaigned by Velyian in led and ridden Connemara, saddle pony, and galloway classes with many ribbons and sashes to their credit. Velyian's fondest showing memories were at the pair's first show when she lost the reins in a ridden class and upon saying "Stop Charlie!" he came to a gentle halt for her to recover them; and of the Toowoomba Royal Show when he was judged champion by an Irish judge who remarked to her that he was the best Connemara he had seen outside Ireland. As well as showing and performing stud duties, Charlie was regularly used for stockwork at Portadown and the Todd's daughters also enjoyed riding him.

Tragically, in 1986 and at only thirteen years of age, Millfields Commodore became very ill with sand colic. Velyian travelled in the back of the truck, trying to comfort him on the way to the vets at the University of Queensland, but when they arrived Charlie had gone into shock and treatment couldn't save him. Velyian was devastated and, although the Todds searched for another Connemara stallion, they eventually decided that he was irreplaceable and shifted their focus to breeding stockhorses with a Thoroughbred stallion over their Connemara mares.

Four stallion sons of Millfields Commodore are included in the studbook: Millfield Cabin Boy imp (99), Connemara Park Andrew (104), Shelford Downs Captain Curragh (105) and Portadown Encore (133). He is also

Chapter 10   The Lavalley Rebel Line in Australia

represented by thirty purebred daughters: Vale Southern Cross (1093), Millfield Seaspray (1130), Shelford Downs Sophomore (1214), Shelford Downs Penelope (1215), Shelford Downs Castanette (1252), Shelford Downs Glencora (1253), Shelford Downs Jenny Wren (1254), Shelford Downs Morning Cloud (1255), Shelford Downs Ramona (1256), Shelford Downs Solitaire (1257), Shelford Downs Sonata (1258), Shelford Downs Bonnie Eileen (1284), Shelford Downs Twinkle (1285), Shelford Downs Valentine (1296), Shelford Downs Sacha (1297), Shelford Downs Astrid (1298), Shelford Downs Rain Cloud (1299), Shelford Downs Gemma (1300), Shelford Downs Solitude (1301), Shelford Downs Brenna (1303), Shelford Downs Rowena (1304), Shelford Downs Selma (1305), Shelford Downs Wilda (1306), Shelford Downs Rana (1307), Shelford Downs Peony (1328), Shelford Downs Lena (1353), Shelford Downs Simone (1369), Shelford Downs Solita (1380), Shelford Downs Starr (1381) and Shelford Downs Rosarana (1383).

Millfield Cabin Boy imp (99): A son of Millfields Commodore, Millfield Cabin Boy was bred by Anne Rolinson in England in 1978, and imported by M Kelly. He was a bay stallion of 13.2hh out of Millfield Fair Lady (UK 15948). Unfortunately he died as a youngster and left no progeny.

Connemara Park Andrew (104): Commodore's second stallion son in the Australian studbook, and his first stallion son to be foaled in Australia, was Connemara Park Andrew, a grey (from brown) pony of 13.3hh. The Wiltshire's transported Connemara Park Trudi (1098) from Victoria to Queensland to visit Commodore and Andrew was foaled in 1978. He was bought from Connemara Park by Delia Cole of Tasmania, classified in 1981 and lightly shown by her, winning the champion Connemara award at both the Launceston and Hobart shows and the stallion class at the 1983 Tasmanian Field Day judged by Elizabeth Petch from the Coosheen Stud in Ireland. Elizabeth Murray of Huon Valley Stud then purchased and used him at stud in Tasmania before she moved to South Australia. In South Australia Andrew continued his showring successes, gaining the champion Connemara Pony stallion sash in 1986 and 1987 at the Adelaide Royal Show.

In 1992, Ann Bush of the Mayo stud leased Andrew and he remained with her until his death in 2002. He sired one stallion son, Achill Fiddler (196), and six daughters: Huon Valley Autumn Tart (1374), Huon Valley Cleo (1417), Mayo Estelle (1591), Ballintapper Hope (1624), Mayo Mary (1631) and Clifden Silver Mist

Connemara Park Andrew (104) in 1992

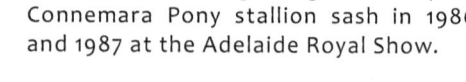

(1704). He also produced a number of geldings and partbreds. One gelding, Clifden Bailey, thoroughly converted his owner Kerry Spiers to Connemaras. She notes that "not only does he excel in any discipline asked of him, eventing, jumping, hacking, he also provides endless joy with trail riding, leading children around on and going to the beach etc. He is such an upstanding horse that every time he leaves this gate I am questioned as to his breed. He is a wonderful ambassador for, and a fine example of the Connemara, which has provided me with the opportunity to meet and discuss the merits of the breed with countless numbers of people who ask me about him!" [9]

Clifden Bailey with Kerry Spiers

Achill Fiddler (196) as a three-year-old

Achill Fiddler (196), Connemara Park Andrew's only stallion son, is a grey (from brown) pony of 13.2hh. He was bred in 2001 by Jane McNicholl of Williamstown in South Australia, out of her mare Cairnhill Fionna (1473). Jane had tried unsuccessfully to use AI on Fionna, so sent her to Connemara Park Andrew, the most local stallion, to try for a pregnancy through natural breeding. The result of this union was Fiddler, who proved to be Fionna's only foal. Fiddler was kept entire to continue Fionna's line, maturing well and passing classification in 2004. He is also the last of Millfields Commodore's stallion line to appear on the CPBSA's stallion list, so I hope that he will produce some good colts to continue this stallion family.

Jane describes Fiddler as "a very true to type pony with great bone and substance, correct limbs, free movement and a quiet temperament". She also notes that he is "definitely a boy, but is very easy to handle". Fiddler was shown lightly but successfully in hand by Jane, and was also started under saddle. At the time of writing he had been purchased by the Lawsons of Burke in New South Wales to use over their Connemara mares.

Shelford Downs Captain Curragh (105) and Portadown Encore (133):

The third son of Millfields Commodore in the studbook, Shelford Downs Captain Curragh, was a grey pony of 13.2hh foaled in 1978 out of Bodenpark Rosethorn

---

9 R48 September 2006

Chapter 10   The Lavalley Rebel Line in Australia

Photo: Tearna Goldston

Portadown Encore (133) led by Allison Hall at the Brisbane Royal Show

imp (1114). Jack Conroy was very impressed with Captain Curragh as a youngster and he was sold to the Bears who presented him for his successful classification. The Bears decided that the ponies would be used as children's ponies rather than for breeding, however, and he was gelded without representation in the studbook.

Portadown Encore is the last of Commodore's stallion sons and was a bay roan pony of 14.1hh foaled in 1986 out of the imported mare Reflection (1102). Cory, as he was known, was shown extensively and successfully as a colt by his breeder, Velyian Todd, and was unbeaten in his led colt classes in 1989. She described him as having a "proud carriage and superb movement" and was encouraged to keep him entire by Anne Rolinson who saw him as a yearling. He passed classification, but a buyer could not be found for him and Velyian decided that he did not have as reliable a temperament as his sire so he was gelded. He was used as a stock pony for a time by the Todd's property caretaker who found him to be one of the best stockhorses he had ridden and was later sold.

Encore did not produce any purebred breeding stock progeny. However, he has one partbred daughter registered, Narrawong Pal, who is owned by the Johnstons of Garnet Stud at Helidon in Queensland and is used for breeding three-quarter-bred ponies.

Glenormiston O'Neill Clanaboy iiu (86)

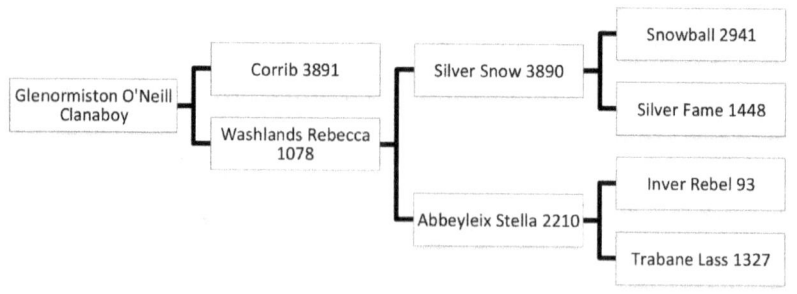

Chapter 10 The Lavalley Rebel Line in Australia

> Glenormiston O'Neill Clanaboy iiu (86)
> ↳ Larrigan (130)

Glenormiston O'Neill Clanaboy was a grey stallion of 13.2hh by Corrib (UK 3891) imported in-utero with his dam and foaled in 1977. He was purchased from Glenormiston Stud by Gary Rozynski who was at the time forming the Noweddie Stud at Pittsworth in Queensland. Gary first became interested in the Connemara Pony as a child when he was given a book with a picture of a Connemara in it. In the 1970s he was breeding Australian Ponies and knew Judy Sterling, a great patron of the Connemara Pony in Queensland. Gary wished to breed a larger pony and of the three colts available at the time, Judy recommended Clanaboy. Gary's aim was to breed pony club mounts with kind temperaments for young teenagers. This was initially done by breeding partbreds from the Australian mares, before some purebred mares were purchased for the stud. Gary believed the ponies should retain their native pony character, and be upstanding, cover plenty of ground, have good bone and show plenty of quality.

Gary describes Clanaboy as having been a gentleman and a charmer, with no vice in him at all. Gary's wife, who "never rode anything", would ride him around the paddocks and visiting children would also use him. He had a special relationship with Rainey Island Joy iiu (1033) but would always come cantering up away from the mares when called, even in a large paddock.

Clanaboy produced one registered stallion son, Larrigan (130), in his breeding career, but this has not been a lasting stallion line. He is represented by nine daughters. These being: Glenormiston Cashelmara (1291), Noweddie Najoy (1333), Noweddie Elke (1399), Amergin Josie Mac (1400), Noweddie Holly (1445), Noweddie Josie (1446), Noweddie Rebecca (1560), Noweddie Natalie (1577), and Noweddie Maylea (1678).

Glenormiston O'Neill Clanaboy (86) with Gary Rozynski at the Toowoomba Royal Show

Glenormiston O'Neill Clanaboy (86) ridden by Sarah Clarke

One gelding son, Noweddie Nicholas, was purchased by Carla Cosgrove as a three-year-old. She broke him to harness and did very well with him in harness classes. After moving to Roma Carla found that there were no harness competitions so started Nicholas under saddle as a

Chapter 10 The Lavalley Rebel Line in Australia

Noweddie Nicholas and Carla Cosgrove

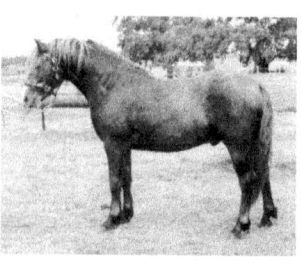

Larrigan (130)

fourteen-year-old and began giving lessons to children on him a month later. In 2008 the long journey was made with Nicholas to Werribee in Victoria to compete at the Hamag EA National Young Dressage Rider and Pony championships. There he became the national champion preliminary, and the runner-up champion novice pony! Quite a feat for a nineteen-year-old pony from Western Queensland.

Larrigan (130): Clanaboy's son Larrigan, was a grey (from black) pony of 14.1½hh. He was bred in 1984 by Ann Bush of the Mayo Stud, who had purchased his dam, the imported mare Easter Journey (1022) in foal. From birth, he was not an easy colt to handle, but "he was such a lovely colt with the potential of being a future stallion" that he was kept entire. His physical potential was realised, with Larrigan being a regular winner in-hand, including champion Connemara stallion at the 1988 Adelaide Royal Show. However he remained very difficult to handle so the decision was made to geld him and he left no progeny. As a gelding, he partnered Catherine Atkinson, and later Carole Benassy, very successfully in hunting and showjumping where he was much admired for his ability and style. In this respect, he has promoted the Connemara Pony very well in South Australia and is remembered fondly for this.

Another colt, the chestnut Noweddie Sojourn, was a full-brother to Larrigan and won many broad ribbons in-hand as a youngster. He was considered a stallion prospect by the Rozynskis who sold him to the Salkelds of Garland Stud in South Australia. Both families thought he was an outstanding colt but he failed classification and died from tetanus after being gelded. This devastated the Salkelds who closed all breeding operations of Garland Stud after this event.

Yarraman Park Toby iiu (94)

Yarraman Park Toby was imported in-utero by the Mitchells of Yarraman Park in Scone, New South Wales. He was foaled in 1976, a buckskin who stood 13.2hh.

Chapter 10   The Lavalley Rebel Line in Australia

Toby was shown extensively, both in-hand and under saddle, for the Mitchells by Tony Oliver-Watkins, one of Australia's great show pony producers and a respected breeder and judge, and was later purchased by him. Toby's impressive array of wins included winning champion led Connemara Pony at the National Stud show four times, champion led Connemara at the Sydney Royal Show three times, and champion led buckskin under 14hh and champion ridden buckskin at the National Buckskin show.

Yarraman Park Toby (94) at the 1981 Castle Hill Show

He was sold on to Betty Hepple of the Pine Tree Stud in North Queensland in 1983 to use over her Inis O'Hara (29) mares. He competed successfully in a huge variety of events for the Hepples, including open led, English saddle classes, western saddle classes, jumping, endurance and harness. Once at a show, a regular competitor commented to them that she could not tell the difference between their two cream ponies. Betty was unsure what she had meant until she realised that the lady had assumed that they competed in the events with two ponies, rather than all with the one pony – a stallion nonetheless!

Toby is represented in the studbook by one stallion son, Yarraman Park Jeremy (117), and by four daughters: Yarraman Park Sweet Sue (1330) and Pine Tree Cadence (1462), and the two bred-up mares Pine Tree Ashes (1460) and Pine Tree Calypso Girl (1461).

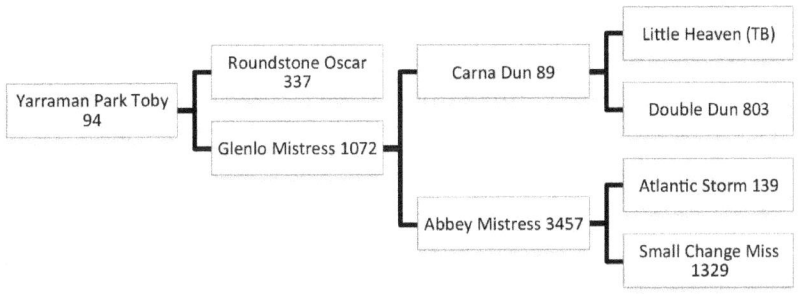

Chapter 10   The Lavalley Rebel Line in Australia

Yarraman Park Jeremy (117) as a young pony.

Yarraman Park Jeremy (117): Yarraman Park Jeremy was a bay stallion of 13.3½hh foaled in 1979 from the imported mare Katie (1014). He was purchased by Mrs Mason of Gardak Stud in Victoria who described him as having "an attractive head, good conformation and being a straight, free mover and smooth to ride".

Jeremy was used briefly by the Roseworthy Agricultural College in South Australia for educating students in stud work but proved to be unsuitable as he constantly walked fence lines. He was not a typical Connemara as he had thrown to the Thoroughbred in his pedigree, so was not used by breeders with purebred mares and was gelded without producing any breeding stock progeny.

Atlantic Rebel imp (107)

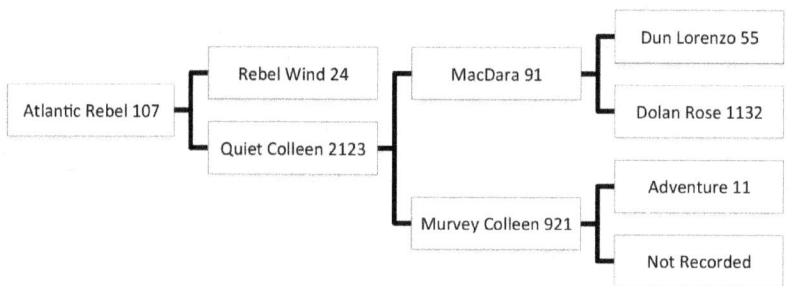

Atlantic Rebel was a grey stallion of 14hh, bred by Thomas Mannion of Roundstone in Ireland in 1967. Atlantic Rebel was raised by Thomas who had him classified at two years old and ran him with a couple of mares before selling him to Michael Clancy. Michael owned him only briefly, selling him on to Sarah Hodgkins of Spinway Stud in England in 1969. Sarah wrote in 1975: "I had never owned a stallion before and was slightly apprehensive as to how I would cope with one. However, he proved to be everything I wanted and with a particularly easy temperament. This he has passed on to his progeny who are all easy and kind to handle."[10]

Atlantic Rebel (107) in South Australia

Although only lightly campaigned, Atlantic Rebel proved himself in the showring, winning reserve champion stallion at the 1972 BCPS Breed Show to Leam Bobby Finn and also winning his class at the BCPS Ridden Show, his first show under saddle. He spent five seasons in England, three with Sarah and two on loan to Lady Hellings,[11] and produced two successful stallion sons in that time, Spinway Corsair (UK 5879) and Lanburn Leemoy (UK 6712), as well as a number of successful daughters and gelding sons.

In 1974, Atlantic Rebel was purchased and imported to Australia by Mr and Mrs Beak of Leura station, Marlborough via Rockhampton in Central Queensland. He remained with them for ten years, running out in 1000 acre paddocks with station mares to add bone, agility and hardiness to the Leura stockhorse breeding program. He was a great success for them. Among Rebel's progeny, all of whom were accepted into the Australian Stockhorse studbook, many won prizes and championships in stockhorse events. Atlantic Rebel did not have access to any purebred mares during this time.

Then in 1984 Mrs Beak contacted Helen Small of Cairnhill Stud in South Australia as she had heard that Helen had lost her stud stallion Noorookoo Harry (47) and asked her if she would like to purchase Atlantic Rebel as a replacement. Helen leapt at the opportunity and Rebel made the long journey to his new home.

Helen, who has described Rebel as being "a lovely ride, with a beautiful temperament, and [he was] a real character",[12] showed him twice in-hand after his arrival in South Australia. At the 1985 Adelaide Royal he won the Connemara stallion class and at the APSB Show he was the supreme Connemara exhibit. He was then retired to light stud duties at Cairnhill for the remainder of his life, as he began to show his age and Helen had sustained a back injury that prevented her from participating in active equestrian activities.[13]

---

10 R14:3
11 R18:3
12 R1 p66
13 R14:3, R18:4, R25:4, R26:3, R1 p66, R7 p52 53 79, R5 p142

Chapter 10   The Lavalley Rebel Line in Australia

During his time in South Australia, Rebel sired three stallion sons: Green Hills Rebel (56), Cairnhill Renegade (140) and Cairnhill Partisan (149). He has seven daughters recorded in the studbook: Lockinge Leonora imp (1104), Mayo Lisa (1444), Exmoor Nutmeg (1467), Cairnhill Fionna (1473), Cairnhill Caitlin (1474), Mayo Tracy (1487) and Lovejoy (1528).

Atlantic Rebel also sired a number of useful geldings and partbreds, including the purebred gelding Cairnhill Woodkern. Before being gelded, Woodkern sired the partbred gelding Cairnhill Fonsie O'Flaherty. Fonsie, out of a Thoroughbred mare, was started by Jane McNicholl of Achill Stud in South Australia and later leased by James Beaton, son of Gill and Greg Beaton of Clifton Stud, who rode him for pleasure as well as taking him to jumping schools and hunting with him. He then moved on to Claire Rowe whose parents, Philip and Ingrid, have Newlands Stud in Victoria – he has really moved in Connemara circles over the years! With Claire, who described him in 2003 as "a pony captured in a horse's body, with a vivid imagination and a calculated sense of humour", he attained the CPBSA's Victorian and National Sporthorse Connemara of the Year, having competed with distinction in dressage, show hunter classes, showjumping and combined training at the top end of pony club.

Cairnhill Fonsie O'Flaherty

Green Hills Rebel (56) at Ballantrae Stud

Green Hills Rebel iiu (56): The first of Atlantic Rebel's stallion sons, Green Hills Rebel, was a grey stallion of 13.2hh imported in-utero with his dam Ballydonagh Belle (1047). Alex and Kit Boyd first became interested in the Connemara Pony after viewing a photograph of Fred Wiltshire with two ponies. They contacted Connemara Park and arranged a visit, viewing Island King and organising the importation of a mare. Green Hills Rebel was foaled in 1973, two days after the arrival of his dam at green Hills in Hawkesdale, Victoria. He was raised by the Boyds, classified and remained at Green Hills as their resident sire until 1981 when he was purchased by Jo Heard for her Ballantrae Stud. However, Rebel stood only three seasons at stud at Ballantrae before his death.

Chapter 10   The Lavalley Rebel Line in Australia

Green Hills Rebel sired one stallion son in his lifetime, Strickland Park Jo's Rebel (175), and four purebred daughters: Ballantrae Lupin (1556), Ballantrae Patsy (1557), Ballantrae Petunia (1659) and Ballantrae Delphinium (1584). One partbred mare by him of note was Greenhills Lollipop. Lollipop, or Cindy as she was known, is another partbred who so impressed her owners that they became true Connemara 'converts'! She was purchased from Greenhills by Melissa Vella who used her at riding club and shows as well as for pleasure riding. Melissa has written that "all who have contact with this pony are impressed with her calmness and sensibility, a definite Connemara trait"[14] and this encouraged Melissa to start Killarney Park stud in Victoria. After competing successfully with another family for a time Cindy was purchased by the Rowes for Claire to try her hand at all manner of equestrian events with safety, enjoyment and success. She certainly fulfilled this role and was recognised by the CPBSA in 1997, winning the Victorian Partbred of the Year and the Jo Heard Memorial Trophy. In Cindy's eulogy in the CPBSA newsletter, Ingrid wrote of her: "She was worth her weight in gold... She fulfilled many things for many people and was always safe, reliable and trustworthy." A wonderful partbred ambassador for the breed!"

Strickland Park Jo's Rebel (175)

Strickland Park Jo's Rebel (175): When Ballantrae Jaffa (1527) was purchased in-foal to Green Hills Rebel by Melissa Smith and Vi Gunn of the Strickland Park Stud, North Creswick, Victoria, in 1995, they received a surprise when Jaffa arrived "with a spunky black colt in tow!" Melissa and Vi decided Jo's Rebel was something special and kept him entire. Strickland Park Jo's Rebel, a grey (from black) of 13.1hh subsequently passed his inspection and has remained at Strickland Park as a stud sire. He has been widely campaigned in-hand and under saddle, with wins in the ridden Connemara class at the Melbourne Summer Royal in 2003, 2004, and 2005 and he has won champion ridden Mountain and Moorland pony at the same show and also the APSB Show. He has been educated during his saddle career by Gail Merygold. Melissa and Vi note that he is a versatile pony under saddle, being both a talented jumper and an exceptional dressage pony.[15]

---

14 R48 1996
15 R50 February 2005

Chapter 10   The Lavalley Rebel Line in Australia

Cairnhill Renegade (140) in 1991

22 year old Cairnhill Renegade ridden by 4 year old Harrison Taylor at Templewood. Cairnhill Cavalier on the left and Rachelle Taylor leading the pair.

Strickland Park Jo's Rebel does not yet have a stallion son representing him in the studbook. At the time of writing he has five adult registered daughters, Strickland Park Carnival (1723), Strickland Park Cheyenne (1787), Strickland Park Tiger Lily (1828), Strickland Park Peek a Boo (1862), and Strickland Park Silver Mist (1863).

Cairnhill Renegade (140): Atlantic Rebel's second stallion son, Cairnhill Renegade, is a bay pony of 13.3½hh foaled in 1985 out of Garland Bayleaf (1247). He was raised as a stallion prospect by Helen at Cairnhill and, having been started under saddle, was sold in 1988 to Rachelle Taylor of the Templewood Horse Riding Centre and Stud, which was set up in the Adelaide Hills of South Australia in 1972. Renegade, appreciated at Templewood for his impeccable manners and temperament and his good straight movement, was used as a stud sire until 1996 when he was gelded. Since then he has been used as a school horse and is a great favourite with both staff and pupils. As a stallion, he was lightly shown, winning numerous ribbons and sashes at agricultural shows. His most notable results were a second place to Glenormiston Jasper in a well-supported stallion class at the 1990 Adelaide Royal show and a fourth place in the open ridden stallion class at the same show, which was a very large class of all breeds.

During his time at stud, Renegade produced one purebred daughter, Templewood Truskmore (1579). He also sired a number of geldings and partbreds. Probably his most successful pairing was with the Clydesdale/Anglo-Arab mare Countess, a cross which produced Templewood Tyrell's Pass, who was used for a number of years as a school horse and then moved on to a very successful show career. Tyrell's Pass's younger brother Templewood Temple Boy, also used initially as a school horse, was sold to Greg and Tanya McKee. He has had particular success in heavyweight hunter classes, taking out this event at the 2006 SAHC championships. At Barastock Horse of the Year in 2007 he was shown in the partbred Mountain and Moorland classes for a second in his led-in class and a third in the ridden – again, very competitive and well-supported classes.

Cairnhill Partisan (149): Partisan was a full-brother to Renegade and a dark liver chestnut or possibly dilute black pony of 13.3hh. Partisan was retained as a stallion prospect by Cairnhill Stud until his purchase as a two-year-old by Sue McTaggart as an outcross stud sire for the Wychwood ponies.

Cairnhill Partisan (149) at 2 years old

Partisan was used only briefly at Wychwood, producing two foals, one of whom is the mare Wychwood Fairy Wren (1601). He was then sold and subsequently gelded without producing a stallion son to represent him.

Chapter 11
The Calla Rebel Line in Australia

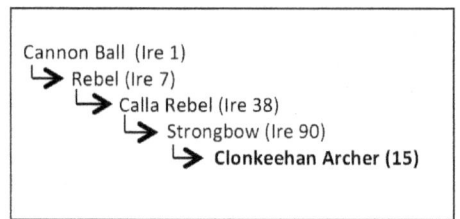

Clonkeehan Archer imp (15)

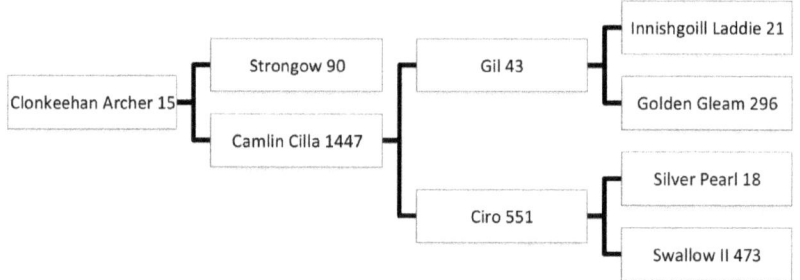

Clonkeehan Archer imp (15)
- Connemara Park Wilfrid (38)
- Barwidgee Target (39)
  - Wychwood Kilbenan (79)
- Connemara Park Timothy (50)
- Domo Cavallo Benjamin (54)
  - Irish Dusk of Canningvale (102)
- Hunter Lodge Ark Royal (60)
- Noorookoo Colin (65)
- Tyn-Y-Rhos Erin (71)
- Hunter Lodge James (85)
- Hunter Lodge Gregory (87)

The stallion Clonkeehan Archer is of particular interest, being the only representative of the Calla Rebel (Ire 38) branch of the Cannon Ball stallion line that was imported to Australia. He was a grey pony of 14hh by Stongbow (Ire 90), bred in Connemara in 1970 by Garnet Irwin. It is assumed that he was purchased as a foal by Miss Frances Lee Norman of Slane and subsequently registered with her prefix. Archer's dam, Camlin Cilla (Ire 1447), was also bred by Garnet and was retained by her for a number of years

Chapter 11   The Calla Rebel Line in Australia

before being given to Miss Norman as a broodmare. In the showring, Cilla's most noteworthy win was the Killanin Cup at the CPBS Annual Show in 1953. Her dam Ciro (Ire 551) won the Archbishop's Cup at the same show. Ciro was one of the mares by Silver Pearl (Ire 18) that kept John Quirke's (Ire 13) influence alive in Connemara Pony pedigrees. She was an exceptional performance mare, competing and winning Connemara races (under the name of Silver Swift), showjumping competitions, in-hand and under saddle, as well as proving her worth as a broodmare. Ciro's dam, Swallow II (Ire 473), has no pedigree recorded in the CPBS studbook and was Garnet's racing mare. She began stud duties very late in her life with Ciro foaled in her twentieth year.[1]

Clonkeehan Archer (15)

Ciro (Ire 551) at the 1951 Royal Dublin Show

Clonkeehan Archer was purchased and imported from Ireland by Fred Wiltshire who was keen on obtaining a pony with Silver Pearl in its pedigree for use in the Connemara Park breeding program. Archer was used by the Wiltshires until most of the ponies were dispersed in 1975 after Fred's death and he was then purchased by the Royles of Hunter Lodge Stud in New South Wales. He was shown lightly by the Royles and won the stallion class at the 1976 Sydney Royal Show. Archer contributed eleven stallion sons to the CPBSA studbook: Connemara Park Wilfrid (38), Barwidgee Target (39), Connemara Park Timothy (50), Domo Cavallo Benjamin (54), Hunter Lodge Ark Royal (60), Noorookoo Colin (65), Tyn-Y-Rhos Erin (71), Candlebark Artur (72), Tyn-Y-Rhos Carna Rebel (75), Hunter Lodge James (85) and Hunter Lodge Gregory (87). This appeared to be a promising start to this stallion family, however it did not continue past the second generation and there are no longer any stallion line representatives at stud in Australia. Archer also sired six registered daughters: Blandings Henrietta (1054), Blandings Juliet (1065) and Blandings Brigid (1118) (all exported to New Zealand); Candlebark Beathag (1122), Green Hills Showgirl (1140) and also the bred-up mare Candlebark Aingealag (2B/010).

---

1 R5 p142, R6 p21, R3 p83

Chapter 11   The Calla Rebel Line in Australia

Connemara Park Wilfrid (38) in 1977

Connemara Park Wilfrid (38): Connemara Park Wilfrid, a grey stallion of 14.¾hh, was foaled in 1973 out of Easter Peak imp (1004). He was bought as a weanling by the Keables in partnership with the Sneddons for Howquadale Stud after they had been impressed with Island King's nature and weight-carrying ability. Howquadale Stud bred only partbreds by Wilfrid, one of whom was a 15hh gelding named Howquadale Remus. Remus, out of a Thoroughbred mare, was the first Connemara purchased by Christa Jones of Gnarwarre in Victoria in 1988. He proved to be a great family mount, carrying Christa as she resumed her riding career, and her son Michael to pony club and eventing. His temperament and ability so impressed the Jones family that they formed the Monahan Stud. At seventeen years of age Remus moved on to Heidi Mestrovic, participating in pony club gymkhanas, ODEs, dressage days and pleasure rides into his twenties. Heidi wrote in a 1999 CPBSA newsletter that "Remus is the most loving, caring, honest horse I have ever encountered... I am lucky to have owned such a beautiful horse".

Connemara Park Wilfrid was also owned for a time by the Woodwards of Candlebark Stud at Broomfield in Victoria and he was described by David in 1984 as: "A magnificent stallion with excellent conformation and very strong bone. He has not been shown since 1980, when he earned reserve champion Connemara stallion at Royal Melbourne and champion Connemara exhibit at Adelaide Expo. He is a versatile fellow, with basic schooling in dressage, some jumping experience (and loads of ability) and skills in stock work with both sheep and cattle. He moves beautifully and has been a pleasure to ride." Wilfrid impressed Lady Hemphill who noted at the Connemara Field Day that he was one of the nicest stallions we had at the time in Australia and that he was very typical and a good, true mover. He was also mentioned by Pat Lyne in *Reflections Through the Mist* who considered him an attractive pony when she saw him at the Adelaide Expo.

Wilfrid is represented by three purebred daughters: Ben Dhui Drishane (1288), Ben Dhui Elphin (1289) and the bred-up mare Howquadale Miffen (2B/032).[2]

---

2 R1 p67-69, R2 p74 78, R6 p110

Chapter 11   The Calla Rebel Line in Australia

Barwidgee Target (39): Barwidgee Target, Clonkeehan Archer's second son, was a grey stallion of 13.2hh foaled in 1973 out of Barwidgee Frederika (1025). He was purchased in 1974 from Barwidgee as a stallion prospect for the foundation of Sue McTaggart's Wychwood Stud in South Australia. Sue first became interested in the Connemara Pony through reading the English Riding Magazine from 1946. In South Australia at the time larger ponies were bred by crossing Shetland and Timor ponies with small Thoroughbreds. Of all the Mountain and Moorland breeds available in the United Kingdom, Sue was particularly attracted to the Connemara Pony due to their height, temperament and jumping ability.[3]

Barwidgee Target (39)

Wychwood Kilbenan (79) as a young pony

Sue found Target to be an exceptional foundation stallion, describing him as a plain, old-fashioned type, with plenty of bone, very good movement and jumping ability, and an exceptional temperament. He was taken to many shows and always did well, including being named reserve champion led Connemara Pony to his half-brother Connemara Park Timothy (50) at the 1983 South Australian APSB Show. Neville Sprod, who was the Master of the Silpark Hunt Club, kept Target for several years and bred some good hunting horses with him. He as then lent to the Roseworthy Agricultural College where he was used to teach the horse course students how to handle a stallion. Due to his temperament and excellent manners, he soon became a favourite with the students and instructors.

During his lifetime, Barwidgee Target produced one purebred stallion son, Wychwood Kilbenan (79), and one daughter, Wychwood Maid Marian (1208). He also sired numerous successful partbreds and gelding sons. For his retirement, he was returned to the McTaggarts and spent his last days at the property Moonaree Station via Port Augusta.

---

3 R51

Chapter 11   The Calla Rebel Line in Australia

Connemara Park Timothy (50)

Connemara Park Timothy

Wychwood Kilbenan (79), Target's son, was a grey (from chestnut) stallion who reached 13.3 or 14hh at maturity and was foaled in 1976 out of Ardan imp (1001). He was purchased by Gwynne Hughes of the cattle station Cliften Hills in Alice Springs as a station sire in order to decrease the height and improve the temperament of the stock horses being produced there. Kilbenan did not produce any purebred breeding stock progeny.

Connemara Park Timothy (50): Clonkeehan Archer's third stallion son, Connemara Park Timothy, was a grey stallion of 13.3hh foaled in 1974 and was also out of Ardan imp (1001). He was bought from the Wiltshires by Colin and Kath Thomas and stood at their property Connemara Hills at Victor Harbor in South Australia until 1981 when he was purchased by David and Diane Searle of Myponga. Timothy was very much appreciated by the Searles, and the following is a quote from Diane in a 1985 CPBSA newsletter: "[Timothy] is very special. He has given us so much love and pleasure over the four years we have had him. He has been a placid, even-tempered horse, even with the children – always ready to gently accept an apple or carrot and to give pony rides. He has, after some education, thank goodness, always been a gentleman to handle, both at home and in the show ring in ridden and led classes. He has won three champion Connemara awards in led-in classes, twelve firsts and twelve second placings. He has given David many hours of pleasurable riding from hacking around the paddocks to the show ring. But David's greatest achievement with Timothy is to ride him as Master's horse on the hunting field where he shows his true passion for jumping. We are very proud to own our beloved Timothy and hope we have many more years of such enjoyment with him and our other Connemaras."[4]

Disappointingly, Connemara Park Timothy also left no stallion sons. However he is represented by four daughters: Earlstone Kellie (1230), Kamara Park Elphin (1365), Cairnhill Chance Encounter (1376) and Templewood Toomervara (1548).

---

4 R51, R26:4

Chapter 11   The Calla Rebel Line in Australia

Domo Cavallo Benjamin (54): Bred in 1973 by Max Stollznow from the imported mare Monkcastle Autumn Mist (1021), Domo Cavallo Benjamin, Clonkeehan Archer's fourth son, was a 14.1hh grey stallion. He was purchased by the Tynans of County Clare Stud and shown successfully in-hand and under saddle in New South Wales, being champion Connemara exhibit at the National Horse and Pony Show in both 1975 and 1976. Frank described him as a pony with a beautiful head and a lovely pony by any standard. He was sold in 1982 to Mr Sam Hamood of the Glenhaven Thoroughbred stud in South Australia.

Domo Cavallo Benjamin (54)

Benjamin produced two purebred daughters, Yarraman Park Emma (1166) and San Ed Petrini (1197). His one purebred stallion son, **Irish Dusk of Canningvale (102)**, was exported from Australia in-utero when his dam, Irish Mist imp (1026), was purchased

Tyn-Y-Rhos Erin (71)

by Sir John and Lady Marshall for their Canningvale Stud in New Zealand. At the time, the Connemara Pony Society of New Zealand had not yet been formed, therefore a small number of New Zealand born ponies are included in the CPBSA's studbook. A grey stallion of 13.3hh foaled in 1978, Irish Dusk, left no stallion sons in New Zealand but did produce eight daughters. Those included in the CPBSA's studbook are Canninvale Bonny Meg (1363) and Canningvale Bonnie Lass (1404).

Hunter Lodge Ark Royal (60), the fifth son of Clonkeehan Archer, was a grey stallion of 13.2hh foaled in 1974. He was bred by Tony Royle out of Connemara Park Mary (1031). Ark Royal was used for breeding at Hunter Lodge but left only one purebred daughter, Hunter Lodge Fedelma (1317).

Tyn-Y-Rhos Erin (71): Tyn-Y-Rhos Erin was Archer's seventh stallion son. He was foaled in 1975 out of Fabian's Rebecca imp (1015), and was a grey (from bay) stallion of 14hh. Su Moore of the Tinderry Stud bought Erin from his breeder, Elisa Philips of Penrith as a weanling. Su first heard about Connemara Ponies when she was attending university and one of her lecturers was eagerly awaiting a foal from a mare she had sent to Connemara Park Arthur (5).

Chapter 11   The Calla Rebel Line in Australia

Erin, described as a weanling by Elisa as being "an outstanding colt with tons of quality and presence, and an excellent show and stud prospect", formed the foundation of the Tinderry breeding program with Su describing him as an old-fashioned sort, with a wonderful laid-back temperament. He was initially used for breeding partbreds but a purebred mare was later purchased for the stud.

Hunter Lodge James (85)

Photo: CPBSA Archive

Erin was used regularly for working stock. He was only shown lightly by the Moores, but on one of these occasions a noteworthy remark was made of him by Lady Hemphill when she viewed him as a two-year-old: "This is what a Connemara Pony should be!" Erin produced one purebred daughter, Tinderry Rosheen (1272), before the Moores lost him at an early age.

Candlebark Artur (72) is one of only three breeding stock progeny of the imported mare My Song (1052) and was bred by the Woodwards in Bungaree, Victoria in 1975. He was grey and stood 14hh. Artur was retained by Candlebark Stud and produced two registered daughters, Yarrandoo Katy (1242) and Candlebark Natasha (1259).

Hunter Lodge James (85): Hunter Lodge James, a grey full-brother to Hunter Lodge Ark Royal, was foaled in 1976 and stood 13.3hh. James was purchased by the Malcolms of Moss Vale in New South Wales to breed ponies for their riding school. The Malcolms were looking for a breed which had a steady temperament suitable for beginners but was also suitable for riders who wished to venture into showjumping and ODEs. They settled on the Connemara Pony. Two bred-up daughters by Hunter Lodge James are recorded in the studbook: Fitzroy Morna (1319) and Fitzroy Pinafore (1346).

Hunter Lodge Gregory (87), Archer's last stallion son, was a grey pony of 14.1hh foaled in 1977 out of Ice Blue imp (1016). Gregory did not produce a stallion son but is represented by one daughter, Cowarral Mariapo (1360).

Noorookoo Colin (65); Tyn-Y-Rhos Carna Rebel (75):

Clonkeehan Archer's sixth and seventh sons, Noorookoo Colin and Tyn-Y-Rhos Carna Rebel, out of Stonely Golden Heather imp (1045) and Connemara Park Ann (1005), did not produce any breeding stock progeny.

Chapter 12 — Conclusion

Chapter 12

In the preceding chapters we have seen how successful each of the imported and imported-in-utero Cannon Ball line stallions has been in laying down a foundation for its own family in Australia. Disappointingly, only ten of these stallions: Island King, Connemara Park Seumas, Tulira Colman, Errislannon Spartan, Toorigal Danny Boy, Blandings Bobby, Millfields Commodore, Abbeyleix Finbar, Shelford Downs Berwick Boy and Atlantic Rebel, still have direct stallion-line male descendants alive and/or standing at stud in Australia. This does not, however, give an overall view of the influence of these stallions, as many are represented in today's ponies indirectly through their daughters or daughters of sons etcetera.

In the next volume of this series we will review all of those imported and imported-in-utero mares that were by Cannon Ball line stallions, and the mare families they have created in Australia. Again, this is purely a method of dividing our Australian pony families into manageable groups for review. The Cannon Ball line does, of course, exist frequently in the back-breeding of all of the ponies present in our studbook.

It is an exciting time for Connemara Pony breeding in Australia with greater access to international bloodlines through frozen semen, and some new imports. An anticipated addition to the Cannon Ball stallion line is the bay colt Sternbergs Lenaro, purchased by the Newton family of Peppertree Connemara Ponies at Tichborne in New South Wales from Sternbergs Connemaras in Germany. Lenaro is by El Larry, a grandson of Killyreagh Kim through his direct sire line. It is planned that Lenaro will be imported in late 2014 after classification in Germany.

Photo: Manfred Grebler

Four month old Sternbergs Lenaro steps out with his dam Lena in Germany

Index

Abbeyleix Finbar (93) 24 30 44 **74-77** (Ch Pic) 155
Abbeyleix Fiona (1151) 16 30 74
Abbeyleix Grey Pearl (1159) 16 130
Abbeyleix Polly (1055) 16
Achill Fiddler (196) 136 **137** (Pic)
Adventure (Ire 11) 26
Airgead (Ire 45) 39
Aisling Park Tanielle (1841) 58
Alannah Kerry (1338) 60
Alnabrone Colleen (Ire 2321) 133
Amergin Josie Mac (1400) 139
An t'Sailchuach (Ire 663) 42
Aran Kilkenny (1185) 102
Aran Medea (1184) 96
Aran Milano (101) 89
Aran Vasari (1321) 72
Aran Vicenzo (PB) 72
Arctic Moon (Ire 2377) 27
Ardagh Maire (1310) 61
Ardan (1001) 5 25 31 47 60 96 121 152
Argenta Megan (1533) 105
Asham Madonna (1850) 85
Ashfield Bay Sparrow (1113) 39
Atlantic Breeze (Ire 2174) 42 (Pic)
Atlantic Rebel (107) 21 44 **142-144** (Ch Pic) 155
Ayle Glory (Ire 2616) 33
Aylesland Silver Velvet (1011) 70 103 112
Ballantrae Acushla (PB) 103
Ballantrae Black Sallee (1795) 130
Ballantrae Bracken 129
Ballantrae Briar 129
Ballantrae Candy (1458) 128
Ballantrae Delphinium (1584) 145
Ballantrae Erica (1428) 128
Ballantrae Fiesta (1554) 128
Ballantrae Flame (1662) 128

Ballantrae Flora (1677) 129
Ballantrae Gazania (1525) 128
Ballantrae Gemma (1555) 128
Ballantrae Gidgee (1612) 130
Ballantrae Gilliflower (1455) 128
Ballantrae Golden Syrup (144) 128 **129-130** (Pic)
Ballantrae Granite (158) 128 129 (Pic) **130**
Ballantrae Heather (1457) 128
Ballantrae Humbug (1456) 128
Ballantrae Jaffa (1527) 128 145
Ballantrae Lupin (1556) 145
Ballantrae Patsy (1557) 145
Ballantrae Petunia (1659) 145
Ballantrae Riff Raff (1589) 128
Ballantrae Ripple (1583) 128
Ballantrae Sparkle (1684) 129
Ballantrae Toffee (1582) 128
Ballantrae Treacle (1429) 70
Ballina Cleopatra (1738) 107
Ballina Melody (1633) 80
Ballintapper Hope (1624) 136
Ballybrack Tullimore (1490) 124
Ballydonagh Belle (1047) 16 144
Ballydonagh Deirdre (Ire 3423) 16
Ballydonagh Kate (Ire 2798) 20
Ballydonagh Rob (Ire 321) 16 20 **23-24** (Ch Pic)
Ballydonagh Sticky (Ire 377) 16 (Pic)
Barolin Aer Lingus (32) 115
Barwidgee Aran (1088) 29
Barwidgee Bugler (25) 102 **108-109** (Pic)
Barwidgee Discus (1160) 49
Barwidgee Drummer (18) 102 **112-113** (Pic)
Barwidgee Fern (1270) 70
Barwidgee Fiddler (34) 102 **110-111** (Pic)
Barwidgee Frederika (1025) 47 151

Index

Barwidgee Honeymead (61) 102 **111**
Barwidgee Kilmain (26) 102 **109-110** (Pic)
Barwidgee Lusitanica (1240) 119
Barwidgee Nandina (1057) 102
Barwidgee Mallow (1186) 129
Barwidgee Mizen (1094) 102
Barwidgee Piper (59) 102 **112-113** (Pic)
Barwidgee Samite (112) **70-72** (Pic)
Barwidgee Shoogle (PB) 102 (Pic)
Barwidgee Silver Dollar (1222) 119
Barwidgee Snowberry (1053) 49 102
Barwidgee Snowdown (23) 102 **103-104** (Pic) 112
Barwidgee Snowdrift (1058) 111
Barwidgee Sonata (1362) 102
Barwidgee Storm (G001) 34 (Pic)
Barwidgee Target (39) 149 **151** (Pic)
Barwidgee Tom Sawyer (120) 70 **73** (Pic)
Barwidgee Velour (1210) 119
Belle Heather (1106) 67
Belle of the Ball (Ire 3122) 123
Benad Katana (1480) 131
Benad Lady Sarah (1532) 131
Ben Dhui Cavatina (1265) 70
Ben Dhui Diccon (123) **97-98** (Pic)
Ben Dhui Drishane (1288) 150
Ben Dhui Elphin (1289) 72 150
Ben Dhui Fanfare (1344) 102
Bergerrone (1492) 49
Betsy Bay (Ire 2075) 118
Bimini Aster (1664) 65
Bimini Cedar (1663) 65
Bimini Elsbeth (1812) 65
Binnowie Eileen (1476) 84
Binnowie Gemini (PB) 118
Binnowie Gemmagh (1746) 84
Binnowie Katie Clare (1748) 84
Binnowie Mandolin (172) **84-85** (Pic)
Binnowie Spotlight (1607) 84

Biwmares Madonna (1681) 83
Blandings Agapanthus (1138) 47
Blandings Amalfi (1546) 107
Blandings Amaranthus (1386) 97 107
Blandings Ambrosia (1235) 97
Blandings Amethyst (1387) 97
Blandings Ardrahan (1281) 111
Blandings Barbados (1534) 64 79
Blandings Beamish (198) **107-108** (Pic)
Blandings Blessington (1388) 64
Blandings Bluebell (1341) 97
Blandings Bobby (44) 16 44 **62-64** (Ch Pic) 96 106 155
Blandings Brigid (1118) 149
Blandings Buttercup (1096) 99 128
Blandings Cean Ruadh 96 (Pic) 97
Blandings Coinneac (1127) 107
Blandings Colleen (1653) 107
Blandings Columbine (1630) 107
Blandings Coriander (1389) 64
Blandings Custard the Dragon (124) 97 **99** (Pic)
Blandins Emerald (1329) 97
Blandings Finola (1390) 64
Blandings Florinda (1391) 64
Blandings Folly (1611) 107
Blandings Foxtrot 107
Blandings Frangipani (1392) 97
Blandings Galway Mary (1236)
Blandings Garrison (80) **117**
Blandings Henrietta (1054) 149
Blandings Holly (1235) 97
Blandings Icing (81) **61**
Blandings Ingrid (1541) 107
Blandings Jade (1260) 64
Blandings Jaipur (1616) 99
Blandings John (150) 63 **64-65** (Ch Pic) 96 106 155
Blandings Jubilation (1171) 63

157

Index

Blandings Juby (1652) 64
Blandings Juliet (1065) 149
Blandings Juniper (1393) 64
Blandings Kashmir (1427) 97
Blandings Kimberley (1261) 64
Blandings Kingston 64
Blandings Lamington (1066) 47
Blandings Marmalade (1238) 97
Blandings Millais (1394) 97
Blandings Millfleurs (1342) 97
Blandings Mufty (1545) 107
Blandings Nutmeg (1395) 97
Blandings Planxty (1181) 63 99
Blandings Poitin (166) **107** (Pic)
Blandings Red Fort (100) 63 **64**
Blandings Red Gum (1654) 65
Blandings Ruby (1226) 63
Blandings Rumba (1544) 64
Blandings Rusheenamarna (1396) 97
Blandings Ryan (157) 63 **65** (Pic)
Blandings Sally (1644) 107
Blandings Sandlewood (1397) 97
Blandings Sapphire (1588) 97
Blandings Seumas (221) **99-100** (Pic)
Blandings Sorbet (1543) 99
Blandings Sylvia (1216) 63 97
Blandings Teresa (1398) 64
Blandings Tiger Lily (1367) 97 107
Blandings Wallflower (1227) 144
Blandings Zircon (92) 63 **64**
Boa (PB) 117
Bodenpark Rosethorne (1114) 137
Boffin Heron (1051) 26 64
Bonny Jean of Canningvale (1195) 63
Boonahburra Carousel (1653) 81
Bridge Boy (Ire 124) 25 **26** (Pic Ch) 118
Buckna (TB) 15
Caballero La Casa Lagrima (PB) 71 (Pic)

Cailin Ruadh (Ire 1476) 133
Cairnhill Caitlin (1474) 144
Cairnhill Cavalier (G198) 147 (Pic)
Cairnhill Chance Encounter (1376) 152
Cairnhill Fionna (1473) 137 144
Cairnhill Fonzie O'Flaherty (PB) 144 (Pic)
Cairnhill Partisan (149) 144 **147** (Pic)
Cairnhill Renegade (140) 144 **146-147** (Pic)
Cairnhill Woodkern (G216) 144
Calla Rebel (Ire 38) 12 **41** (Ch) 148
Calla Roan (Ire 196) 41
Calmore Swagman (UK 5329) 26 **27** (Pic Ch) 101
Camlin Cilla (Ire 1447) 148
Candlebark Aingealag (2B/010) 149
Candlebark Artur (72) 149 **154**
Candlebark Beatha (68) **60-61** (Pic)
Candlebark Beathag (1122) 149
Candlebark Eamhair (1135) 47
Candlebark Eiliah (1180) 60
Candlebark Leitis (1190) 111
Candlebark Lili (1192) 111
Candlebark Lucrais (1245) 60
Candlebark Macrigh (49) **60**
Candlebark Mairi (1308) 60
Candlebark Marsale (1223) 60
Candlebark Mudlark (1120) 96
Candlebark Natasha (1259) 154
Candlebark Sharon (2B/009) 96
Canningvale Bonnie Lass (1404) 153
Canningvale Bonnie Meg (1363) 153
Cannon Ball (Ire 1) 5 **10-12** (Pic Ch) 44
Canrower Lass (Ire 1977) 26
Capparis Casanova (197) 55 57 (Pic) **58**
Capparis Champagne Charlie (188) 66 **67** (Pic)
Capparis Enya (1720) 66
Capparis O'Grady (201) 58 (Pic) **59**

Index

Capparis Patsy's Luck (1688) 66
Capparis Rachelle (1689) 66
Capparis Solitaire (1719) 66
Carawah Briar Rose (1576) 56
Carna Bobby (Ire 73) **14-16**
(Pic Ch) 24 26 46 63 96
Carna Dolly (Ire 442) 15 (Pic)
Carna Dun (Ire 89) 5 7 16 21 26 68
Cashel Kate (Ire 2030) 16(Pic) 20 23
Celtic Basil (224) 86 (Pic) **87** (Pic)
Celtic Cymbal (1737) 87
Celtic Driftwood (1465) 70
Celtic Fairy Tale (1855) 112
Celtic Fiddlesticks (1732) 87
Celtic Kathy O'Hara (1793) 87
Celtic Marjoram (1782) 87
Celtic Rosemary (1706) 87
Celtic Santolina (1711) 87
Celtic Seadrift (1707) 87
Celtic Silver Finn (147) 70 **73-74**
Celtic Silver Thread (1372) 70
Celtic Spice (1733) 87
Celtic Storm Cloud (1510) 70
Celtic Sweet Ashrinn (1692) 87
Celtic Sweet Candy (1783) 87
Celtic Sweet Katie (1761) 87
Celtic Thyme (1587) 87
Celtic Tipperary Fling (134) 70
Celtic Touch and Go (1469) 70
Celtic Winter Snow (131) 102 **112**
Charlie (Ire 2) 41
Cheviot White Clover (UK 17231) 134
Chiltern Curlew (Ire 619) 133
Chiltern Gemini (1074) 104
Chiltern Martina (1128) 22 65
Chiltern Saffron (1101) Prologue (Pic)
Chiltern Variation (1129) 22
Chittering Gully Cameo (1351) 49

Chittering Gully Fantasy (1328) 49 88
Chittering Gully Guinevere (1352) 49
Chittering Gully Shadow (G106) 115
Chittering Gully Sweet Whisper (1454) 49
Chittering Gully Windsong (1377) 49
Cil Ciarain (Ire 78) **14**
Ciro (Ire 551) 149 (Pic)
Clairvale Cenedra (1685) 76
Clairvale Cuiliuir (1755) 87 99
Clairvale Eibhlin (1837) 94
Clairvale Padraic (240) **94** (Pic)
Clifden Bailey 137 (Pic)
Clifden Silver Mist (1704) 136
Clonkeehan Archer (15) 42 44 **148-149** (Pic)
Clonkeehan Auratum (Ire 104) 5 7 15 37
Clonterna Honeysuckle (1017) 111 112
Clough Rebel (Ire 33) 68
Cocum Hawkstone (Ire 570) **18-19** (Pic Ch) 69
Cocum Raindrop (1103) 19
Coleby Horatio (UK S12) 134
Colleen Bawn (Ire 159) 15 22 (Pic)
Colmaur Colleen (1656) 64
Colmaur Kasey (163) 63 **65-67** (Pic)
Connemara Boy (Ire 9) 5 7
Connemara Park Andrew (104)
135 **136-137** (Pic)
Connemara Park Ann (1005)
47 96 100 115 154
Connemara Park Arthur (5) **47-49** (Pic) 153
Connemara Park Billy (9) **52** (Pic)
Connemara Park Bonnie (1059) 96
Connemara Park Bruce (20) **61**
Connemara Park Garry (37) **60**
Connemara Park George (45) **61**
Connemara Park Guy (58) **61**
Connemara Park Hilda (1062) 96
Connemara Park James (8) **50** (Pic) 125 131
Connemara Park Joybelle (1132) 47

Index

Connemara Park Judy (1024) 61 65 96
Connemara Park June (1030) 96
Connemara Park Justin (17)
Connemara Park Kathleen (1082) 96
Connemara Park Kenneth (2) 131
Connemara Park Leonie (1099) 47
Connemara Park Mac (11) **61**
Connemara Park Margaret (1077) 47
Connemara Park Mary (1031) 47 153
Connemara Park Maureen (1087) 33
Connemara Park Michael (51) 60
Connemara Park Paul (24) **59**
Connemara Park Peter (10) **54** (Pic)
Connemara Park Richard (27) 95 **96-97** (Pic) 106
Connemara Park Rita (2B/001) 131
Connemara Park Russell (4) **61**
Connemara Park Sally (1006) 47
Connemara Park Seumas (3) 26 44 **95-96** (Pic) 155
Connemara Park Sheba (PB) 112
Connemara Park Timothy (50) 149 151 **152** (Pic)
Connemara Park Trevor (19) 95 **96**
Connemara Park Trudi (1098) 47 136
Connemara Park Wilfred (38) 149 **150** (Pic)
Coomel Prima Donna (1043) 27
Coosheen Finn (Ire 381) 16 **24** (Pic) 30 74
Coosheen Laura (Ire 1084) 24
Cootehill Cream Puff (1683) 65
Cornamona of Millfields (UK 13864) 133 (Pic)
Corrib (UK 3891) 30 **39-40** (Pic Ch) 139
Corrib Bridget (1340) 121
Corrib Park Ballymac (162) 90 **91-92** (Pic)
Corrib Park Camilla (1509) 56
Corrib Park Cherub (1627) 91
Corrib Park Clarissa (1628) 91
Corrib Park Katie Clare (1508) 90
Corrib Park Kelly (159) 90 **91** (Pic)

Corrib Park Mactavish (145) **57** (Pic)
Corrib Park Macushla (1568) 90 99
Corrib Park Micaela (1507) 76
Cottenham Sailor (UK S15) 134
County Clare Celtic Song (1073) 110
County Clare Mickey (21) 39 44 **120-121** (Pic Ch)
County Clare Rebel (1067) 52
County Clare Superstar (1041) 52
Cowarral Mariapo (1360) 154
Cowslip of Calla (Ire 1008) 40
Creg Lassie (Ire 1737) 118
Cregmore Colm (84) 114 119
Cregmore Dun (Ire 223) 25 44 **114-115** (Ch Pic)
Cregmore Galway (62) 29 44 **118-119**
Crystal Shannon (1513) 56
Cunderdin Ann Oakleigh (1085) 117
Cunderdin Dolphin (1183) 117
Cunderdin Rory Richard (55) 34 44
Curra Melody (1484) 105
Currachmore Cashel (Ire 1128) 69 (Pic)
Curraglen Whisper (1749) 105
Cushatrough Lass (Ire 1650) 68 69 (Pic)
Daddy Cool (PB) 113
Dancing Queen (PB) 113
Dancing Spanner (Ire 1750) 37
Dangan Lady (1050) 63
Dark Warrior (PB) 113
Derrada Fanny (Ire 182) 30
Derry Boy (Ire 30) 94
Derryowen Seagull (1145) 39
Despatch (PB) 117
Diamonds (1146) 38
Dolan Rose (Ire 1132) 21
Domo Cavallo Benjamin (54) 149 **153** (Pic)
Domo Cavallo Petra (1109) 54
Domo Cavallo Praize (63) **54-57** (Pic) 82
Doon Lass (Ire 1311) 46

Index

Doon Paddy (Ire 95) 18 37
Doon Reaghaun (Ire 1461) 19
Dooyher Lass (Ire 188) 13
Drimeen Dun (Ire 1449) 121 123 (Pic)
Dun Aengus (Ire 120) 42
Dundrum (PB) 5 (Pic) 101
Dun Belle (Ire 779) 133
Dylanglen Diamond Tiara (1695) 76
Dynamite 11
Eaden Calypso (1150) 27 64 101
Earl of Doon (DEN 33) 75
Earlstone Kelly (1230) 152
Easter Journey (1022) 37 140
Easter Mask (1003) 54 59
Easter Peak (1004) 60 61 150
Easter Sparkle (1007) 49
Easter Strand (1008) 34 109 113
El Larry 155
Eloura Mickey Finn (PB) 125
Emerald Cornelian (1048) 32
Emerald Valley Lilly Pilly (1709) 99
Emerald Valley Monsoon (1713) 99
Emerald Valley Pride of Erin (1493) 56
Emerald Valley Revelation (1486) 56 86
Equus Blondie (1283) 130
Errisbeg Rose (Ire 2895) 21
Errislannon Asphodel (1018) 60
Errislannon Alainn (1027) 36
Errislannon Cailin (1029) 36
Errislannon Coltsfoot (Ire 115) 122
Errislannon Columbine (Ire 1023) 49
Errislannon Daisy (Ire 2533) 122 123 (Pic)
Errislannon Dana (Ire 4769) 122
Errislannon Diamante (Ire 6026) 36 (Pic) 122
Errislannon Sparkler (Ire 210) **35-36** (Ch Pic) 127 131
Errislannon Spartan (Ire 30) 36 44 **121-124** (Ch Pic) 155

Exmoor Caitlin (1596) 52 78
Exmoor Grania (1609) 78
Exmoor Irish Jack (178) 78 **79-80** (Pic)
Exmoor Jamaica (1613) 78
Exmoor Molly Malone (1839) 80
Exmoor Nutmeg (1467) 144
Exmoor Polly Waffle (1648) 130
Exmoor Silver Finn (G217) 78
Exmoor Silver Swallow (1249) 119
Exmoor Sinead (1595) 78
Fabian's Rebecca (1015) 61 153
Fairyhill Madonna 3 (Pic)
Faro (PB) 102 (Pic)
Farravane Boy (Ire 71) 68
Feldale Mouse (PB) 56 (Pic) 57
Finchampstead Fascinatin' Rhythm (UK 216) 69
Finchampstead Martha (1147) 18
Finola of Leam (Ire 3036) 17 24 30 74
Fitzroy Cluan (1318) 60
Fitzroy Morna (1319) 154
Fitzroy Pinafore (1346) 154
Flash Girl (Ire 1771) 69
Forest Flower (Ire 2692) 42
Four of Diamonds (1070) 57
Furnace Lass (Ire 366) 35
Galway Park Clare (1042) 96
Galway Park Finesse (1441) 70
Galway Park Maura (1108) 102
Galway Park Theresa (1149) 115
Garafin (Ire 3350) 116
Garafin Boy (28) 26 44 **116-117** (Ch Pic)
Garland Bayleaf (1247) 132 146
Garland Celebration (1187) 108
Garland Grey Feather (1209) 132
Garland of Blossom (1217) 108
Garland Marele (PB) 108
Garland Shannon (40) 102 **112-113** (Pic)

Index

Garland Silver Willow (1366) 94
Garnet Helena (1669) 92
Garnet Lovely Lyric (1718) 92
Garnet Morin (1750) 92
Garnet Oracle (207) 98 (Pic) **99**
Garnet Oseille (1792) 92
Garnet Panache (1834) 92
Garnet Penny (1852) 92
Garnet Phineas (206) **92** (Pic)
Garnet Phoenix (208) **92-93** (Pic)
Garnet Portrait (1814) 92
Garnet Prelude (1810) 92
Garnet Quantum Leap (1815) 92
Garnet Quelle (1824) 92
Garnet Quicksilver (211) 92 (Pic) **93**
Gentle Breeze of Millfields (Ire 2648) 133 134 **(Pic)**
Gil (Ire 43) 13 **14** 40
Glengarry Patsy Malone (1536) 59 76
Glen Nelly (Ire 1344) 28
Glenormiston Abbey Lara (1475) 56
Glenormiston Adare (1726) 56
Glenormiston Aedin (1803) 76
Glenormiston Aislinn (1799) 56
Glenormiston Alanna (1440) 56
Glenormiston Amelia (1670) 56 57
Glenormiston Araminta (1424) 76
Glenormiston Ballycara (1640) 56
Glenormiston Bridie O'Loan (1269) 55 85
Glenormiston Carrilon (PB) 119
Glenormiston Cashel (1747) 76
Glenormiston Cashelmara (1291) 139
Glenormiston Catriona (1496) 76
Glenormiston Celebration (1672) 56 89
Glenormiston Celtic Pride (218) 55 **59** (Pic)
Glenormiston Celtic Prince (205) 55 **59** (Pic)
Glenormiston Ciara (1679) 56
Glenormiston Ciaran 56 (Pic)

Glenormiston Clare (PB) 56
Glenormiston Clementine (1520) 76
Glenormiston Clemma (1724) 80
Glenormiston Clonakilty (1780) 76
Glenormiston Clonmel (1638) 56 57
Glenormiston Cloonlara (1710) 76
Glenormiston Cloonshee (1742) 76
Glenormiston Cornamona (1698) 76
Glenormiston Cuchulainn 57
Glenormiston Diamond Lil 57
Glenormiston Diamonds Forever (1420) 55
Glenormiston Dolly (1497) 56
Glenormiston Dulcinea (1570) 59 76
Glenormiston Fenella (1447) 76
Glenormiston Fiona (1699) 76
Glenormiston Fineen (212) 76 **87-88** (Pic)
Glenormiston Finnian (148) 76 **82-83** (Pic)
Glenormiston Finola Grey (1410) 76
Glenormiston Fintan (151) 76 **83-84** (Pic)
Glenormiston Fintona (1606) 76
Glenormiston Fintra (1806) 76
Glenormiston Fionnabhair (1770) 76
Glenormiston Fionnuala (1641) 76
Glenormiston Firrene (1846) 76
Glenormiston Flashy Diamond (1808) 56
Glenormiston Flora (1639) 76
Glenormiston Flurry Knox 85 **89** (Pic)
Glenormiston Freedom (137) 76 **81** (Pic)
Glenormiston Innisheer (PB) 57
Glenormiston Jasper (135) 76 **78-79** (Pic) 81
Glenormiston Jessie Diamond (1495) 56
Glenormiston Katie Corkery (1199) 55
Glenormiston Kerima (PB) 116
Glenormiston Kilty Finn (114) 76 **87-88**
Glenormiston Kinsale (1785) 76
Glenormiston Kitty O'Day 99
Glenormiston Laura (1439) 56
Glenormiston Lauren (1694) 56

Index

Glenormiston Lillee O'Brien (1233) 55
Glenormiston Lizzie Diamond (1571) 76
Glenormiston Macadamia (1220) 57
Glenormiston Macroom (1409) 76 91
Glenormiston Maggie Macnamara (1234) 102
Glenormiston Maisie MacInealy (1267) 70
Glenormiston Mallow (1415) 76
Glenormiston Mary Murphy (1292) 76
Glenormiston Mavourneen (1374) 76
Glenormiston McInnerney Muskerry (95) 78
Glenormiston Mellerick (PB) 76
Glenormiston Molly Malone (1244) 108
Glenormiston Mr Macnamee (115)
76 **77-78** (Pic)
Glenormiston O'Neill Clanaboy (86) 40 44 **138-140** (Ch Pic)
Glenormiston Patrick (PB) 55 (Pic) 56
Glenormiston Rosaleen (1673) 76
Glenormiston Rosalie (1809) 56
Glenormiston Roscrea (153) 89
Glenormiston Roskeen (1700) 76
Glenormiston Rossleague (1725) 80
Glenormiston Rusheen (1620) 58
Glenormiston Slipper (164) 76 **85** (Pic)
Glenormiston Snow Fox (213) 76 **87-88** (Pic)
Glenormiston Tess (1776) 76
Glenormiston Theresa Diamond (1438) 76
Glenormiston Treasa (1804) 76
Glenormiston Willy Diamond (121) 55 **57** (Pic)
Glenrose Roisin (1838) 92
Glentrasna Grey (Ire 1154) 94
Glory Boy (31) 26 44 **117-118** (Ch Pic)
Golden Gleam (Ire 296) 14 (Pic) 40
Golden Glimmer (Ire 297) 14
Gold Flake (Ire 1324) 31 33
Gold Rose (Ire 1437) 33
Gracefield Park Aladdin (200) **81-82** (Pic)
Gracefield Park Atlantic Swirl (210) 80

Gracefield Park Majestic Dancer (PB) 81
Gracefield Park Mr Ed (234) 81 **82** (Pic)
Grange Solitary Swan (1112) 23
Grayswood Doon Bridge (Ire 5829) 8 (Pic)
Greaney Rebel (Ire 186) 31 **39** (Ch Pic)
Green Hills Final Fling (1660) 80
Green Hills Lollipop (PB) 145
Green Hills Rebel (56) 44 **144-145** (Pic)
Green Hills Shannon (1271) 119
Green Hills Showgirl (1140) 149
Grey Swan (Ire 457) 25
Harknow (PB) 110 (Pic) 111
Hattondale Aspen (1516) 60
Heather Bell (Ire 15) 35 133
High Trees Kerry Blue (1083) 32
Hillside Rover (ID) 5
Hillview Ailin C'Ait (1482) 51
Hillview Ailin Patrice (1518) 51
Hillview Finnian (152) **51**
Hillview Irish Mist (1643) 51
Hillview Little Tori (1658) 51
Hillview Shevalli (1822) 51
Hillview Trojan (183) **51-52** (Pic)
Hillview Vallen (1610) 51
Hinton Bush Law (UK 6765) 27
Home Vale Diamond (1593) 83
Home Vale Emerald (1599) 83
Home Vale Fiddlesticks (176) 82 (Pic) **83**
Home Vale Nicholas (PB) 103
Home Vale Perfection (1219) 83 104 105
Home Vale Quantas (106) 1 (Pic) **104-105** (Pic)
Home Vale Samantha (1371) 104
Home Vale Serenade (1370) 104
Home Vale Sinbad (PB) 103
Home Vale Talisman (125) 104 **105-106** (Pic)
Home Vale Tracey (1402) 104
Home Vale Velvet (1411) 104
Home Vale Webster (136) 104 **106-107** (Pic)

Index

Home Vale Yeltor (1501) 104
Home Vale Zadia (1512) 104
Howquadale Miffen (2B/032) 150
Howquadale Remus (PB)
Hunter Lodge Arc Royal (60) 150
Hunter Lodge Blixen (1126) 121
Hunter Lodge Fedelma (1317) 153
Hunter Lodge Gregory (87) 149 **154**
Hunter Lodge James (85) 149 **154** (Pic)
Huon Valley Autumn Tart (1374) 136
Huon Valley Cleo (1417) 136
Huon Valley Lady in the Snow (1239) 104
Ice Blue (1016) 115 154
Inis O'Hara (29) 42 83 141
Innishgoill Laddie (Ire 21) 12 **13** (Pic Ch)
Inver Bridge (Ire 459) 18 30
Inver Rebel (Ire 93) 18 **30-31**
Irene (Ire 624) 26
Irish Beauty (Ire 669) 14
Irish Dusk of Canningvale (102) **153**
Irish Mist (1026) 39 153
Island Baron (Ire 327) **37** (Ch Pic)
Island Duke (Ire 208) 22
Island King (1) 5 16 44 (Pic) **45-47** (Ch Pic) 155
Islehurst Bornado (PB) 61
Jabiru Galway Jester (113) 109 **110**
Jabiru Jennifer Clare (1405) 109
Jabiru Jo's Pride (1248) 52
John Quirke (Ire 13) 149
Julie (Ire 2246) 100 101 (Pic)
Just Lately (PB) 79
Kahean Snowblossom 108
Kamara Park Elphin (1365) 152
Karingal Flying High (PB) 50
Karingal Patrice (PB) 125
Katie (1014) 52 142
Kemill Hill Alicia (1413) 124
Kemill Hill Amie (1479) 124

Kemill Hill Bridgina (1119) 33
Kemill Hill Dermot (189) 126 **127** (Pic)
Kemill Hill Doon (1322) 124
Kemill Hill Halligan (1768) 123 **126-127** (Pic)
Kemill Hill Neuala (1875) 126
Kemill Hill Niamh (1768) 126
Kemill Hill O'Reilly (138) 123 **125-126**
Kemill Hill Rosheen (1323) 124
Kemill Hill Siobhan (1224) 124
Kemill Hill Spinnaker (91) 123 **124-125** (Pic)
Kemill Hill Stephanie (1324) 124
Kemill Hill Tinka (1155) 51 124
Kemill Hill Veracious (G291) 126
Kettledrum (PB) 119
Kiahma Susi (1730) 98
Kildare (PB) 47 (Pic)
Kilkieran Kirsten MacNeill (1574) 78 92
Kilkieran Michael's Miss (1498) 78
Kilkieran Rinamee (1449) 78
Killarney Park Spinifex (1537) 107
Killyreagh Kim (Ire 308) 16 **20-21** (Pic) 155
Kings Ransom (Ire 584) **21**
Kingstown (Ire 2532) 37 (Pic)
Kinvara Morning Light (36) 96 **100**
Kirtling Brigadoon (Ire 625) 18 **19-20**
 (Pic Ch) 89 133
Kirtling Haze (1028) 54 82
Knock Ina (1039) 16 124 126
Kooringa Park Benelong (PB) 56
Lagoonside Alleluia (1540) 73
Lagoonside Barnabas (142) 70 **72-73**
Lagoonside Trinity (1690) 81
Lanburn Leemoy (UK 6712) 143
Larrigan (130) 139 **140** (Pic)
Lavalley Rebel (Ire 24) 12 **30** (Ch) 40 94 120
Leam Bobby Finn (Ire 297) 16 **17-18**
 (Pic Ch) 30 74 143
Leam Dooneen (Ire 4384) 19 (Pic)

Index

Leam Lassie (Ire 1838) 25
Lefroy Abaigeal Mackilveen (1551) 50
Lefroy Ailin Dwane (128) 50 (Pic) **51**
Lefroy Keara O'Kinderlan (1343) 50
Lefroy Niall McBrady (126) **50-51**
Lefroy Prudence O'Hederman (1538) 50 126 127
Lefroy Una MacGilna (1481) 50
Lisavalla Rose (1049) 64 117
Little Heaven (TB) 5 37
Little Model (PB) 5
Lockinge Leonora (1104) 144
Lonsdale Moonwind (NZ S57) 60
Lor Sparrow (Ire 1264) 23
Lovejoy (1528) 144
Lydican Dun (22) 44 **115** (Pic)
Macaroon of Calmore (1079) 77 101
MacDara (Ire 91) 21 26 122
Macushla (PB) 47
Marble (Ire 254) 35 (Pic)
Marco Polo of Clonkeehan (Ire 236) 26-27 (Pic)
Marric Cortina (PB) 118
Maureen's Cuckoo (Ire 8700) 23
May Boy (ID) 5
Mayo Estelle (1591) 136
Mayo Lisa (1444) 144
Mayo Mary (1631) 136
Mayo Tracy (1487) 144
Meadowbank Stormgirl (1506) 56
Melanita (PB) 115
Mervyn Pookhaun (Ire 528) 16
Michmel Fine Girl (PB) 56
Millfields Cabin Boy (99) 44 134 135 **136**
Millfields Commodore (69) 33 44 53 **132-136** (Ch Pic) 155
Millfields Coronach 34
Millfields Coronet (UK 17254) 133 134 (Pic)

Millfield Fair Lady (UK 15948) 136
Millfields Festival 134
Millfields March Winds (48) 36 44 **131** (Ch Pic)
Millfields Sapphire (UK M00483) 123
Millfield Seaspray (1130) 134 135
Millfields Viking (41) **130** (Ch Pic)
Miravale Firefly (1566) 131
Miravale Star Gazer (1485) 131
Mitchell Connemara Ma-Ria Park (1290) 49
Monahan Ballad (1542) 98
Monahan Bridie (1539) 98
Monahan Deanna (1590) 98
Monahan Encore (1602) 98
Monahan Gumnut (173) **98-99** (Pic)
Monahan Gypsy (1655) 98
Monahan Harrison 97
Monahan Hullabaloo (1697) 98
Monahan Irish Melody (1736) 98
Monahan Jessie Belle (1735) 98
Monahan Keely (1744) 80
Monahan Limerick (199) **80**
Monahan Mozart (228) 79 (Pic) **80**
Monahan Nightingale (1789) 98
Monahan Oaks (1833) 80
Monahan Odele (1831) 80
Monahan Pistacio (1867) 80
Monahan Quickstep (1866) 80
Monkcastle Autumn Mist (1021) 153
Moonie Argentina (1225) 53
Mountain Birch (Ire 1537) 94
Mountain Lad (Ire 32) 5 7
Moyglare Samson (Ire 329) 42
Mungala Aisling (1651) 86
Mungala Anasta (1813) 59
Mungala Ceitein (1650) 86
Mungala Emerald Isle (165) 76 **85-86** (Pic)
Mungala Fenella (1597) 76

165

Index

Mungala Lacey (1702) 86
Mungala Pocheen (1629) 76
Mungala Siobhan (1575) 78
My Song (1052) 154
Mylerstown Huckleberry Finn (89) 18 44 68-70 (Ch Pic) 72
Mylerstown Peach (Ire 7474) 68
Narrawong Pal (PB) 138
Naseel (Arabian) 5
New Song Autumn 80
Noorookoo Colin (65) 149 **154**
Noorookoo Harry (47) 143
Noorookoo Spice (2B/036) 59
Noreen Ban (Ire 2355) 14 52
Noreen Grey (Ire 2287) 29
Noweddie Elke (1399) 139
Noweddie Holly (1445) 139
Noweddie Josie (1446) 139
Noweddie Najoy (1333) 139
Noweddie Maylea (1678) 139
Noweddie Natalie (1577) 139
Noweddie Nicholas 139 140 (Pic)
Noweddie Rebecca (1560) 139
Noweddie Sojourn 140
Oakdale Clonkilty (1229) 131
Oakdale Fanny Hill (1064) 34
Oakdale Inniskillen (1228) 131
Oakdale Millhara (1218) 131
Oakdale Aran Isle (PB) 70
Oakdale Tara (1277) 131
Oakleigh Mermaid (1036) 117
Orphan Dolly (Ire 1747) 36
O'Shea (PB) 47
Our Smokey (Ire 2969) 114 119 (Pic)
Oxenholm Dulcinea (1232) 78
Oxenholm Tiffany (1268) 56 85 88 89
Patsy Fagan (Ire G58) 114 115 (Pic)
Peggy 28 29 (Pic)

Phylmar Annette (PB) 121
Phylmar Sophie (1220) 121
Phylmar Tammy (PB) 121
Pine Tree Ashes (1460) 141
Pine Tree Cadence (1462) 141
Pine Tree Calypso Girl (1461) 141
Portadown Encore (133) 135 **137-138** (Pic)
Portadown Irish Rose (1412) 55
Prince Llewellyn (Welsh Cob) 11
Rainy Island Joy (1033) 139
Rainy Island Leprechaun (35) **49-50** (Pic)
Rainy Island Song of Joy (1282) 49
Rebel (Ire 7) **12** (Pic) 14
Rebel Wind (Ire 24) 31 **34-35** 100
Reflection (1102) 138
Renvyle Rebel (1002) 25 61
Ridgeway Dream (1173) 63
Rio Irish Rose (PB) 124 (Pic)
Rio Shirhl (PB) 125
Riverdance (PB) 113
Robinhill Blackberry (70) **49-50**
Robinhill Blueberry (1174) 49 91
Robinhill Lara (PB) 49 (Pic)
Robinhill Reverie (2B/020) 49
Robinhill Silver Jubilee (1182) 49
Robinhill Sterling Silver (53) 34 44 **132** (Ch Pic)
Robinhill Timoshay (PB) 49
Rory of Millfields (Ire 158) 31 **33-34** (Pic) 130
Rosenaharley Rowley (Ire 775) 69
Rosmuck (Ire 865) 94
Roundstone Oscar (Ire 337) **37-38**
Roundstone River (Ire 4746) 38 (Pic)
Rowenglen Caitlin (1535) 61
Rupari Baronia (1696) 72
Rupari Candy Tuft (1765) 72
Rupari Bridie (PB) 71
Rupari Meemanii (158) 71

Index

Rupari Ronan (143) 71 **72-73** (Pic)
Rupari Storm Girl (1657) 72
Rupari Sumar (PB) 71
Salette Honeycomb 72 111
Salette Innis Bo Finne (1368) 70
Sandy Park Kathleen Mavourneen (1202) 19
Sandy Park Molly Malone (1203) 63
Sandy Park Peggy O'Neill (1349) 97
Sandy Park Rosie O'Grady (1350) 64
San Ed Cara (1134) 47
San Ed Patrini (1179) 91 153
Scarteen of Calmore (UK 12600) 27
Seacliffe Camille (1489) 131
Seacliffe Lady Kate (1517) 131
Seacliffe Summer Winds (1565) 131
September Song of Millfields (1010) 108 112 113
Sheelin Grove Seumas Victor (180) 76 **87-88**
Shelford Downs Ascension (1175) 53
Shelford Downs Astrid (1298) 136
Shelford Downs Berwick Boy (96) 20 44 **89-90** (Pic Ch) 109 155
Shelford Downs Bonnie Eileen (1284) 136
Shelford Downs Brenna (1303) 136
Shelford Downs Captain Curragh (105) 135 **137-138**
Shelford Downs Castanette (1252) 136
Shelford Downs Clairwood (1176) 16
Shelford Downs Dearliza (1177) 53
Shelford Downs Gemma (1300) 136
Shelford Downs Glencora (1253) 136
Shelford Downs Jenny Wren (1254) 136
Shelford Downs Lena (1353) 136
Shelford Downs Michelle (1117) 50 121
Shelford Downs Morning Cloud (1255) 136
Shelford Downs Pegeen (1302) 90
Shelford Downs Penelope (1215) 135
Shelford Downs Peony (1328) 136
Shelford Downs Pollyanna (PB) 53
Shelford Downs Rain Cloud (1299) 136
Shelford Downs Ramona (1256) 136
Shelford Downs Rana (1307) 67 (Pic) 136
Shelford Downs Revelation (1141) 53
Shelford Downs Rosarana (1383) 136
Shelford Downs Rowena (1304) 136
Shelford Downs Royal Star (1178) 49
Shelford Downs Sacha (1297) 136
Shelford Downs Selma (1305) 136
Shelford Downs Simone (1369) 136
Shelford Downs Solita (1380) 136
Shelford Downs Solitaire (1257) 136
Shelford Downs Solitude (1301) 136
Shelford Downs Sonata (1258) 136
Shelford Downs Sophomore (1214) 135
Shelford Downs Sparkle (PB) 53
Shelford Downs Starr (1381) 136
Shelford Downs Twinkle (1285) 136
Shelford Downs Valentine (1296) 136
Shelford Downs Wilda (1306) 136
Shipton Nadir (UK 14614) 101
Silver (PB) 109
Silver Bridle (Ire 394) 68
Silver Mill (1038) 16 132
Silver Pearl (Ire 18) 149
Silver Rebel (Ire 841) 68 69
Silver Sultan (6) 118
Skibbereen (ID) 5
Sliabh na mBan (Ire 227) 116
Smack the Pony (PB) 66 (Pic) 67
Smokey (Ire 1198) 114 (Pic) 119
Smokey Duncan (Ire 871) 119
Smokey Jane Grey (Ire 7477) 119
Snowball (UK 2941) 7 33
Somerville Park Pollyanna (PB) 81 (Pic)
Speculation (Ire 295) 26
Spinway Cailin (Ire 6311) 122

Index

Spinway Comet (Ire 935) 122
Spinway Corsair (Ire 5879) 143
Spinway Fantasy (1143) 21
Springfield Abbigail (1592) 83
Springfield Darina (1634) 83
Springfield Devereux (169) 76 **86-87** (Pic)
Springfield Eryleen (1646) 83
Springfield Gemmagh (1676) 83
Springfield Grace (1675) 83
Springfield Irinagh (1686) 83
Springfield Kylemore (1858) 98
Star of Fahy (1453) 28
Sternbergs Lenaro 155 (Pic)
Stonely Golden Heather (1045) 154
Strickland Park Carnival (1723) 146
Strickland Park Carousel (1703) 65
Strickland Park Cheyenne (1787) 146
Strickland Park Diamond Lil (1832) 65
Strickland Park Irish Dancer (1708) 65
Strickland Park Irish Mist (1829) 65
Strickland Park Jo's Rebel (175) **145-146** (Pic)
Strickland Park Lucy (1665) 65
Strickland Park Peek a Boo (1862) 146
Strickland Park Silver Mist (1863) 146
Strickland Park Tiger Lily (1828) 146
Stroller (PB) 5
Stongbow (Ire 90) **41-42** (Pic) 148
Swallow II (Ire 473) 149
Sweet Sue (1012) 26 53 60
Sycamore Antarctica (1451) 106
Sycamore Blossom (1491) 106
Sycamore Delight (1531) 106
Sydserff Brig-O-Doon (83) 20 44 67
Tallamara Misty Lady (1337) 131
Tawmara Angee (1163) 60
Tawmara Island Boy (77) 52 **53-54**
Tawmara Katie (1463) 60
Tawmara Mitzi (1359) 60

Tawmara Primrose (1133) 60
Tawmara Suesanna (1197) 60
Tawmara Yolandi (1320) 60
Templewood Rose of Tralee (1608) 71
Templewood Temple Boy (PB) 146
Templewood Toomervara (1548) 152
Templewood Truskmore (1579) 146
Templewood Tyrell's Pass (PB) 146
The Admiral (Ire 201) **16** 20 23
Thistleton (TB) 5
Thunderbolt (Ire 178) 122
Tiercel Galloping Major (103) 22 44 **93-94** (Pic Ch)
Tiercel Mystical (UK 569) 33 (Pic)
Tiercel Witch Hazel (UK 15949) 93 94 (Pic)
Tinderry Donna (1379) 105
Tinderry Enya (1642) 105
Tinderry Jinden (1605) 105
Tinderry Norah (1522) 105
Tinderry Merlin (PB) 109
Tinderry Rosheen (1272) 154
Tintagel Guinevere (2B/003) 96
Tintagel Kathleen (1221) 97
Tooreen Laddie (Ire 86) 13 **25** (Ch)
Tooreen Ross (Ire 99) **25**
Toorigal Danny Boy (33) 36 44 **127-129** (Ch Pic) 155
Toorigal Emma (1136) 47
Toorigal Hannah (1243) 54
Toorigal Melody (1207) 49
Toorigal Purdie (1164) 108
Toorigal Robyn (1137) 108
Toorigal Sarah (1124) 121
Toorigal Sean (57) **49-50** (Pic)
Tralee Ethereal Star (1874) 67
Truska Pimpernell (Ire 618) **21-22** (Pic Ch)
Tulira Aileen (1115) 29

Tulira Colman (7) 26 27 43 (Pic) 44 69 **100-103** (Ch Pic) 105 155
Tulira Finn MacCool (Ire 715) 28
Tulira Fuchsia (1131) 29 88
Tulira Grainne (1111) 29
Tulira Heather (Ire 4851) 28
Tulira Highball (Ire 750) 101
Tulira Mairtin (Ire 214) 25 **28-29** (Pic Ch)
Tulira Mary Lou (1157) 29
Tulira Nimble Dick (Ire 426) 29 (Pic)
Tulira Silver Gull (Ire 1193) 29
Tully Lad (Ire 48) 16
Tylani Artell (146) 90 **91**
Tyn-Y-Rhos Carna Rebel (75) 149 **154**
Tyn-Y-Rhos Ele (1205) 115
Tyn-Y-Rhos Erin (71) 104 149 **153-154** (Pic)
Tyn-Y-Rhos Ria (1154) 115
Tyn-Y-Rhos Sir Anthony (74) **115**
Vale Southern Cross (1093) 134 135
Waterproof (Ire 1162) 39
Wattle Hills Christmas Eve (1844) 92
Wattle Hills Dochas (1435) 56
Wattle Hills Golden Wedding (1436) 56
Wattle Hills Laurel Wreath (1313) 55
Wattle Hills Liberty (1375) 76
Wattle Hills Marde Gras (1524) 56
Wattle Hills Medlar (1434) 56
Wattle Hills Primera (1314) 55
Wattle Hills Question (1354) 76
Wayfarer (Ire 1210) 25
Whalton Sandune (UK 4411) 19
Whitecrofts Bridie (1585) 125
Wild Lassie (Ire 1894) 32
Wildwych Dreamtime 89
Wildwych Eclipse 89 (Pic)
Wildwych Judas Hascarrots 80
Windward (1196) 36
Windy (Ire 782) 34 100

Winter (TB) 5 7
Wisbridge Erinmore (Ire 484)**32-33** (Ch Pic)
Wisbridge Golden Rebel (Ire 130) **31-32** (Pic Ch) 34 94
Wisbridge Golden Virginia (UK 14305) 33
Wisbridge Silver Birch (K 4888) 94
Wisbridge Whiskey Flake (UK 4486) **32** (Ch)
Wise Colleen (Ire 2372) 22
Wise Cuckoo (Ire 2714) 22
Wise Cygnet (Ire 544) 21 **22-23** (Pic Ch)
Wise Sparrow (Ire 2270) 23
Wychwood Blue Wren (1854) 87
Wychwood Fairy Wren (1601) 147
Wychwood Kilbenan (79) 151 (Pic) **152**
Wychwood Maid Marian (1208) 151
Yarraman Park Amy (1086) 121
Yarraman Park Emma (1166) 153
Yarraman Park Four Bells (1210) 108
Yarraman Park Henrietta (1191) 52
Yarraman Park Henry (43) **52-53** (Pic)
Yarraman Park Jeremy (117) 141 **142** (Pic)
Yarraman Park Polly (1278) 52
Yarraman Park Sarah (1231) 98
Yarraman Park Sophie (1081) 117
Yarraman Park Sugar (1168) 38 129
Yarraman Park Sweet Sue (1330) 141
Yarraman Park Toby (94) 38 44 **140-141** (Ch Pic)
Yarrandoo Eily (1241) 119
Yarrandoo Katy (1242) 154

Reference List and Recommended Reading

R1 : Connemara Milestone. Produced by: Central Victorian Activities Group of the CPBSA Inc. Editors Heather Storey, Jean Vanstan, Catriona Storey. Echuca Offset Printers. 1989.

R2 : Connemaras in Australia. Produced by: CPBSA. Editors: Sally Withers, Sue Dodds and Christa Jones. 2001.

R3 : Connemara Pony Breeders' Society 1923-1998. Elizabeth Petch. 1998. Published by Connemara Pony Breeders' Society. Printed by Litho Press Co.

R4 : Shrouded In Mist. Pat Lyne. 1984 Orphans Press Ltd.

R5 : Out Of The Mist. Pat Lyne. 1990. Orphans Press Ltd.

R6 : Reflections Through The Mist. Pat Lyne. 1993. Orphans Press Ltd.

R7 : The English Connemara Pony Society 1947-1997. Pat Lyne. 1997. Orphans Press Ltd.

R8 : As I See It. Pat Lyne. 2006.

R9 : Connemara Seaboard Of The Horses. Ursula Bruns.

R10 : The Connemara Pony. Anne Rolinson. J. A. Allen an imprint of Robert Hale Ltd. 2000.

R11 : Calmore Days. Susan Bowen. 1997. Printex.

R12 : Thunderbolt – His Life and Times 1963-1995. Pat Lyne. 1995. Orphans Press Ltd.

R13 : Connemara Chronicle. The ECPS. 1974. Vol 1. Editor Pat Lyne.
: 1 – 'Keymark Stud Advertisement' by Mr and Mrs Bigger. P50.
: 2 – 'Carna Dun 1948-1973' by Garnet Irwin. P39.
: 3 – 'Hyndon Slipper' by Pat Lyne. P27.
: 4 – 'Snowball 1941-1972' by Valentine Richardson. P37-38.

R14 : Connemara Chronicle. The ECPS. 1975. Vol 2. Editor Pat Lyne.
: 1 – 'Carna Bobby' by G.E.P. P67-68.
: 2 – 'Creg Coneera 1947-1974' by Cynthia Duff. P68.
: 3 – 'Atlantic Rebel' by Sarah Hodgkins. P63

R15 : Connemara Chronicle. The ECPS. 1976. Vol 3. Editor Pat Lyne.
: 1 – 'A Pony In A Thousand' by Valentine Boucher. P13-19.
: 2 – 'Around Our Studs No.2' by Pat Parker. P29.
: 3 – 'English Connemara Breed Show 1975' by Honor Parry. P39-41.
: 4 – 'MacDara (91) 1949-1975' by Pat Lyne. P69.
: 5 – 'Whalton Sandune' by Pamela Forman. P9.
: 6 – 'Sean of Leam' by Iona Philp. P70.
: 7 – 'News 1975' by Pat Lyne. P6-8.
: 8 – 'Peg Labouchere' by Pat Lyne. P21.
: 9 – 'Stallion Review – Millfields Commodore' by Pamela Forman. P11.

Reference List and Recommended Reading

R16	:	Connemara Chronicle. The ECPS. 1977. Vol 4. Editor Pat Lyne.
R17	:	Connemara Chronicle. The ECPS. 1978. Vol 5. Editor Pat Lyne.
	:	1 – 'Around Our Studs No.4 – The Calmore Stud' by Pat Parker. P13.
	:	2 – 'English Connemara Breed Show 1977' by Cynthia Muir. P47-49.
	:	3 – 'Dun Aengus (1958-1977)' by S.B. P53.
	:	4 – 'Clonkeehan Auratum 1954-1976' by Marie Levigne. P54-55.
	:	5 – 'Progress' P25
R18	:	Connemara Chronicle. The ECPS. 1979. Vol 6. Editor Pat Lyne.
	:	1 – 'Between The Shafts' by Rosalind Harris. P27-29.
	:	2 – 'Connemara Gleanings' by Pat Lyne. P61-65.
	:	3 – 'The Leys Stud' by Pat Parker. P19-21.
	:	4 – 'Stallion Review – Spinway Corsaire' by Pam Forman. P15.
R19	:	Connemara Chronicle. The ECPS. 1980. Vol 7. Editor Pat Lyne.
	:	1 – 'Events and News 1979' by Pat Lyne. P15.
	:	2 – 'Connemara Gleanings' by Pat Lyne. P75-77.
	:	3 – 'Stallion Review – Silver Snow' by Pam Forman. P19.
R20	:	Connemara Chronicle. The ECPS. 1981. Vol 8. Editor Pat Lyne.
	:	1 – 'Editorial' by Pat Lyne. P9-18.
	:	2 – 'Connemara Gleanings' by Pat Lyne. P87-89.
	:	3 – 'Stallion Review – Macnamara' by Pat Forman. P21.
	:	4 – 'Island Duke 1963-1980' by Pat Lyne. P35.
R21	:	Connemara Chronicle. The ECPS. 1982. Vol 9. Editor Pat Lyne.
	:	1 – 'Stallion Review – Truska Pimpernel' by Pam Forman. P23-24.
R22	:	Connemara Chronicle. The ECPS. 1983. Vol 10. Editor Pat Lyne.
	:	1 – 'Cocum Hawkstone' by Pam Forman. P23.
	:	2 – 'The Leam Stud' by Pat Parker. P27.
	:	3 – 'Stallion Profiles – Corrib' by Pat Lyne. P33.
	:	4 – 'Did You Know?' by Dr Nicola Hall. P57.
	:	5 – 'Presidents Lunch and Stallion Parade' by Nicholas Palmer. P11-14.
	:	6 – 'Keirin of Leam' by Pat Lyne. P33.
R23	:	7 – 'Old Favourites – Laura of Leam' by Pat Lyne. P84.
	:	Connemara Chronicle. The ECPS. 1984. Vol 11. Editor Pat Lyne.
	:	1 – 'Did You Know?' by Dr Nicola Hall. P45.
	:	2 – 'In Reply... to 'Early Detection of Promising Stallions'' by Susan Bradley. P83-84.
	:	3 – 'MacNamara 1960-1983' by Pat Lyne and Blanche Miller. P29.
	:	4 – 'Stallion Review – Atlantic Sentinel' by Pam Forman. P19.
	:	5 – 'Australian News' by M Kelly. P136-137.
	:	6 – 'New Zealand' by Stephanie Brooks. P144-145
R24	:	Connemara Chronicle. The ECPS. 1985. Vol 12. Editor Pat Lyne.
	:	1 – 'Truska Pimpernel and Thunderbolt' by Pat Lyne. P26-27.
	:	2 – 'English Connemara Breed Show 1984' by I. M. Yoemans. P29-31.

Reference List and Recommended Reading

	:	3 – 'Did You Know?' by Dr Nicola Hall. P57-65.
	:	4 – 'Field Day Lockinge Manor, Wantage' by Nicholas Palmer. P10-12.
	:	5 – 'Truska Pimpernel and Thunderbolt' by Pat Lyne. P26-27.
R25	:	Connemara Chronicle. The ECPS. 1986. Vol 13. Editor Lady Hellings & A Healing.
	:	1 – 'Around Our Studs – The Leaze Stud' by Pat Parker. P21-22.
	:	2 – 'Thunderbolt' by Pat Lyne. P103.
	:	3 – 'Australian News' by S McTaggart. P136-138.
	:	4 – 'Atlantic Rebel' by Sarah Hodgkins. P138-139.
R26	:	Connemara Chronicle. The ECPS. 1987. Vol 14. Editor A Healing.
	:	1 – 'Kirtling Brigadoon' by Pam Forman. P23.
	:	2 – 'Thunderbolt' by Nicholas Palmer. P22-23.
	:	3 – 'Spinway Corsaire' by Sarah Hodgkins. P12.
	:	4 – 'News from Australia' by Suzanne McTaggart. P169.
R27	:	Connemara Chronicle. The ECPS. 1988. Vol 15. Editor A Healing.
	:	1 – 'English Connemara Pony Society Stallion Parade and Inspection Seminar' by John O'M Meade. P15.
	:	2 – 'Whalton Sandune 1963-1987' by 'E.S'. P63.
	:	3 – 'Stallion Review – Atlantic Swirl' by Pamela Forman. P22.
	:	4 – 'Millfields Stud' P32-34.
R28	:	Connemara Chronicle. The ECPS. 1989. Vol 16. Editor A Healing.
R29	:	Connemara Chronicle. The ECPS. 1990. Vol 17. Editor A Healing.
	:	1 – 'Stallion Review – Wisbridge Erinmore' by A L Healing. P13.
	:	2 – 'Leam Bobby Finn' by Miss A. L. Healing. P17.
R30	;	Connemara Chronicle. The ECPS. 1991. Vol 18. Editor A Healing.
	:	1 – 'Eileen Thomas' by John Meade. P11.
	:	2 – 'Errisbeg Rose' by Sarah Hodgkins. P65-66.
	:	3 – 'Thunderbolt – The Progeny' by Nicholas Palmer. P43-47.
	:	4 – 'Errislannon Daisy' by Stephanie Brooks. P167.
R31	:	Connemara Chronicle. The ECPS. 1992. Vol 19. Editor Lady Scott.
R32	:	Connemara Chronicle. The ECPS. 1993. Vol 20. Editor Lady Scott.
	:	1 – 'Clifden Show 1992' by 'N.W.P'. P155-158.
	:	2 – 'Kid You Know' by Dr Nichola Hall. P61-65.
R33	:	Connemara Chronicle. The ECPS. 1994. Vol 21. Editor Pat Lyne.
	:	1 – 'Leam Bobby Finn 1967-93' by John and Phyllis Meade. P25.
	:	2 – 'Did You Know?' by Dr Nichola Hall. P87.
	:	3 – 'Stallion Review – Mahogany' by Nicholas Palmer. P18-19.
R34	:	Connemara Chronicle. The ECPS. 1995. Vol 22. Editor Lady Scott.
R35	:	Connemara Chronicle. The ECPS. 1996. Vol 23. Editor Lady Scott.
	:	1 – 'Thunderbolt' by Lady Scott. P15.
R36	:	Connemara Chronicle. The ECPS. 1997. Vol 24. Editor Lady Scott.
	:	1 – 'A Pony For All Seasons' by Susan Bowen. P23.
	:	2 – 'Did You Know?' by Dr Nichola Hall. P63-68.
	:	3 – 'Tulira Nimble Dick 1970-1995' by Beatrice Milleder. P232.

Reference List and Recommended Reading

	:	4 – 'Junior Roundabout' by Julia Spacey Woods. P101-107.
	:	5 – 'Vale – Tiercel Witch Hazel' by Benita Sanders. P57.
R37		Connemara Chronicle. The ECPS. 1998. Vol 25. Editor Lady Scott.
	:	1 – Australia' by John Tennant. P233-234.
R38		Connemara Chronicle. The ECPS. 1999. Vol 26. Editor Lady Scott.
	:	1 – 'Cocum Hawkstone' by Lady Scott. P25.
R39		Connemara Chronicle. The ECPS. 2000. Vol 27. Editor Lady Scott.
	:	1 – 'The Strong But Gentle Connemara' (From Horse and Hound March 25th 1977) by Liz Harries. P201.
	:	2 – 'Atlantic Sentinel 1966-1999' by Elizabeth Beckett. P27.
	:	3 – 'Laurel 1969-1999' by Sue Williams. P23-24.
R40		Connemara Chronicle. The ECPS. 2001. Vol 28. Editor Lady Scott.
	:	1 – 'Mahogany' by Zoya Hellings. P35.
	:	2 – 'Australian News' by Sue Clarke. P222-224.
R41		Connemara Chronicle. The ECPS. 2002. Vol 29. Editor Lady Scott.
R42		Connemara Chronicle. The ECPS. 2003. Vol 30. Editor Lady Scott.
	:	1 – 'The Shipton Stud' by Pat Parker. P36-37.
R43		Connemara Chronicle. The ECPS. 2004. Vol 31. Editor Lady Scott.
	:	2 – 'Laurin and Swirl' by Ginette Mason. P173.
	:	3 – 'A Perfect Match.. Island Duke – Arctic Moon' by Lady Scott. P114.
	:	4 – 'Australian News – Glenormiston Ciaran' by Annette & Kate Gardiner. P221.
R44		Connemara Chronicle. The ECPS. 2005. Vol 32. Editor Lady Scott.
	:	1 – 'Perfect Match Atlantic Sentinel – Shipton May Queen' by Doreen Halliday and Carolyn Moore. P134-135.
	:	2 – 'A Perfect Match MacNamara – May Retreat' by Blanche Miller. P136.
R45		Connemara Chronicle. The ECPS. 2006. Vol 33. Editor Lady Scott.
	:	1 – 'Wisbridge Erinmore' by Valentine Richardson and 'MS'. P25.
	:	2 – 'A Gentle Breeze From Connemara – the Story of a Stud' by Anne Rolinson. P133-136.
R46		Connemara Chronicle. The ECPS. 2007. Vol 34. Editor Lady Scott.
R47	:	Connemara Mare Families by Jenny Hagenblad. http://www.connemaraponny.org/mares/mares.htm
	:	1 – Winnie IRE 141
	:	2 – Silver Grey IRE 143
	:	3 – Fag an Bealach IRE 209
	:	4 – Sliabh na mBan IRE 227
	:	5 – Roundstone Lass IRE 235
	:	6 – Cuach na Coille IRE 236
	:	7 – Bog Oak IRE 287
	:	8 – Red Granite IRE 306
	:	9 – Retreat IRE 320
	:	10 – Silver Spray IRE 328

Reference List and Recommended Reading

	:	11 – Gray Beauty IRE 358
	:	12 – Furnace Lass IRE 366
	:	13 – Silver Bridle IRE 394
	:	14 – Killary Maid IRE 424
	:	15 – Callowfeenish Dolly IRE 437
	:	16 – Lady Jane IRE 455
R48	:	CPBSA Newsletter
R49	:	Michael O'Malley Letters
R50	:	BRAG Newsletter
R51	:	Connemaras in South Australia by Sue McTaggart

www.ingramcontent.com/pod-product-compliance
Lightning Source LLC
Chambersburg PA
CBHW070316240426
43661CB00057B/2665